ICELAND

NATURE'S MEETING PLACE

A March afternoon at Onundarfjordur in the remote West Fjords.

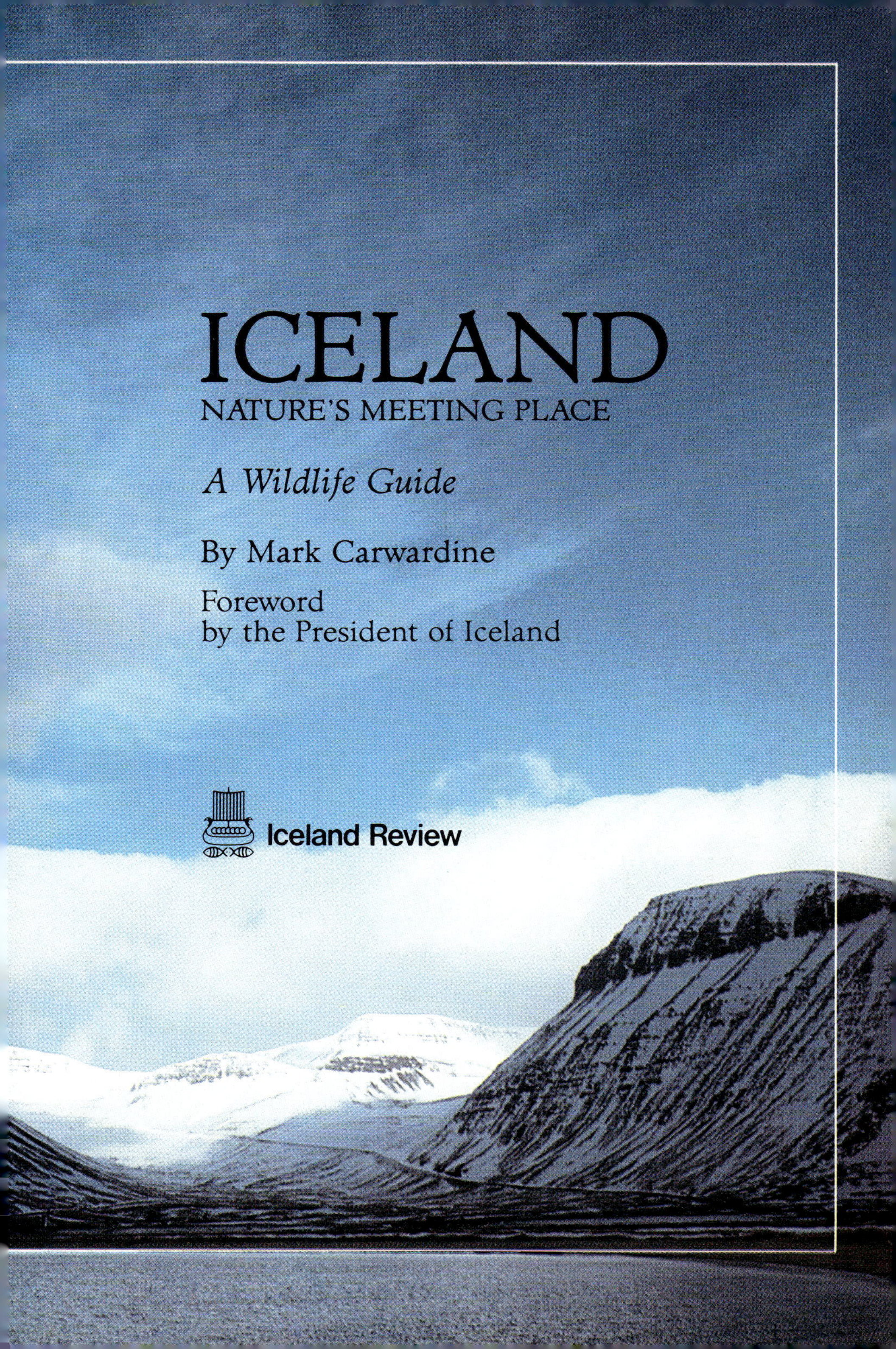

ICELAND

NATURE'S MEETING PLACE

A Wildlife Guide

By Mark Carwardine

Foreword
by the President of Iceland

Iceland Review

For Debbie

Iceland — Nature's Meeting Place
Text © by Mark Carwardine
Design: Gudjón Sveinbjörnsson
Front cover design: Fanney Valgardsdóttir
Typesetting: Leturval, Reykjavík
Lithos: Prentmyndastofan Ltd., Reykjavík
Printed in Italy
Published in 1986 by Iceland Review ©
Reykjavík, Iceland

FOREWORD

BY VIGDÍS FINNBOGADÓTTIR, PRESIDENT OF ICELAND

People who are born and bred in the enchanting atmosphere of this unique island in the North Atlantic are always pleased when outsiders observe and appreciate the charms of its nature. This book is a concise guide to the various features of Icelandic nature, to all those aspects of the country that have helped to mould the character of its inhabitants and give them a special view of life and a separate identity. We Icelanders are deeply conscious of this identity, which is the foundation of all our culture. On the strength of our awareness of this identity we are convinced that we have a contribution to make, something unique to give to other people.

One of the most striking harbingers of spring in Iceland is the Arctic tern. This agile flier undertakes a journey of 17,000 kilometres in order to spend the summer in our company for the purpose of ensuring the continued survival of the species. We always welcome the Arctic tern when it appears, and we also welcome the appearance of a book that throws a light on our northern island and can act as a guide to its natural marvels.

Looking westward to Myrdalsjokull from Asar.

PREFACE

My first visit to Iceland, in 1981, was under rather unusual circumstances. A young male walrus had beached himself on the coast at Skegness, in England – over a thousand miles from where he should have been in the Arctic – and I somehow became involved in an extraordinary plan to take him back home. So it was that I found myself in Reykjavik for the first time, helping to canvass the assistance of Icelandair, the Icelandic Government and the Iceland Defence Force in returning 'Wally', as he became known, to his native Greenland.

Wally was successfully deposited with some walrus friends; and I returned to England spellbound by the spectacular country, Iceland, through which we had passed.

Two things about the country in particular struck me during that first fleeting visit. One was the magnificent unspoilt scenery and the wealth of wildlife; the other was the complete lack of information available on either. It is my hope that this book will play a part in filling that gap.

I have returned to Iceland innumerable times since 1981, while researching for this book, and have come to know and appreciate the country, its wildlife and its people. I hope the product of those visits will encourage and help more people to discover the 'jewel of the north' for themselves.

Mark Carwardine

At Nordura, salmon vie with the splendour of the landscape for the visitor's attention.

ACKNOWLEDGEMENTS

Many people have assisted with the production of this book by providing advice, helping with research, reading drafts and in other ways. There are far too many to mention them all here, but I would like to express my thanks to everyone.

I would like to begin by thanking the President of Iceland, Vigdis Finnbogadottir, for contributing a foreword to this book and for the interest she has shown in the project.

In particular, in Iceland, I am indebted to Aevar Petersen and Erling Olafsson at the Icelandic Museum of Natural History in Reykjavik; Sigrun Helgadottir at the Nature Conservation Council; Arnthor Gardarsson at the University of Iceland; Johann Sigurjonsson at the Marine Research Institute; Thoroddur Thoroddsson and Helgi Hallgrimsson at the Museum of Natural History in Akureyri; Kristjan Jonsson at Reykjavik Excursions; Bernard Scudder at Iceland Review; and Birgir Olafsson at Icelandair in Reykjavik. They all happily put up with my frequent requests for help, often at short notice, and my regular knocking on their doors.

In the UK, in no particular order, I would like to thank George Medley, Craig Johnson, Pat Torrie, Simon Zisman, Lorraine Agass, Peter Martin and a long line of Carwardines, notably Betty, David, Adam and Vanessa, for helping in different ways; and the many secretaries, especially Jane Atkinson, at the World Wildlife Fund who spent their evenings slaving over hot word processors.

I am particularly indebted to Johann Sigurdsson, Regional Manager for Icelandair in London, for his generous assistance, enthusiasm and encouragement, and to his ever-helpful secretary, Pat McKenzie. Special thanks also go to my publisher, Haraldur J. Hamar, for his assistance, patience and unerring faith in the fact that I would eventually produce a completed manuscript.

Last but by no means least, I would like to thank Debra Taylor for all her help and tolerance during the three years in which this book has dominated my life.

Needless to say, I take full responsibility for the interpretation of all the information and advice I have received.

M.C.

A meadow in Vatnsdalur near Thingeyrar, North Iceland.

CONTENTS

CHAPTER 1

JEWEL OF THE NORTH

65 million years ago, a small planet hurtling through space at 72,000 kilometres an hour collided with the earth. It burst into the North Atlantic, punctured the oceanic crust and made a hole about 100 kilometres across.

The impact, according to one intriguing theory, resulted in destruction of almost unimaginable ferocity, like a thousand nuclear wars. Tidal waves swept the oceans, volcanoes erupted and earthquakes shook the continents and whipped the seas. A massive dust cloud developed and shrouded the earth, blocking out the sun and changing the climate. All the mighty dinosaurs were killed in the catastrophe — so were three quarters of every other species living in that prehistoric world.

But all was not lost. Perhaps by way of consolation, the tremendous impact is supposed to have triggered a series of events which led to a new volcanic island, Iceland, emerging from the sea.

Like any other volcanic island, Iceland is basically a pile of lava on the ocean bed

ICELAND
0
50
100 km
800m
100m
0
Arctic Circle
Grimsey
Hornbjarg
Raufarhofn
Thorshofn
Vopnafjordur
Bolungarvik
Isafjordur
Dranga-
jokull
Flateyri
Thingeyri
Bildudalur
Patreksfjordur
Holmavik
Hunafloi
Skagastrond
Saudarkrokur
Blonduos
Siglufjordur
Olafsfjordur
Dalvik
Akureyri
Eyjafjordur
Husavik
Asbyrgi
Dettifoss
Krafla
Myvatn
Laxa
Jokulsa a Fjollum
Flatey
BREIDAFJORDUR
Hvammstangi
Blanda
Egilsstadir
Seydisfjordur
Neskaupstadur
Eskifjordur
Stykkisholmur
Budardalur
Olafsvik
Snaefells-
jokull
Odadahraun
Askja
Hveravellir
Hofs-
jokull
Sprengi-
sandur
Snaefell
Kverkfjoll
Djupivogur
Langjokull
Kjolur
Hvitarvatn
Reykholt
Borgarnes
FAXAFLOI
Hvalfjordur
Hvita
Akranes
Thingvellir
Gullfoss
Geysir
Thjorsa
Thorisvatn
VATNAJOKULL
Hofn
REYKJAVIK
Gardabaer
Kopavogur
Hafnarfjordur
Skalholt
Skafta-
fell
Keflavik
Njardvik
Selfoss
Hekla
Landmanna-
laugar
Reykjanes
Grindavik
Thorlakshofn
Kirkjubaejarklaustur
Ingolfshofdi
Thorsmork
Myrdals-
jokull
Westmann Islands
Vik
Dyrholaey
Surtsey

Preceding pages: Aerial view over the Laki area, to the south-west of Vatnajokull.

that has grown sufficiently high for the tip to rise above the water surface. The asteroid collision theory is just one of several quite different theories suggested in recent years in attempts to explain how such a pile appeared. No other country in the world illustrates so completely within its borders the geological dictum that the present is a key to the past. It is simply a matter of selecting the right key.

If anyone ever decided to drain the Atlantic Ocean, for example, it would be possible to see Iceland resting on a ridge on the seabed. It is one of the few places on earth where such a "submarine ridge" actually rises above the surface of the sea. That is a clue in itself. The island also has plenty of volcanoes, geysirs, hot springs and boiling mud to hint at its origin. In fact, the whole landscape speaks aloud of the dramatic elemental forces which move continents, form oceans and build mountains – the scientists, however, have yet to agree on their meaning.

Geologically speaking, Iceland is a very young country. No rocks over 20 million years have been found on the land, and none over 65 million years have been found from the shelf under the present sea level. Large areas are thought to have been built up within the last million years or so and, indeed, it is still growing. The emergence of a new island, now known as Surtsey, off the southern coast, proved that to a startled world only twenty years ago.

The present day landscape of Iceland is a product of the building up through this vivid volcanism on the one hand and by weathering, erosion and transport by very

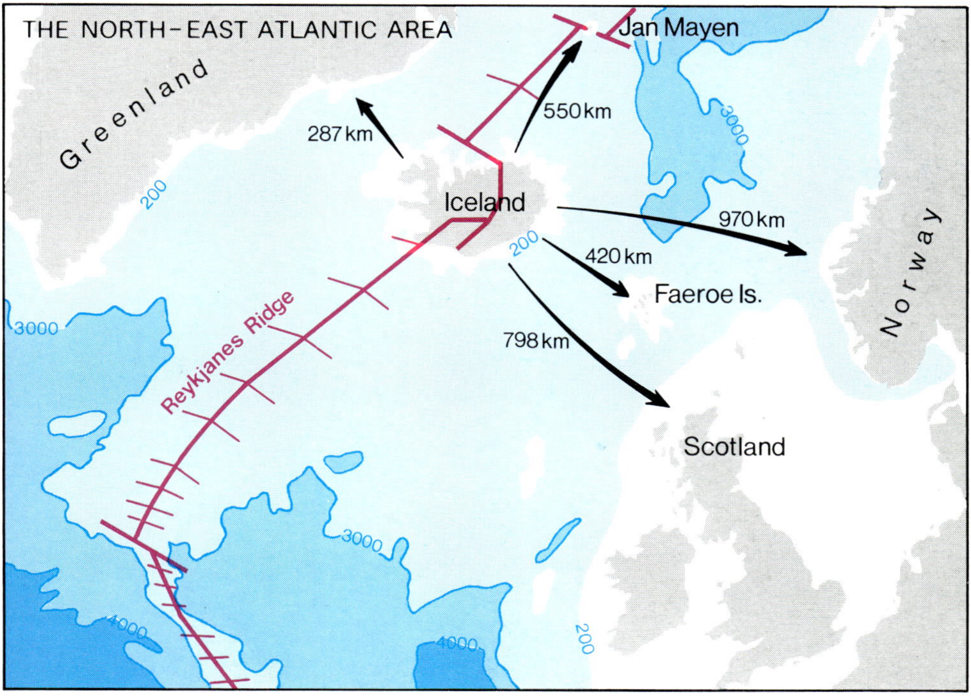

powerful external agencies such as frost, rain, wind, rivers, glaciers and surf on the other. It is a land of contrasts, one of the few places on earth where you can observe volcanoes side-by-side with vast ice-caps spreading into lava fields only recently red-hot and glowing in the night; where you can see Europe's largest glacier, largest waterfall and largest geysir; where you can plunge into a hot thermal spring, even though the land around may be covered in snow; where you can find unnavigable rivers and even where you can find lunar landscapes which provide training grounds for astronauts.

The Republic of Iceland, sitting in the extreme north of the Atlantic Ocean, with its northern shore just short of the Arctic Circle, is the westernmost landmass of Europe. Lying midway between New York and Moscow, it has a total area of just over 100,000 square kilometres (making it the second largest island in Europe and the third largest in the Atlantic) and yet the whole country's population is a mere fraction of either of those cities. The reason is simple: most of the 300 kilometres from north to south and the 500 kilometres from east to west is uninhabitable. No less than 73% of the land is covered with glaciers, lava fields and other wasteland — and 60% is over 400 metres above sea level.

Greenland is the nearest landmass, 287 kilometres away, with the Faroes (418 kilometres), Scotland (798 kilometres) and Norway (970 kilometres) a long way behind. Partly because of this isolation, it was the last European country to be settled.

According to the old Icelandic Sagas, Ice-

The Icelandic flag at the site of the ancient Althing, in Thingvellir, south-west Iceland.

land was given its name by a disgruntled Norwegian Viking. Floki Vilgerdarson was one of the first people to attempt a permanent settlement on the newly discovered island 1100 years ago, in the 860s. During his first summer there Floki, who was a keen angler, became so absorbed in fishing that he forgot to make hay for winter feed to feed his stock. Though not surprised, he was annoyed when most of his animals died, and decided to return to Norway. Before leaving he climbed a mountain and saw a fjord filled with drift ice, which gave him the idea of the name. He thought ill of the land and he wanted to give it an uninviting name. He did, however, later revise his views – and came back to Iceland to settle permanently.

Floki was not the first person ever to have visited Iceland, though. Irish monks, or hermits, were there in the 8th century, but they soon left with the arrival of pagan Norsemen and their Celtic slaves from Britain. From early times these monks had been seeking out uninhabited islands "in order to serve God untroubled by worldly affairs"; but they left Iceland because they "did not wish to live among heathens".

Despite the fact that the Norsemen were faced with an effectively uninhabited volcanic island, well off the main trade routes of the Viking ships that quartered the northern seas at the time, they were the people who systematically settled during the period 870–930 AD. Among them was another famous early Icelander, Ingolfur Arnarson, who fled Norway after a killing. He settled in a bay where he saw steam rising from hot springs, and called the bay Reykjavik (the Icelandic "reykur" means "smoke"). With this act, in 874, Iceland's real history and settlement begins.

The exact proportions of these two nationalities, Norwegian and Celtic, among the Icelanders today is not known. On the one hand, there are almost no traces of Celtic influence on the Icelandic language (though a number of cultural items may be traced to Ireland) while, on the other, blood group investigations show a close similarity between those of the Irish and Icelandic peoples.

As soon as they arrived, the pioneers began to organise themselves and consequently formed a state without parallels at the time. Although the last European country to be settled, Iceland is the seat of the oldest democracy in northern Europe. About 900 AD, when China was a great Empire and the rest of Europe was the spoil of princelings and robber barons, the Icelanders were busying themselves making laws – and breaking them.

They formed their own parliament, called the Althing, and each year the whole community of Norsemen met in a natural amphitheatre in Thingvellir, in the southwest. Legend has it that the site was chosen because the farmer who originally owned the land had killed one of his slaves, and had been outlawed. Justice was seldom so fair in other slave-owning cultures – and never was there such a remarkable beginning to democracy.

At the time, people were relatively well off, had time and ships to travel abroad, and spent many hours composing poems and writing. But in the 13th century times worsened – there was no wood left in the country for shipbuilding – and Iceland became dependent on foreign ships. It was not long before the Icelanders had to forfeit their independence and face centuries of foreign rule. The climate worsened as well, with the so-called "little ice age" in the seventeenth century, and conditions became very bad. Often living in very critical circumstances, they were intermittently ravaged by natural cataclysms, plagues and starvation. Famine was imminent whenever the hay crop or the fish catch failed and people became less resistant to epidemic diseases such as smallpox and the plague. Conditions reached an all-time low in the 18th century. 18,000 people had died in the period 1707–9 alone, due to the worst smallpox epidemic in the country's history. Poisonous gases and ash from volcanoes killed three quarters of all the livestock and thousands of people died from starvation. But the 34,000 record low population (since early in the settlement period) pulled together – and the Icelanders began their fight for survival and independence.

Despite very adverse living conditions during most of the nineteenth century, the population began at last to grow. By 1925 it had reached 100,000 and then doubled again in only 42 years.

Such a dramatic history could not have failed to mould their character and, today, Icelanders are proud of their country and proud of their cultural heritage. They are a very independent people, whose Viking ancestors trailblazed the North Atlantic Sea routes to the New World 1000 years ago and nearly 500 years before Christopher Columbus. But, disgruntled as he was, Floki Vilgerdarson was not a typical Icelander. There is an old saying that Iceland is not a land of ice – the friendliness of the people has melted much of it. Not only are they friendly to visitors, but they give the impression of being the best of friends with everyone else in the country. In Reykjavik, at least, they all seem to know one another!

This may well be true, since Iceland is the most sparsely populated country in Europe, with a national average of only two inhabitants per square kilometre (Norway comes a distant second with thirteen) and a grand total of only sixty towns and villages. Most settlements are limited to the narrow coastal belt and the valleys and lowland plains of the south. Since more than half the nation lives in the capital region of only 50 square kilometres, the rest of the country, more than four fifths of its area, is more or less devoid of human habitation. In fact, it has been estimated that no more than one million people have ever lived in the country since its discovery.

The change from a completely rural to a predominantly urban population has taken place in less than a century. These days, only a proverbial handful of the population lives in rural districts, although until this century most people still derived their livelihood from fishing and farming. Agriculture is still important but it is now mechanised and employs a continually shrinking number of people. Despite this and the fact that only about 20% of the country is suitable for agriculture, Iceland is self-sufficient in meat, poultry and dairy products. But only about 8% of the working population is actually employed in these industries today. The same principle applies to the fisheries – which employ only 14% – even though fishing and fish production account for over 70% of Iceland's exports.

Iceland has changed dramatically in the last century. After hundreds of years of foreign rule, in 1874, the Danish King granted it a separate constitution with a small measure of self-government. It marked the thousandth anniversary of the settlement. From this point there was no turning back – the event proved to be highly significant – both politically and economically. Home rule was granted in 1904, independence (though still in union under the Danish crown) came in 1918, and in 1944 the final goal was reached with the establishment of the new Republic of Iceland. 678 years of foreign rule had ended.

Today, the Icelanders are proud of the fact that, although their country is a vital member of NATO, they have no military force other than a few fishery protection and coastguard vessels.

Iceland relies entirely on NATO and the 1951 defence agreement with the United States, which maintains one of the lowest profile bases in the world at Keflavik, the site of the international airport. Iceland is of crucial strategic importance to the West as it guards both the Greenland and Faeroe gaps through which all Soviet submarines must pass if they wish to enter the North Atlantic. There are currently about 5,000 US personnel and their families at Keflavik.

Iceland today is a modern society. It has one of the highest per capita incomes of any nation in the world – and one of the highest car ownerships in Europe – as well as high standards of education and health. Even life expectancy is among the highest in the world, for both men and women, being 73.9 and 79.5 years respectively.

Despite this gradual migration towards towns, and rapid changes in the space of 100 years, many aspects of the countryside will long be dear to the hearts of Icelanders. Many of the people who are now town-dwellers still confess to a feeling that they

Downtown Reykjavik. A view to the north-east across the bay which marks one of the Icelandic capital's natural borders.

are "transplanted farm folk", as they put it.

Like most of Iceland's towns, the capital Reykjavik grew from a rural habitation beside a good natural harbour. Located on a broad, sweeping bay in the south-west corner of the country, the city is surrounded by a ring of impressive mountains, including a spectacular glacier-shaped volcano, thought to be extinct, far across the bay.

"Reykjavik" literally means Smoky Bay. But, just as the country's name is a chilly misnomer (in the summer, at least), so Reykjavik is practically a smokeless city. So much so that you can quickly get a tan, in comparatively cool weather, simply because the air is so clean and pollution free. Indeed, on cloudless days it is possible to see the Snaefellsjokull glacier across Faxafloi Bay, over 140 kilometres away.

The name owes its origin to the presence of hot springs in the area, breaking through the surface of the earth's crust and emitting clouds of natural steam and mist. Those springs have long since been tamed and put to practical use, with huge pipelines bringing in abundant supplies of naturally heated water to provide all the houses with central heating. What look like large petrol tanks in and around the city are, in fact, hot water storage tanks. Consequently, but to confuse matters even more, Reykjavik has recently acquired a new nickname — "The Smokeless City"!

Modern Reykjavik is a far cry from the desolate anchorage our friend Ingolfur chose, when he stepped ashore more than eleven centuries ago. On the site of that first farmhouse now stands the most

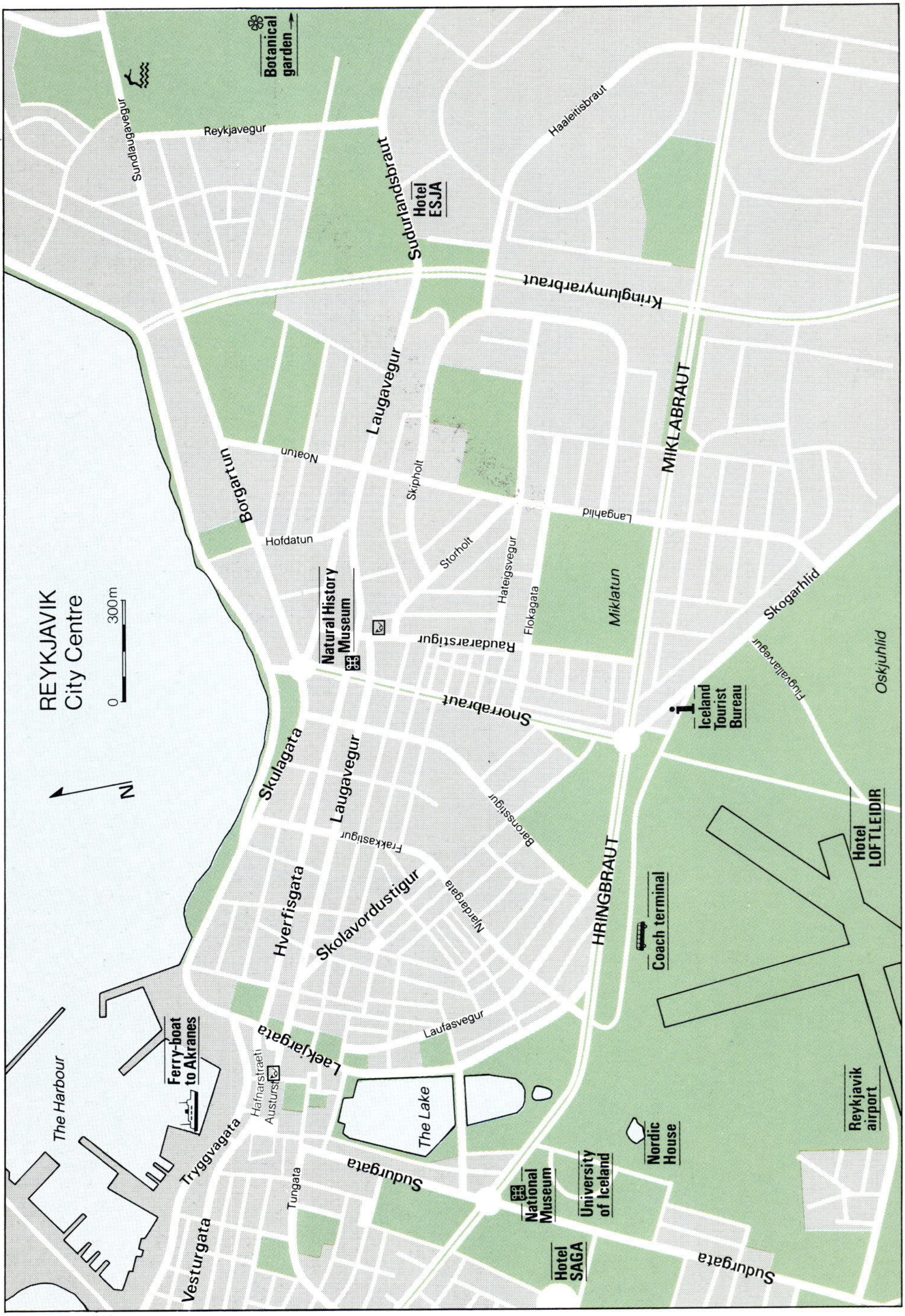
REYKJAVIK
City Centre
0
300m
N
The Harbour
Ferry-boat to Akranes
Tryggvagata
Vesturgata
Hafnarstræti
Austurstr.
Tungata
Lækjargata
The Lake
Sudurgata
National Museum
University of Iceland
Nordic House
Hotel SAGA
Reykjavik airport
Hotel LOFTLEIDIR
Coach terminal
HRINGBRAUT
Laufasvegur
Njardargata
Skolavordustigur
Hverfisgata
Frakkastigur
Laugavegur
Baronsstigur
Skulagata
Snorrabraut
Iceland Tourist Bureau
Flugvallarvegur
Oskjuhlid
Skogarhlid
Miklatun
Flokagata
Hateigsvegur
Raudararstigur
Natural History Museum
Storholt
Skipholt
Langahlid
MIKLABRAUT
Hofdatun
Borgartun
Noatun
Laugavegur
Kringlumyrarbraut
Sudurlandsbraut
Hotel ESJA
Haaleitisbraut
Reykjavegur
Sundlaugavegur
Botanical garden

Aerial view of Akureyri, the "capital" of north Iceland.

northerly metropolis in the world, with a population of 90,000 living within 300 kilometres of the Arctic Circle. It is a bustling city with brightly-coloured houses, attractive shops and excellent restaurants.

It is effectively the centre of the Icelandic nation. From becoming an independent township with 302 inhabitants as recently as 1786, it is now the administrative, commercial and cultural heart of Iceland. It is home to the official government institutions, libraries and museums, higher education and research centres, professional theatres and orchestras, law courts, open-air swimming pools and sports stadiums, shipping lines, air and bus companies, factories and processing plants.

The "capital" of north Iceland is Akureyri, with a population of about 13,000. It is the country's second most important town, beautifully situated at the head of Eyjafjordur on the north coast. Built on a flat spit of land it is rapidly spreading up to the base of the mountains behind. As a residential centre it is little more than 200 years old, but its history as a trading station dates back to before the 16th century. Akureyri has a fishing industry, with herring processing and fish freezing plants, and is one of the country's main manufacturing centres. Now known as the "Town of the Midnight Sun", it is Iceland's main winter sports centre, with a spectacular ski area amongst the pyramid-like peaks, Sulur and Hlidarfjall, above the town. It is particularly famous for its public park, which has living examples of almost every known species of Icelandic vascular plant.

Lone farm buildings in Arnarfjordur, in the western fjords.

Isafjordur is another important town, the largest in the western fjords. Originally called Eyri, it has a long history and a very good harbour. But it is only linked to the rest of the country by road in summer – travel is over high mountain tracks – and they are blocked by snow in winter. Isafjordur ski area, at Seljalandsdalur, is considered among the best in Iceland and it has an important fishing and fish processing industry.

Outside the main towns, lone farm buildings in valleys or along the coast are typical amongst the unwelcoming terrain. Between these dwellings, there are massive glaciers, powerful gushing hot springs that send columns of superheated water high into the air, hundreds of volcanoes (many of them active), vast lava fields like the surface of the moon, fast-flowing rivers, lakes and impressive waterfalls. But, most of all, there is unlimited elbow room. Only 235,000 people live in a country almost half the size of the United Kingdom. The interior, which has an average height of 500 metres above sea level, consists of mountains and high plateaux devoid of man. The highest point in the country is Hvannadalshnjukur in the south-east, reaching 2119 metres above sea level.

Volcanic peaks break into the skyline all over the country and lava fields cover over 10% of the total land area.

As the two great continents of North America and Northern Europe gradually drift apart, the so-called Atlantic Rift, which runs through Iceland, causes spectacular volcanic activities and earthquakes. Iceland sits directly on one of the Earth's major geological faults.

Some 150 to 200 volcanoes have erupted

Hekla, nearly 7,000 years old, was renowned throughout the Catholic world in the Middle Ages as the abode of the damned.

since the end of the Ice Age — thirty of them since settlement of the country — and more than twenty are still active today. Nowadays, on average, an eruption takes place about every five years. Few spots on the globe rival such activity — something like a third of the world production of lava in the last 500 years is "made in Iceland"!

Nearly every type of volcano is found in the country. Lava-producing fissures, forming so-called crater rows, are the most common. In 1783 one of these, the twenty mile long crater-row Lakagigar (which has about 100 separate craters) poured out the biggest lava flow known to have been produced by any single volcano in the world. The gases and ashes from this eruption poisoned massive areas of grassland, causing great havoc to farmers, and eventually resulted in one of the country's worst ever famines and thousands of deaths.

But probably the most famous Icelandic volcano is Hekla. At least 6,600 years old, it was renowned throughout the Catholic world in the Middle Ages as the abode of the damned. Since its first recorded eruption in 1104 Hekla proper has erupted sixteen times and has caused enormous damage throughout a massive section of the country. At the outset of one particular eruption, in March 1947, the eruption column rose to an astonishing 30,000 metres and the lava covered 100 square kilometres. The eruption lasted no less than thirteen months. Hekla recently erupted on a much smaller scale in 1980.

The most dramatic recent volcanic eruption started on the night of 23rd January 1973 on the only inhabited island of the Westmann group, known as Heimaey. In a staggering rescue operation, the entire population of 5,300 was safely moved to the mainland in the space of a few hours. But damage to Heimaey itself was devastating. The eruption lasted until May, by which time half the town was submerged in lava and the rest was covered in thick layers of ashes.

By comparison earthquakes, albeit frequent, are rarely harmful. Minor earth tremors are recorded somewhere in the country virtually every day but the most recent really disastrous earthquakes struck the southern lowlands as long ago as 1784 and 1896. There was another sizeable one in 1934.

The scene of this endless tug-of-war between opposing forces, and the extreme contrasts inherent in Iceland, are nowhere more striking than at the places where fire and ice co-exist. Volcanoes are often situated right underneath glaciers and ice-caps, spectacular sights in themselves. Some of the country's most active volcanoes are hidden under the vast expanse of Vatnajokull, in the south-east, the largest ice-cap in Iceland. Indeed, at 8,400 square kilometres, Vatnajokull is greater in size than all the glaciers and ice-caps of mainland Europe added together. Its maximum thickness is 1000 metres, in places reaching 120 metres beneath sea level. Since Iceland's climate is milder than it once was, during the last few decades most of the country's ice has markedly thinned and retreated. Indeed, some of the smaller caps have all but vanished. Nevertheless, almost all types of glacier are still to be found there, ranging from small cirques to extensive plateau ice-caps. In all, they cover an area of 11,800 square kilometres, or 12% of the total area of the country.

Iceland is also richer in hot springs and solfataras (areas of high-temperature activity) than anywhere else in the world. The temperature gradient on the bedrock is on average two to three times the global average. The main high-temperature areas are Torfajokull, east of Hekla (with a total power output equivalent to 1,500 megawatts) and Grimsvotn, in the Vatnajokull glacier. There are no fewer than 800 hot springs, or low-temperature areas, in Iceland, where the average temperature of the water is 75°C (167°F). The biggest hot spring of all, Deildartunguhver, has a flow of 150 litres (40 gallons) of boiling hot water per second. 78% of all homes in Iceland are heated with water from these hot springs.

Some of the hot springs are spouting springs, or geysirs, the most famous of which is Great Geysir in Haukadalur in the south. This is the one from which the international word "geysir" or "geyser" is derived. It has been known to eject a water column to a height of 60 metres but, sadly, Great Geysir now erupts on a smaller scale — on Sunday afternoons only — and prompted by the addition of soap! But it is surrounded by other, smaller but more active, geysirs.

Rivers in Iceland are extremely numerous and tend to be very full due to heavy rainfall and abundant glacial meltwater. Most of them stem from glaciers and are consequently heavily laden with debris and are rather turbid and grey in colour. Swift currents make most of them, if not all, unnavigable. Along the length of these rivers are many impressive waterfalls, typical of the young landscape. The most famous of these are Gullfoss (32 metres), Dettifoss (44 metres) and Skogafoss (60 metres).

Iceland's coastline, 6,600 kilometres of fjords and headlands, forever being battered by the unruly North Atlantic, also shows a series of land forms of infinite variety, from sandy expanses and rocky headlands to sheer cliffs. There are numerous islands around the coasts, only some of which are inhabited. The largest are

Dramatic shoreline near Vik, on the southernmost point of the country.

Heimaey in the Westmann Islands to the south (with a population of about 5,000), Hrisey to the north (population 300) and Grimsey on the Arctic Circle (population 70).

Like the geology, the Icelandic climate is full of contrasts and surprises. Iceland sits between two very different air masses (of polar and tropical origin) and is affected by the confluence of two different ocean currents. Consequently, the weather is characterised by constantly alternating calms and storms, thaws and snows and generally good and bad weather. It is both impossible and foolhardy to make predictions — they are nearly always contradicted by the reality of events.

In very general terms, the climate is warmer than might otherwise be expected, thanks to the warm waters of the Gulf Stream. Strictly speaking, Iceland is said to enjoy a cool, temperate, oceanic climate. January is the coldest month although, as the locals will proudly tell you, the average daily temperature in Reykjavik (0°C or 32°F) is higher than in New York or Vienna at the same time of year! In July, temperatures rise to a mean of 12°C (55°F) but they can reach much higher. Akureyri is nearly always a few degrees lower. The wettest regions are in the south and south-east; and coastal areas tend to be fairly windy. The weather is generally much more stable in the north, which really has a continental-like climate.

One thing is certain. If you meet Iceland during a bad spell, the Icelanders will cheerfully tell you that they have never known the weather to be so bad for the time of year! Besides, the weather is so changeable that the old adage "if you don't like the weather in Iceland, just wait a minute" is so true that there is no cause for despair. Rain and snow rarely dampen the spirits of the Icelanders — they go bareheaded and umbrellaless in the worst of weather, always confident that it will improve very soon.

The best time to visit is between May and October because, not only is the weather

Nowhere else in Europe offers such a wide variety of natural wonders as the Lake Myvatn area. The region is littered with a range of pseudo-craters, volcanoes and (shown here) colourful muddy sulphur pools.

Iceland is famous for its spouting springs, or geysirs. Strokkur, in Haukadalur in the south, erupts every few minutes.

likely to be at its best, but there is also virtually continuous daylight. In the height of the summer even the lighthouses are switched off since in Reykjavik only two hours separate sunset from sunrise and in the north the sun barely sets at all. The really dark period, with only three or four hours of daylight, lasts from mid-November until the end of January.

In autumn and early winter it is often possible to see the Northern Lights, while early spring and late autumn offer some of the longest and most beautiful twilights anywhere in the world.

May to October is also the best time of year for ornithologists, botanists, mammologists, entomologists and any other bobble hat-wearing, binocular-carrying and field guide-using group of people.

Iceland is an exciting place for all these natural history enthusiasts. Not only is the setting spectacular, and the wildlife abundant, but there is the excitement of the unknown as well. Only 100 years ago there were no roads of any description anywhere in the country. It was not until 1973 that the ring road around Iceland's coastline was completed and there are still many areas of the interior which are inaccessible other than by helicopter. Consequently, the natural history of Iceland is not well known compared with other European countries. New discoveries are being made all the time and there are plenty of opportunities for visiting naturalists to join in the excitement.

So, if you are looking for penguins (they are in the Antarctic!), Eskimos or igloos, long stretches of sun-drenched golden sand or candy floss and thirty six varieties of ice-cream, then Iceland is certainly not the place to go. But if you are looking for 100,000 square kilometres of some of the most unforgettable and previously inaccessible areas of the world — where you can drive or walk for hours, days or weeks without seeing a single soul — or if you are looking for a menagerie of interesting wildlife, or simply a "comfortable adventure", then Iceland, Europe's most beautifully kept secret, is where you will find it.

CHAPTER 2

GREEN ICELAND

One of the main characteristics of the flora of Iceland is its paucity of flowering plants — only about 520 species occur in the country altogether. This is partly because the climate is unfavourable for vegetation, with low temperatures in the summer, a long hard winter and a generally short growing period. It also has something to do with the fact that, not so long ago, indeed only about 20,000 years ago, most of the country was entirely covered with the glaciers of the last Ice Age. Icelandic botanists believe that less than half — possibly as few as a quarter — of the vascular plants around today are glacial survivors. No doubt the isolation of Iceland, stuck out in the middle of the sea miles from anywhere, provides limited possibilities for immigration from other land masses, and also keeps numbers low.

It seems that some scientists cannot accept such a short list — even though many of the species which do occur are particularly interesting — and there have been several attempts to make it longer! There is still a great deal of controversy, but most

Preceding pages: Although a striking feature of Iceland is the nakedness of its land, some parts of the country are luxuriantly green.

At the time of the settlement, Iceland was "wooded from the shoreline to the mountain slope". Today, this wood at Hallormsstadaskogur is one of only two sizeable woods left.

specialists agree that about 520 is the most accurate figure. In the past, nearly 200 "species" of hawkweed and over 100 "species" of dandelion have bumped up the numbers — but nearly all of them turned out to be varieties or, at best, sub-species.

Despite all these problems, Iceland did once have a great deal, if not a great variety, of vegetation, covering more than half its total land area. There were no wild herbivorous mammals in the country at all and, for all the years since the end of the last Ice Age, the vegetation had evolved relatively undisturbed by grazing animals. Then man arrived.

Farming has been the principal employment of Icelanders since the land was settled in the 9th century. The first people to arrive brought large numbers of livestock with them from their Norwegian homes — mostly cattle — but also sheep, horses, pigs and goats. Grazing areas were utilized to the full and the vegetation, chief protector of Iceland's easily-eroded soils, began to deteriorate. Vast areas of woodland were cut for fuel and charcoal-making, and burned to improve grazing, the deterioration became worse and, in many areas, soil erosion set in. At the same time, the climate became colder and ash and pumice from several great volcanic eruptions added to the devastation.

The disappearing vegetation was noted as early as the 1120s, when the Book of Icelanders ("Islendingabok") is thought to have been written. It commented that "at the time of the settlement, Iceland was wooded from the shoreline to the mountain slope". But the trend was allowed to continue and, if anything, it actually speeded up.

American soldiers, unfortunately unaware of this fact, were enticed to Iceland during the Second World War with the promise that "there is a virgin under every tree". They arrived to find that the birch trees, which once blanketed almost half the total vegetated area, had all but disappeared. Today, the original stands have been reduced to mere remnants of what they once were. Less than a quarter of Iceland is covered in vegetation of any kind — and trees comprise barely 1% of this. While some birch are scattered in a few sheltered places in the valleys of the lowlands, only two sizeable woods are left — the biggest is at Hallormsstadaskogur in the east — the other being Fnjoskadalur in the north. Birch are the only trees which occur in any numbers (mostly downy birch) — and the tallest of these are hardly twelve metres high. The bulk of the woods is increased with some shrubby species such as rowan and tea-leaved willow.

Developing tourism and ever-increasing travel threaten the surviving and still-vulnerable vegetation even more these days. Driving on untouched ground, for example, puts pressure on sensitive land which can take years to recover — if erosion does not remove the topsoil first.

The resultant nakedness of the land, with large areas of bare rock, stony deserts, sandy wastelands and lava fields, is a very striking feature which distinguishes Iceland in many ways from other countries in Europe. Extensive areas, especially on the highland plateau of the interior, have always been almost bare of vegetation, as have large areas around the ice-caps and in front of the glaciers. New lava flows and ash from volcanoes have sometimes covered great areas of land and killed or damaged all the vegetation. And, largely due to Iceland's latitude, the natural upper limit of continuous vegetation cover is found at a rather low altitude: thick cover is never found much above 700 metres. Above this height, the land is reserved for a few scattered individuals of hardy arctic-alpine species, along with some lichens and mosses. The tree-line is even lower, averaging no more than 200—400 metres. So Ice-

land's plants have always had to contend with hardships, long before man ever arrived. Man's artificial changes have simply been too dramatic, too rapid and too serious, even for Iceland's hardy species.

But what the flora lacks in quantity it makes up for in quality. Situated in the Atlantic, mid-way between Europe and America, and lying on the boundary of the Arctic and boreal regions, Iceland does have an extremely interesting and varied flora. What is more, provided that sheep and other grazing animals can be kept away from the buds and saplings, birch and various evergreens can still thrive there — and are being re-introduced to suitable areas as part of a major reafforestation scheme — so the potential for retrieving the original luxuriance is still there.

The Icelandic flora is of fairly mixed origin but could be described as north European in character. About two thirds of the vascular plants are dicotyledons and the remaining third monocotyledons — a proportion very similar to that found in most northern countries. Perhaps ironically, considering all the damage that has been done, about 100 species are thought to have originated as man-made introductions, both accidental and intentional, from other countries in Europe. Most of the species which are known to occur are also found in Scandinavia, some 350 of them are found in Britain, and only about 275 from Greenland.

Overall, it has a relatively small western element (the proportion of plants with their main area of distribution west of Iceland) compared to the dominating eastern element. But, despite the north European influence, just over 100 species are also found in America. A few of these grow in Iceland and nowhere else in Europe. These are lyngbye's sedge, a tall and beautiful plant, often found growing densely and forming a fairly broad zone of vegetation around estuaries and areas flooded by rivers every year; arctic riverbeauty, which is a purple willowherb growing densely on gravelly river banks, in river gorges or in

Preceding pages: Iceland's striking landscape is unlike any other found in Europe, as this aerial view over Langisjor, to the west of Vatnajokull, shows.

Cotton grass is so common in some areas that it blankets the ground.

Cushions of moss campion add colour to the Icelandic countryside.

gravelly dried-out river beds in many parts of the country; northern green orchid, which has sweetly-scented flowers and lives on grassy slopes in lowlands all over the country; sea rocket, which is common in the south-west, south and north-west; arctic wintergreen, which is found at a few sites in the north; marsh felwort, which has an attractive overall bluish tint and is occasionally found on river banks over most of the country; and broad-leaved willow, a variable species growing all over the country. Recent work has questioned whether or not the broad-leaved willow is a true American species after all, but it has been included here for its obvious interest, even though it is a controversial subject among many botanists.

It is probably more accurate to describe the vegetation as oceanic sub-arctic in character. Although the mainland of Iceland is situated just south of the Arctic Circle, it still supports the largest area of ice in Europe and, consequently, much of the plant life is arctic. Probably as many as a third may be characterised as arctic-alpine species. This is interesting because it means that many of the common Icelandic plants are the sought-after rarities from further south, in Scotland for example.

Although there are a number of rare and local species, over 30 of which are officially protected by law, and a considerable number that have a restricted distribution, the floral differences between different parts of the country are not as great as might be expected. The north is obviously where most of the arctic species, such as alpine whitlow-grass, mountain heath and arctic harebell, occur in greatest numbers but most other plants are widely distributed.

Yet there are many factors likely to be influencing their distribution patterns. There are great variations in temperature, rainfall and wind, largely according to the altitude or distance from the coast and the warm Gulf Stream. Frost action, glacial melt-water and snow cover in winter are also important ecological factors in most parts of the country. Why more plants do not have restricted distributions within Iceland due to some of these ecological factors is an interesting phenomenon.

The lowlands are characterised by grasslands and heaths, with intermittent and frequent bogs and marshes. For this reason, grasses and sedges are far and away the commonest groups in the country, with nearly 100 species between them.

The bogs are extensive and cover large areas of Iceland. Apart from the sedges, horsetails and various dwarf shrubs are among the commonest plants in these areas, as well as rushes and cotton-grass which blanket the ground in some places. But this may soon change with today's extensive and large-scale operations to drain the bogs, in order to replace the natural vegetation with grasses for livestock grazing. Outside the central highlands, many bogs have already been drained for cultivation, mostly with the help of subsidies from the State amounting to some 70% of the total cost. The highlands themselves have so far escaped most of this damage — and harbour a few outstanding tundra-like bogs.

Low-growing shrubs are dominant on the heathland, especially heather, crowberry, bog whortleberry, bearberry and dwarf birch, which often cover large areas of both heathland and moorland.

The grasslands and wet meadows are full of beautifully-flowered members of the pink, saxifrage, rose and daisy families. Depressions at lower altitudes are often covered in flowers of these families. Herbs also add some colour, including lady's bedstraw, and there are enormous numbers of hawkweeds and dandelions, probably commoner in terms of sheer numbers than any other species in Iceland.

Iceland has about 1,000 different species of mosses, liverworts and lichens.

Ridges, covered with gravel and stones, often rise above the surrounding level stretches of grasslands, heaths and bogs and many species grow scattered between the stones. Among these are mountain avens, thyme, moss campion, thrift and alpine mouse-ear, all of which are common.

Another interesting, though more unusual, habitat is the warm soil around Iceland's hot springs, which is particularly favourable for vegetation and provides a home for characteristic species found nowhere else in the country. These include adder's tongue spearwort, redleg, marsh

pennywort, water speedwell, marsh cudweed and other species of characteristically southern origin. Commonly, some bacteria and algae are also found — living actually in the hot water itself.

Another unusual habitat lies in the interior. Vascular plants that are more often associated with the coast, such as thrift and sea campion, are often found in Iceland growing on the sand dunes of the central desert.

The many wetlands are also good for plants — Lake Myvatn, for example, has some of the richest vegetation in the country along its shores. Certainly the most evident of these plants (though, ironically, rarely found at Myvatn!) is cotton-grass, or bog-cotton, which imparts a special look to wetlands in late summer, with its fluffy heads. Cotton-grass is so common in many areas that, for years, it provided a ready supply of its wool-like material for use as candle and lantern wicks.

Faced with such a variety of conditions and habitats in a comparatively small space, visitors, who rarely have as much time as they would like, can have problems identifying plants in Iceland. The fact that many of the indigenous species flower for extremely short periods does not help either. They never seem to be in the right stage of flower or fruit when you see them! A worthwhile visit, therefore, is to the Botanical Garden in Akureyri (there is a similar, though much smaller, one in Reykjavik) which was founded by the ladies of the town in 1912. It boasts living examples of almost all the native vascular plants of Iceland and, since most of them are labelled, provides an excellent opportunity to get to grips with the more difficult species.

To stretch the identification skills even more, Iceland has a considerably longer list of non-flowering plants. These include about 550 different species of bryophytes, the mosses and liverworts, which are more abundant in Iceland than anywhere in northern Scandinavia or Greenland. They are particularly common on the older lava-flows and form an almost continuous carpet in the absence of vascular plants.

Eventually, these are replaced by dwarf shrubs and, later on, by birch. But there are some beautifully developed young moss carpets in the south (almost entirely of **Racomitrium lanuginosum**, with some **Racomitrium canescens**) and in the Budahraun and Myvatn areas, with luxuriant growths of ferns, herbs and grasses in some of the sheltered crevices and depressions to add to the spectacle.

The Iceland moss (**Cetraria islandica**) is particularly famous but the sword moss (**Bryoxiphium norvegicum**) is probably a more interesting species found virtually nowhere else in Europe. In Iceland it was discovered at Lake Kleifarvatn, 25 kilometres south of Reykjavik, and has since been found all over the country in the new volcanic zone, from the south-west to the north-east. But not all Iceland's mosses are arctic species. On the contrary, there are even more temperate bryophytes than there are temperate species in the vascular groups.

Iceland also has about 450 different species of lichens, generally Scandinavian in character, which join the mosses on some of their lava carpets and in many parts of the otherwise bare mountains.

About 250—300 mushroom species are known to exist in the country. Many of them are edible, very few are poisonous and none are deadly poisonous. There are about 200 species of seaweed, with a luxuriant littoral growth of them around most of Iceland's coastline. On the whole, these species are very similar to the algae along the coasts of north Norway, but one species in particular — "söl" — is interesting because it used to be eaten by some Icelanders. There is a considerable difference, possibly due to varying water temperatures, between the species found in the north-east and east, which are primarily of arctic origin, and those found in the south-west and south, where the arctic species are replaced by warm boreal water varieties. There is also a considerable difference between the inner parts of the fjords and the outer coast. These spatial differences are in stark contrast to the generally wide distribution of terrestrial plant species.

CHAPTER 3

ICELAND IN THE AIR

There are enormous numbers of birds in Iceland. Many millions of them converge on the country each spring to breed, forming some of the most spectacular nesting colonies to be seen anywhere in the world. And it has some of the most remarkable urban birds in Europe: Reykjavik with its own small colony of arctic terns, nesting right in the city centre, and Akureyri with its harlequin ducks.

Iceland is also ideally situated for vagrant and migrating species, which have attracted almost as much interest among ornithologists as the breeding colonies. An organised effort to collect and store information on rare visitors can be traced back to 1937, when Finnur Gudmundsson (late curator of the Icelandic Museum of Natural History) began getting naturalists in various parts of the country to send him information on birds seen, or the specimens themselves.

Then, early in 1980, a group of bird watchers in cooperation with the Museum established an unofficial committee to deal

with all these records. The aim of the committee is to collect records of rare birds in Iceland, check their validity and publish annual reports on their findings. Each of the eleven members consider rare bird reports independently and if two or more of them do not accept a record it is therefore not published.

The records show that on average, three to four new bird species have been added to the Iceland list every year since the early 1940s.

Most of these are accidentals, arriving from both sides of the Atlantic only once or, at most, just a handful of times. Some will probably never be seen again – the chances of seeing another yellow-bellied sapsucker, for example, are just about nil – but it is exciting to think that at the right time of year virtually anything can turn up. It is by no means uncommon for visiting birders on holiday to discover a "new" species for Iceland, an honourable claim to fame in the world of ornithology.

Other migrants are more regular visitors recorded annually but still in fairly low numbers, including ruff, grey plover, pomarine skua (mostly from boats out at sea) and great shearwater, which is a summer visitor possibly occurring in greater numbers than once believed. All these migrants and accidental visitors have so far bumped the Iceland bird list up to over 300 species. But compared with other European countries, Iceland has very few resident species. Because of its northerly latitude, daylight hours are very short in winter – so resident birds have to overcome the problem of severely limited feeding times – as well as the usual winter hardships. Many inevitably avoid such seasonal rigours by migrating.

In contrast, several species are nevertheless common in winter – but have never, or only rarely, attempted to breed. The blackbird is among these and has attempted to breed only twice. This may partly be explained by the fact that some species cannot cope with the lack of suitable habitats (especially the absence of real woods), the general scarcity of insect life and the unpredictable weather. Among the commoner nesting passerines which have overcome these problems, only the raven, snow bunting, redpoll and Icelandic wren are resident, while the meadow pipit, white wagtail, redwing and wheatear, albeit common, are summer visitors. The starling has been established only since about 1940, but as a breeding bird its distribution is still restricted.

But an increasing number of visiting birds are making breeding attempts and, in the last 60–70 years, the number of nesting species has increased considerably. 73 species are now known to be regular breeders. Several more are breeding irregularly, or regularly but rarely, including the fieldfare (which is a common winter visitor) and house sparrow, though none of them is anywhere near settled permanently. Swallows nest irregularly, but have undoubtedly been doing so for several centuries. Coots, lapwings and collared doves have all bred a few times. Shoveler, tufted duck, pochard, lesser black-backed, herring, common and black-headed gulls, short-eared owl and wood sandpiper have all colonized since the beginning of the century as well but these are all now firmly established.

This all suggests, perhaps because of its relative isolation, that Iceland has not yet been fully settled zoologically. The country's changing climate may also be an influence. It has been getting gradually warmer in Iceland since 1950 so, if the rise in temperature continues, we may expect to see further additions to the breeding list in coming years. It is an exciting prospect.

But, above all, it is the individual abundance and tameness of the well-established breeding birds, together with a handful of "Icelandic specialities", which really make Iceland such a popular destination for bird watchers from all corners of the globe.

There is a strange mixture of arctic, temperate, American and European species. Several American birds are found in Iceland but nowhere else in Europe, making it the easternmost outpost of these New World species. Similarly, lying in the middle of the ocean, it is the westernmost outpost of several Old World species. There are also a number of Icelandic birds which

Preceding pages: Many millions of birds converge on Iceland each spring to breed, many others occur as vagrant or migrating species.

The arctic tern, photographed here at Hafnarfjordur Harbour, is the only breeding tern in Iceland, but nests in enormous numbers.

have been described as separate subspecies or races, including the merlin, black guillemot, water rail and black-tailed godwit, and found in no other country in the world. For example, the Iceland wren, the smallest breeding bird in the country (and perhaps nowhere more numerous than at Oraefi) is a sub-species of the common wren found exclusively in Iceland while the Iceland falcon, the most celebrated of all Iceland's birds, is a race of the gyrfalcon, found only in this country.

The best time of year to visit Iceland for bird watching is during May, June and early July to view the seabird colonies, breeding waterfowl and other wetland birds, and the resident birds of prey. These are undoubtedly the three main attractions. Any time from August through to October, or late March, April and May, can be good for migrants and rarities, particularly in the south-west.

Seabirds

The cool, rich waters surrounding Iceland provide bountiful fishing for enormous populations of seabirds. No fewer than 23 species nest in Iceland, many of them in astronomical numbers: fulmar, storm petrel, Leach's petrel, gannet, kittiwake, shag, cormorant, arctic tern, manx shearwater, arctic skua, great skua, eider, little auk, razorbill, common guillemot, Brunnich's guillemot, black guillemot, puffin, common gull, herring gull, lesser black-backed gull, great black-backed gull and glaucous gull.

Despite their collective name, not all of

them nest by the sea, though some, such as the gannets and kittiwakes, are exclusively oceanic. Arctic terns can often be seen fishing on lakes a long way inland, while fulmars regularly nest on inland cliffs (but always fly to the sea to feed). Skuas also nest, in fairly large colonies, inland. There are records of nesting as far as 120 kilometres from the nearest coast, for example at Thjorsarver, Central Iceland, though this involved only one pair.

Although seabirds often congregate in dense colonies at localized spots, precise estimates of their numbers are very difficult. Counting nests is often either impractical or impossible, because they are either hidden or inaccessible. Similarly, counting individual birds has its problems as they are constantly flying around!

The easiest species to census are those nesting on level ground or in distinct colonies, such as gannets, shags and cormorants. Even colonies of this kind that are difficult to reach can be counted by aerial photography.

Nevertheless, the whereabouts of all seabird colonies in Iceland is not documented and some populations fluctuate considerably from year to year. Population figures given in this section are therefore mostly "guesstimates" (though many are based on actual counts), but do give an indication of relative abundances.

Similarly based on largely incomplete evidence are the many theories about the winter quarters of Iceland's seabirds. There has been a fairly large-scale research programme during the last decade involving the ringing of large numbers of seabirds, and some, such as the puffin, fulmar and arctic tern had been ringed in appreciable numbers before. But there are still many gaps in our knowledge and the comments on some species are necessarily based on unproven theories.

The emblem of Iceland, the puffin, is perhaps the best known of all the country's seabirds. It is also one of the commonest — there are believed to be between eight and ten million pairs of them — which is more than at any other single location anywhere else in the world.

The puffin nests in greater numbers in the Westmann Islands than at any other single location anywhere else in the world.

Icelandic for puffin is "lundi" or "prófastur", a term otherwise used to denote a churchman of high rank, and no doubt referring to the bird's dignified looks. Amusing and fussy characters, they insist on nesting sites protected from surf action but with a sea view, and are only really happy with lush grass all around and thick soil underneath. Puffins nest on grassy slopes on the top of islands or islets, and on the grassy ledges of cliffs, all around Iceland's coasts. Normally, they dig burrows in the soil, though occasionally they lay their eggs in boulder screes or under rocks. They dig through the turf with their powerful beaks and webbed claws, burrowing deep holes often two metres in length in which to lay their single egg. The young bird, when it hatches, is then protected in the tunnel from bad weather and enemies such as skuas and gulls.

The largest puffin colonies are found in the Westmann Islands to the south and the islands of Breidafjordur in the west. They are very precise birds, arriving at the nesting cliffs after their annual migrations from the high seas south and south-west of Iceland or even, in the case of first year birds, sometimes from Newfoundland, nearly always between April 17th and 24th! They even return to the exact holes they occupied the previous year.

Immediately on arrival they set to work cleaning and tidying up the old nests. They also work very hard in their search for food for the offspring, flying back and forth from the sea with beakloads of up to ten or more small fish neatly arranged in a row. After such a hectic summer, they leave their cliff ledges in August or September and eventually fly back to their winter

quarters — a journey which can take as little as three weeks. The young puffins, however, are often delayed. After leaving the sanctuary of their nests they easily get confused and aim for the bright lights of nearby towns, such as Vik or Heimaey, landing, somewhat bemused, amongst the houses. It is a favourite and exciting pastime of Westmann Islands children to spend some of their summer and early autumn evenings collecting puffins from the streets ready to release them from the beaches next morning. The one who saves the most becomes the "Puffin Fledgling King" for a year.

All six species of auk that inhabit the North Atlantic breed in Iceland. While the puffin is the commonest, the little auk, at the other end of the scale, is represented by just two nesting pairs. They once nested at several points on the mainland, particularly on the Langanes peninsula in the north-east, and are still very common further north in Greenland and Spitzbergen. But today, in Iceland, little auks nest only among boulder screes on the island of Grimsey in the north. They are well protected by law — you need a permit just to approach the breeding area — but, for once, the main problem is thought to be one of climate. Little auks are really high arctic birds, preferring the kind of weather human visitors like to avoid, and Iceland is at the southern extreme of their natural breeding range. So they have probably suffered due to the climatic improvement in Iceland of recent years.

Nevertheless, while they are very rare breeders, in winter they visit in large numbers from the north. It is thought that these individuals come from Spitzbergen, but no-one is really sure. Their numbers vary considerably depending on the state of the sea ice, but most winters they can be seen along the north and east coasts without too much difficulty. In particularly bad weather they are occasionally wrecked some way inland.

The remaining four auks all occur in good numbers. Common guillemots are probably the commonest, and Brunnich's are also numerous. Iceland is one of very few places in the world where the two overlap — since the Brunnich's is usually a more northerly species. The common guillemot exhibits two different colour forms: the bridled (with a white eye ring and trailing stripe) and the unbridled. The proportion of each varies from colony to colony, but there is a general trend whereby the bridled form becomes increasingly more common towards the south. 50% of the common guillemots in the Westmann Islands are bridled, compared with only 10% in the northern colonies. The total population is about two million pairs, compared with some 1.6 million for

A bridled guillemot, one of two different colour forms of the common guillemot found in Iceland.

Fulmars gather in their hundreds or thousands around fishing boats, processing plants and the whaling station at Hvalfjordur (seen here feeding on a fin whale carcass).

Brunnich's. Both species are also common in Icelandic waters during winter.

Razorbills come next, with slightly under one million pairs, breeding on cliff ledges all around the country. Although few have been ringed in Iceland, it is likely that they winter in the Faeroe Islands.

The black guillemot, or tystie, is considerably rarer than the others, with a maximum of 100,000 breeding pairs (and most likely considerably less), and does not nest in such dense colonies. It prefers a more solitary way of life than any of its relatives. Although it is well dispersed around most of the country's coasts and islands, its distribution is thought to have been adversely affected by mink, though it is still uncertain whether or not this has led to an actual decline in the overall population number. About a third of the young birds winter in Greenland, while the breeders are thought to stay near their breeding areas, rarely moving more than a few kilometres away. Icelanders in olden times used to think the whole population disappeared into sea caves during the winter. They were unaware of the seasonal change from a black coat with a white patch on each wing in summer to a white winter coat! Incidentally, the Icelandic subspecies has very faint black lines on the white wing patches, though they are extremely difficult to distinguish in the field. This variety is only found in Iceland and Greenland. As with all black guillemots, only their bright red feet and bills retain their colour throughout the year.

Black guillemots are settled in their nesting areas by the end of March, even though they do not actually lay eggs until about two months later. The one or two young hatch out after about four weeks. The next four weeks for the young birds are spent eating – they prefer bright red butterfish – with twenty or more meals a day. The adults have to drop and retrieve these fish repeatedly before returning to the nest, as they are able to survive out of water longer than most other species. Even so, it is still common to see butterfish alive and wrig-

More than ten per cent of the world's gannet population nests in Iceland — some 22,000 pairs.

gling when being swallowed by an eager young guillemot. They seem happy with the technique, though, and use it for other species of fish as well.

Another cliff-nester, the fulmar, was once only found on Grimsey. But the population began to expand southwards (from Spitzbergen to the UK) in the mid-1700s and the species is now a very common breeder all around Iceland even, in the Markarfljot canyons, about 50 kilometres inland. The total population is now well over one million pairs. They gather in their hundreds or thousands around fishing boats, processing plants and the whaling station at Hvalfjordur.

They were very common at the beginning of the century and enormous numbers were killed by Icelanders for food. But suddenly, in 1936, psittacosis appeared and threatened to kill many of the bird catchers, as it had already done in the Faeroes. The taking of fulmars was forbidden by law in 1940 and, although the ban was later lifted, fulmar-catching has not really caught on again.

With 22,000 breeding pairs, the gannet is — on a world scale — another very common breeding bird in Iceland. Compared with millions of auks, such a population may seem rather small, but it amounts to more than 10% of the world population. The gannet is the largest seabird of the North Atlantic, with a wingspan of nearly two metres, and roams widely between both sides of its shores. Breeding, however, is restricted to only a few colonies, usually on isolated offshore islands and stacks. There are only about 40 such gannet colonies in the whole world, and only half of them have more than 1,000 pairs.

There are two separate gannet "breeding stations" in Iceland, and one of these (in the Westmann Islands) is divided into four separate colonies. The other, by far the most well-known, is Eldey, south-west of the Reykjanes peninsula, which is the third largest gannet colony in the world (behind St. Kilda and Grassholm in the United Kingdom). It has been a nature reserve since 1940 and provides a home for up to 16,000 nesting pairs.

Four other sites, at Raudinupur in the north-east (where small numbers still nest), Drangey and Grimsey in the north, Geirfuglasker off the Reykjanes peninsula and Sulustapi in the north-west, were all once gannet stations of various sizes but are now more or less extinct. Two were destroyed by earthquakes (one as recently as 1934); the others disappeared largely at the hands of man.

Icelandic gannets travel southwards along European coasts in winter, all the way to north-west Africa. They were once highly prized as indicators of shoals of herring and other fish, due to their conspicuous hunting method of spectacularly diving into the water after their prey from as high as 50 metres. Nowadays, though, electronics have made the gannet redundant in this function.

To visiting bird watchers, three more seabird species hold a particular interest in Iceland: the manx shearwater, Leach's petrel and storm petrel. It is the most northerly breeding station of all three, though they are rarely seen due to their nocturnal habits. Iceland is a kind of meeting point for them — manx shearwaters (which appear in May) and storm petrels (which are the last seabirds in Iceland to breed, during July) have their main breeding grounds in Britain — while Leach's petrels have their stronghold on the other side of the Atlantic, in Newfoundland. The shearwaters belong to the same race as those which nest in Britain and are believed to follow much the same migratory pattern, spending the winter off the South American coast, south of the Equator. Similarly, the petrels are thought to join their British counterparts in South Africa.

Until 1977, the Westmann Islands were

thought to be the only breeding place for these birds. But both petrels have since been discovered nesting at Ingolfshofdi and there have been unconfirmed reports from Reynisfjall. The total maximum breeding populations have been estimated at 10,000 pairs each, but sceptics suggest that a figure of 1,000 may be more reasonable.

The arctic tern is another special Icelandic attraction. It is the only breeding tern in the country, nesting in enormous numbers around the coast and, for example at Lake Myvatn, several places inland, with up to a million pairs in all. Large colonies are found at Vik in the south, Hellissandur in the west and on Hrisey Island in the north. Arctic terns are very popular with the Icelanders, being the harbingers of spring and a never-ending source of wonder. The majority of Iceland's birds seem to spend the winter off the southwest African coast, but some travel on further, a total of some 17,000 kilometres, to Antarctica.

The slavonian, or horned, grebe is Iceland's only resident grebe.

The great skua, along with its cousin the arctic skua, nests along coastal areas around Iceland.

In complete contrast, many shags and cormorants have been ringed in Iceland but few recoveries have come from abroad. In winter, the cormorants spread all around the Icelandic coastline, while shags congregate mostly in the western half of the country. Both species nest almost exclusively on the mainland's west coast and on the islands of Breidafjordur and Faxafloi. Cormorant numbers have declined since the beginning of the century, now standing at less than 4,000 pairs, and the breeding range too has decreased. Shooting is thought to be partly to blame but

also, particularly in the north, ice may have scraped and destroyed the benthic fauna in the littoral zone where they find most of their food. There are considerably more shags, with a total of 7,000 breeding pairs.

As far as gulls are concerned, the kittiwake is a particularly common species, with somewhere between 100,000 and one million breeding pairs. It usually nests on vertical cliffs and, among many other species, noticeably favours the enormous bird cliffs on Grimsey and the Westmann Islands. It is a pelagic bird and disperses, mostly to northern Greenland waters, in winter.

Most of the other gulls are new immigrants: common, herring, lesser black-backed and black-headed (though not strictly a seabird) have all colonized Iceland since 1920. The great black-backed gull has been present much longer and is very common throughout the country, while glaucous gulls are restricted almost exclusively to the Breidafjordur area as nesting birds, though they can be seen all along the west coast and all around Iceland in winter. Incidentally, despite its name, the Iceland gull does not nest in Iceland at all (its main breeding grounds are in western Greenland) but it is a very common winter visitor.

Arctic skuas are very common throughout the country (though more so in the south), while great skuas mostly inhabit the vast fluvio-glacial outwash plains in the south and south-east. The majority of Iceland's 12,000 or so nesting pairs of great skuas are to be found in this area, notably on the Skeidararsandur sands, in and around Skaftafell National Park, in the south-east, during May and early June. This is their biggest breeding ground in the northern hemisphere.

Birds of Prey

In addition to nearly a dozen visiting birds of prey which have been recorded in Iceland, there are three resident species — the Iceland falcon, merlin and white-tailed

Above: The larger and whiter form of the gyrfalcon, the Iceland falcon, is found nowhere else in the world. Approximately 200 pairs breed in the country altogether.

Below: Ptarmigan are one main food of the gyrfalcon. Every winter, the toll on them is so heavy that their numbers are reduced by up to a third.

eagle — plus two species of owl. This is a small number of nesters compared with other countries, partly because of the isolation of Iceland and partly because the small mammals and birds in their diet are not particularly plentiful.

The merlin is the most common bird of prey in Iceland; with the exception of the central highlands, it is found all over the country. It is also the only truly migratory bird of prey in Iceland — most of them leave in autumn for western Europe — but some do remain for the winter.

The size of the population is unknown precisely, but there has almost certainly been a decline in recent years. The cause is not clear. The Icelandic merlin is a special sub-species, **Falco columbarius subaesalon.** It is found mostly on heaths and moorland, usually avoiding forests and mountain areas. It feeds mainly on redwings, meadow pipits, wheatears and waders, as well as occasional young arctic terns and ptarmigan, and in winter often chases snow buntings into towns.

The larger and whiter form of the gyrfalcon, the Iceland falcon, (believed by many scientists to be an entirely separate race from the birds in Scandinavia) is found nowhere else in the world. It is the national bird of Iceland and its mobility and powerful character have attracted attention from all over Europe for centuries. In aristocratic circles, a prize of a falcon from Iceland was regarded as a special privilege by winners of contests, and their value was so high that royalty used them as diplomatic gifts and as ransom in exchange for prisoners. They were used for hunting and regularly trained by the nobility of Denmark, Norway, Germany, France, England and other countries. Up to 200 birds were being exported every year at one time.

In the sixteenth century, the King of Denmark claimed ownership of all gyrfalcons in Iceland. He hired out the right to catch them and this became a considerable source of income for the Danish Crown. He benefited greatly from giving falcons to other Heads of State as tokens of friendship. Even two centuries later, when pirates from the North African coast were plundering ships sailing through the Mediterranean, Danish ships were allowed to sail unimpeded. But interest in falcon hunting dwindled greatly in Europe towards the end of the eighteenth century and such royal capture died out soon after.

Perhaps surprisingly, it is still a widely distributed bird, with an estimated 200 pairs breeding in the country altogether, and can be seen almost anywhere, even in Reykjavik. Gyrfalcons have been fully protected by law since 1913 except for a ten year period, from 1930—40, when the protection was lifted and there were a number of foreign expeditions to Iceland to capture the birds. Approaching too close to their nests is prohibited, as is photographing the birds at their nests except with special permission from the Ministry of Culture, which is granted only after consultation with the Bird Protection Committee. Such laws are obviously difficult to enforce, but on several occasions in recent years people have been caught and found guilty of removing chicks and eggs from nests. But trade in the birds is now an extensive underworld business, despite the threat of fines of many thousands of dollars. Stuffed gyrfalcons are popular as ornaments in some parts of the world, the eggs are highly sought-after by collectors and young birds are much prized by falconers.

Gyrfalcons are most common around the north-west peninsula, where they nest on cliffs near lagoons in the lowlands; in Skagafjordur in the north; and near Husavik. The exact sites within these three areas are not named for obvious reasons. They choose uncushioned ledges or abandoned ravens' nests on which to lay their eggs. Sometimes these nests aren't even aban-

doned — but it is futile for the hapless ravens to try repossession — they simply have to build again. The young falcons leave in July, when they are two months old, and stick together for a while before assuming their independence.

Gyrfalcons are best known for their manoeuvring ability in the air, a skill the Icelandic birds use to the full in hunting their main diet of other birds, chiefly ptarmigan.

During late autumn and winter they often move to the coasts, but most choose to follow the ptarmigan flocks. During winter, the toll on ptarmigan is so heavy that Iceland falcons reduce their numbers by up to a third each year. Indeed, the two species' numbers tend to fluctuate together — which gave rise to an old Icelandic legend that the ptarmigan is the Iceland falcon's sister. They do separate for a while in midsummer, when the ptarmigan is at its scarcest and the falcons search for other prey such as wading birds, only returning late in July when the new broods have formed into large flocks once again.

Thirty or more pairs of white-tailed eagles now nest fairly regularly in Iceland, mostly along the north-west peninsula, at Faxafloi and in Breidafjordur, and they can occasionally be seen in the east in winter. But eagles have declined considerably in the last two centuries and are no longer the common sight they used to be. Only in the last ten years or so have the numbers begun to pick up once again, thanks to a concerted effort by the Bird Protection Society in Iceland. 1984 was the best season for decades, with total population estimates placed between 115 and 120 eagles at the end of the year. 28 nests provided a total of 25 fledglings — a further 9 pairs established territories but did not nest — and no less than 8 of the surviving eaglets were hatched in areas where nesting was unknown ten years ago.

Their numbers did not begin to decline significantly until the latter part of the 19th century. There was popular prejudice against eagles as scavengers but, more importantly, there was a massive campaign of extermination because of the damage they were believed to do to breeding eider ducks and lambs. The Eider Duck Breeding Society was established in 1885 for the express purpose of completely exterminating eagles and other so-called predators and scavengers, and a large reward was paid for every eagle killed.

During the first half of the nineteenth century, the white-tailed sea eagle population reached a peak of almost 300 pairs. They were found all over the country — not only around the coast, as now — but also near lakes and rivers, such as Thingvallavatn, Myvatn and the Laxa. By 1920, there were just ten pairs left, almost all at Breidafjordur.

White-tailed sea eagles have declined in numbers in recent years and are no longer the common sight they used to be.

In 1913 a law was passed for the eagle's protection, but such legislation has proved difficult to enforce. Not everyone respects the law and the killing continued. By 1959 there were still only 11 pairs breeding and another seven or eight non-breeding pairs in the entire country. Young sea eagles, under about one year old, live to a large extent on carrion and the main cause for the poor success was attributed to the laying of poisoned baits for foxes. In 1964, this was prohibited – but today the greatest threat comes from poison laid by breeders of eider ducks to eliminate scavengers. But the greatest problem for eider breeders comes from Iceland's vast population of great black-backed gulls – and a far more feasible alternative for dealing with them would be the burying of waste.

The actual proportion of different foods taken depends enormously on where in Iceland the birds are. But for the most part they take lumpfish, salmon, fulmar, eider, puffins and gulls.

It cannot be denied that eider forms a large part of the eagle's diet. But the eider stock in Iceland is around half a million, so it is ridiculous to conclude that about 100 eagles have any effect on the stock size. They are often accused of disturbing breeding eider; but egg-laying does not decrease – the birds simply move further away from where the eagles are nesting. The remains of lambs are sometimes found by eagle nests, but most of them are thought to be taken as carrion, after the lambs have died from other causes.

Little is known about either species of owl, though both are certainly rare and rarely seen. Short-eared owls are the commoner of the two (though by no means actually common), found mostly on low-lying moorland and in the valleys. They are among a handful of birds which have settled and bred in the country during the climatic amelioration in the first half of this century. The first nest was found at Rangarvallasysla in 1912 – before then it was known only as an irregular visitor. These days, the birds nest sparsely in lowland areas all over the country, usually on heathland, though the population is still small. Also, the average clutch size in Iceland is usually much lower than abroad. It is not clear what happens to short-eared owls in winter; they are probably partly migratory birds, and at least one ringed in Iceland as a young bird has been recovered in Britain. Several birds are, however, known to be resident.

Snowy owls are resident but extremely rare, restricted to certain wild and largely inaccessible parts of the central highlands. They have long been known as rare visitors to Iceland and were not recorded nesting until 1932, at Skjalfandafljot. No nest has been recorded since the middle of the 1960s but they are thought to breed in the oases sheltered by the south-eastern corner of the large Hofsjokull glacier and in a few other places. It is quite possible that breeding does go unnoticed. Like the gyrfalcon, snowy owls usually prey on Iceland's only gallinaceous bird, the ptarmigan, as well as goslings and waders in spring and summer.

Wetland Birds

Iceland has a rich variety of wetlands, including extensive bogs, marshes and inland waters. Together with the shallows and intertidal areas of an extremely indented coastline, they provide excellent habitat for breeding birds and feeding grounds for species migrating between the Canadian Arctic and Greenland, and Western Europe. They also provide important wintering grounds for species such as the sea ducks.

Together, they make Iceland's wetlands internationally important, especially as several sites hold up to 50,000 breeding, feeding, moulting or nesting individuals of each of several species. Nowhere in Europe is there a greater concentration of breeding waterfowl than in Iceland. Some even say it is the greatest haunt anywhere in the world.

Among the fabulous throng is a significant proportion of the world's population of pink-footed goose, once a mysterious species which occupied the minds of naturalists for years. There are two distinct populations of these birds. One breeds in Spitzbergen and winters in the Low Countries, Denmark and Western Germany. The other breeds in Iceland and Greenland and winters entirely in the UK. The mystery was that by no means all the wintering birds could be accounted for in their homes further north. Breeding grounds had been known in Spitzbergen since 1855 and Greenland since 1891, but it wasn't until 1929 that the species' main breeding ground was discovered — in Iceland. In addition to about 4,000 pairs in several fairly well-known sites in other parts of the country, an enormous site was discovered hidden at Thjorsarver, a small area south of Hofsjokull. Expeditions to the area in recent years estimate a population of between 10 and 11,000 breeding pairs.

The greylag goose is the only other species of goose that nests regularly in Iceland, replacing the pink-foot in the low-lying areas. Three other species, the barnacle, brent and white-fronted, are regular and common passage migrants though, with the exception of the barnacles (which have a very small population anyway) they do not breed.

Mute swans have never occurred in Iceland naturally — but they did breed in the country for nearly twenty years. One pair, a gift from Hamburg, was introduced to Lake Tjornin in the centre of Reykjavik in 1958 and immediately began to breed fairly successfully. Numbers reached a peak of almost 50 several years later, nesting at various localities around the capital. No-one knows why, but after that they began to decline and the last one was seen in 1977.

Although Bewick's swans have occurred, the only breeding swan today is the whooper swan — Iceland is one of the few places where it can still be called a common breeding bird — with between 5 and 7,000 pairs. It is particularly numerous on lake-dotted high ground on the borders of the central highlands. Large numbers of non-breeding birds spend the summer in Iceland feeding, gathering in large flocks in bays or on lakes. Their breeding counter-

The pink-footed goose was once shrouded in mystery — it was not until 1929 that the main breeding ground was discovered — in Iceland.

Iceland's only breeding swan is the whooper swan. It is one of the few places where it can be called a common breeding bird.

parts are not so sociable and prefer a large area of lake to each pair. In October, they begin to leave Iceland, migrating south to Britain and elsewhere for the winter.

Among the ducks, the commonest species are tufted duck, scaup, mallard and wigeon with 5,000 pairs or more each; the common pochard is a new immigrant and, while it does occasionally breed, is still rare. The gadwall is fairly abundant in places such as Lake Myvatn and, among the surface-feeding ducks, teal, pintail and shoveler all breed but are less common.

Three others of particular interest are the Barrow's goldeneye, the harlequin and the American wigeon, all American species. The Barrow's goldeneye is found nowhere else in Europe, but has a wide geographical distribution from the Rocky Mountains in the west to Iceland in the east. In America it nests in hollow trees, whereas in Iceland it nests in fissures and holes in lava. It is only found nesting regularly in two places in Iceland: Lake Myvatn (where it occasionally also nests in old houses, barns made of lava and blocks of turf, and in nestboxes) and the river Laxa. In contrast, the harlequin (whose male is one of the most spectacular of all ducks) is widely distributed in Iceland, although in summer it is confined to swift-flowing rivers and mountain streams. The American wigeon has been recorded nesting in the country since an adult male, a female and three downy young were discovered in 1901, though this record is now not considered authentic. Today it appears only as a vagrant. The frequent occurrence of these American birds in Iceland is not sur-

Above: The almost exclusively marine eider duck is the most abundant duck in Iceland. The female is superbly camouflaged for incubating her eggs among the rocky terrain.

Below: The male harlequin is one of the most spectacular of all ducks. It is an American species, though widely distributed in Iceland.

prising, since European wigeon ringed in the country have been recovered many times along the eastern seaboard of North America.

In addition to the harlequin, which winters at sea off Iceland's coasts, and the Barrow's goldeneye, which spends most of its time inland, there are three other species of sea duck. The common scoter breeds in the north-east by lakes on moorland, but winters in coastal waters; and the long-tailed duck breeds both inland on wetlands and by the coast, nearly always wintering offshore. Finally, there are over 200,000 pairs of the almost exclusively marine eider duck, making it the most abundant duck in the country. There is a particularly large colony to the north of the River Laxa, shortly before it meets Skjalfandi Bay, but there are no fewer than 250 major colonies throughout the country in all. The high-priced down has been collected from eider nests, while incubation is underway and after the young have hatched, for centuries. Reykjavik and its environs is a particularly good area to see eider — they gather off the coast in enormous numbers late in the summer.

Also around the coasts, particularly in sea lochs and fjords, is the red-breasted merganser. It is a common bird throughout the year in Iceland. Goosanders also occur — but are much rarer — and normally frequent inland lakes or fast streams or rivers.

The most characteristic waders of the country are the golden plover and whimbrel. Their cries and calls can be heard all over the vast moors, heathlands and lowlands. Redshank, snipe, dunlin, oystercatcher, ringed plover, red-necked phalarope and, to a lesser extent, purple sandpiper, are all fairly common breeders; the black-tailed godwit is fairly common in the southern boggy lowlands (and has spread to the west, north and east fairly recently); and turnstone, knot and sanderling are common passage migrants on their way to and from Greenland and Arctic Canada.

Perhaps the species of most interest is another American bird, the grey phalarope. In Iceland it is not a numerous bird, with only about 50—60 pairs, but it can be seen with luck. Elsewhere in Europe, it breeds in the high Arctic — only on Spitzbergen, where it is abundant, and Bear Island.

Other wetland species include resident water rails, which are very rare everywhere except in a few swamps in the south-east; coot have bred several times but are still struggling to get properly established; grey herons and curlews are fairly common winter visitors; and there is one resident grebe, the slavonian or horned grebe, which is at its greatest density on Lake Myvatn, where about 250 pairs nest.

Finally, two divers are found in Iceland. The well-distributed red-throated diver usually chooses small pools and tarns. The great northern diver nests on the larger lakes and ponds. The latter is particularly common on mountain lakes, but rarely more than one pair is found nesting at each stretch of water. They prefer solitude, being impatient of too-close neighbours, whatever the species! They build their nest right at the water's edge — their feet are so far back on the body that they cannot walk at all — so they can slip directly from incubating their eggs or feeding their young back into the water. Their feet are, instead, well placed and ideally suited for swimming. In winter, great northern divers spend most of their time around the coasts.

CHAPTER 4

DOWN TO EARTH

Before Iceland was settled in the 9th Century, the arctic fox was the only terrestrial mammal in the country. But the early settlers brought dogs, horses, sheep and cattle with them and, much later, pigs, goats and cats. Over the years brown rats, black rats, house mice and the long-tailed field mouse have all been accidentally introduced by man as well. Reindeer were imported from Norway in the late 18th Century and snowshoe hares and musk ox were both introduced a little over 100 years later, though they quickly disappeared. Most recently mink, introduced for fur farming, have escaped and settled.

While all this has been happening, polar bears have continued their occasional visits aboard ice floes from further north. But they have never been settled permanently, as far as it is known.

So out of a total of fifteen terrestrial mammals which can be seen in Iceland today, the only truly native resident is the arctic fox. Man is responsible for the presence of no fewer than thirteen out of fourteen of the remainder. It has been claimed that the European otter (**Lutra lutra**) occasionally occurs, but this has never been verified. There are many reports, the majority from the late 1930s, of otters being sighted during bad weather in the eastern fjords. It is just possible that they visit Iceland from Norway on ice floes or pack ice – other species, such as polar bears and arctic foxes are known to travel between Greenland and Iceland in this way.

Polar Bear

The most recent polar bear to be seen in Iceland was in 1978, at Adalvik on the north-west peninsula, where it stayed for several weeks. Before that, one turned up on Grimsey, in the north, in 1973. More recently, footprints were found in the snow near Straumnes in 1981 but they "disappeared" before scientists could verify them as polar bear. Many others have been seen on drift ice by Icelandic trawlermen – who see them within the 200-mile fishing limit most summers – including a possible half

Preceding pages: Out of a total of fifteen land mammals which can be seen in Iceland today, man is responsible for the presence of no fewer than thirteen.

Polar bears have probably never been true residents of Iceland – and are very rarely seen today – but over past centuries many thousands have visited from further north.

a dozen or more in 1984 alone. The total number is unknown, as most do not get reported.

Although bears have probably never been true residents of Iceland, over past centuries many thousands have turned up around the north, north-west and east coasts, after drifting for weeks on ice floes from Greenland or trekking for hundreds of miles on sea ice. Most often seen in very bad winters, when the Arctic pack ice stretches far enough south to connect Iceland's coastline with Greenland, each new arrival has been carefully recorded by the Icelanders for hundreds of years. In 1274,

for instance, there were 22, in 1275 there were 27. The very first visit recorded was in 890 when one of the early settlers met a mother and two cubs near a lake now known as Hunavatn, the "bear cubs lake".

Polar bear skins were highly prized for the altars and pulpits of cathedrals and churches, where priests used them to keep their feet warm. But, most of all, the bears' dignity, majesty and rarity made them coveted as mascots in the courts of kings. In Iceland, the king decreed that all pelts must be sold to royal officials, or elsewhere only by permission. But all over Europe it was as companions and pets that they were most welcome. Kings should "keep and esteem them as the great treasures of this world", declared one Icelandic bishop, St. Thorlak.

Harold the Fairhaired of Norway was the first European king to have a polar bear, caught for him by an enterprising hunter around AD 880 when a mother and her two cubs had drifted ashore on Iceland's coast. King Harold was overcome; he gave the hunter an ocean-going ship filled with a cargo of wood. Needless to say, it wasn't long before every king in Europe wanted a polar bear, and there was great competition amongst hunters to get them and amongst the sovereigns themselves to own them. The King of Denmark quickly outdid King Harold — for his bear, he gave a trading vessel, a sizeable sum of money **and** a gold ring. There were other, less tangible, rewards too. A canny Icelandic priest named Isleifur was made Bishop of Iceland in exchange for a bear, after a clever bit of wheeling and dealing.

The interest in polar bears at that time was enormous. They were very highly esteemed in both Greenland and Iceland. Even so, most visiting bears today are shot soon after arrival. Occasionally they are able to stroll far into the country unseen by man — but are then killed later in the summer or autumn when they return from the interior to the coast. They are not popular with farmers, particularly with reports earlier this century of up to 30 bears visiting Iceland in great "ice-years" and killing horses and sheep.

Reindeer

The first reindeer appeared in Iceland in 1771, when 13 were transported from Finnmark, in Norway. Three survived the journey and were released. A further 70 animals were introduced from the same area during the period 1777—1787. They were released in three main regions: the Reykjanes peninsula in the south-west, Eyjafjordur and Thingeyjarsysla in the north, and Vopnafjordur in the east. It had been planned to bring in Lapp families at the same time to teach Icelanders how to tame and use the animals, as in northern Scandinavia, but the plan did not come off. No attempts were made to retain the animals in domestication in Iceland and they quickly became completely feral.

During the first few years after introduction, the numbers increased very rapidly, reaching a peak of many thousands around the middle of the 19th Century. The numbers then declined rapidly until less than 200 were left around 1940, all living in the eastern interior, in the highlands north of Vatnajokull. The reindeer in the north and south-west had disappeared completely by the 1930s, though some of them had probably moved eastwards and got mixed up with the other animals. Numbers in the eastern population, however, have increased rapidly once again and the population has now stabilised at a little over 3,000, kept in check by hunting, hard winters and competition for food from sheep and horses. Still found to the north and north-east of Vatnajokull, the largest numbers are concentrated around Snaefell and along the eastern fjords south to Hornafjordur.

But the increase to today's figure was by no means steady. In January 1972, it was reported that the number of wild reindeer in eastern Iceland, having increased during the period 1965—69, had dramatically dropped again — by over a third — during the ensuing two years. But the numbers increased again, from 2,111 in 1972 to today's figure.

There have been several explanations for these dramatic fluctuations. Hunting pres-

sure from man is thought to have been low in old times — indeed the decline of the population continued despite long periods of total protection. Today, limited hunting under official supervision is allowed from 1st August to 15th September. The most likely explanation is the difficult snow conditions limiting access to grazing in winter. This could also account for the fact that they have not survived elsewhere in Iceland. During the summer most of the animals stay inland, at the usual sites north-east of Vatnajokull, but in September some of them migrate to the lowland and coastal areas where they spend the winter. In recent years, some of the coastal animals have remained around some of the fjords for the summer and do not migrate.

Rodents

Only four species of rodent occur in Iceland: brown rat, black rat or ship rat, long-tailed field (or wood) mouse and house mouse. Three of these species (all except the long-tailed field-mouse) occur almost only in urban areas, and of these only the brown rat is well established. The house mouse is very rare in Iceland and by no means firmly settled. The black rat does not really have a firm foothold either but it does occur sporadically in Reykjavik and perhaps in other ports. It was first recorded in 1919, though possibly arrived as early as the middle of the 18th century; two nests with young were discovered in 1926 and many more came on board Icelandic trawlers sailing between England (Grimsby and Hull) and Reykjavik during the following years. The brown rat also occurs mostly in built-up areas and, although common in the country as a whole, is found very little away from man. It probably arrived in Iceland around the middle of the 18th century and was certainly in Reykjavik by 1865. It had spread all over Iceland by the end of the 19th century. In the vicinity of coastal towns, brown rats are often seen looking for food, a variety of invertebrates mostly, on seaweed-covered beaches. The house mouse lives almost entirely in houses though it, too, is occasionally seen on beaches. Nothing is known about its colonization of Iceland, but it probably came with man very early on, soon after the settlement. These days it is common in most built-up areas. The long-tailed field mouse is the only species which occurs all around the country and is not necessarily bound to human habitation. Although they are found on every farm, and sometimes go into homes during very cold spells, the majority thrive without being dependent on man — though they probably arrived in Iceland with him as early as the 800s. They are found wherever there is vegetation, and even in lava fields and rocky areas. A maximum of 160 mice per hectare has been recorded in some places — not surprisingly, they can form an important part of the diet of predators such as mink, short-eared owls and foxes.

Snowshoe Hare and Rabbits

Despite a surprising number of reports to the contrary — and a special Icelandic law dating back to 1914 for its protection — the snowshoe or mountain hare does not occur in Iceland. There have been several attempts to introduce it as a game species, however. The first was in 1784 at Hvalfjordur, but none survived the winter. The next attempt was in 1869, on Videy Island, which once harboured an important eider colony. The locals thought they were disturbing the eiders — so killed the lot. Two hares were also unofficially introduced to the Westmann Islands around the turn of the century; one was very quickly killed but the other survived on its own for many years. They have never occurred anywhere else in Iceland and consequently have not been seen in the country for over 70 years. Many rabbits have escaped from farms over the years and have survived in the wild for short periods, but they never settled permanently.

Musk Ox

Three unsuccessful attempts have been made to introduce the musk ox to Iceland,

Preceding pages: Reindeer were introduced to Iceland in 1771. A population of about 3,000 still lives to the north and north-east of Vatnajokull.

The American mink was introduced to Iceland for fur farming in 1931. A few animals escaped and it is now a common animal around the coast and near freshwater.

primarily to boost farming activities. The first attempt was in 1905, when seven calves were transported from a high arctic area of Greenland. They all died the first year, probably because the lush green valley in which they had been released in the south-west of the country was entirely unsuitable. A small expedition in 1929 brought back seven more animals; six died of disease almost immediately and the sole survivor succumbed to the same disease in the spring of 1931. Another seven were released at Thingvellir in 1930 but none of them survived longer than three years.

Mink

The American mink was introduced to Iceland for fur farming in 1931. A few animals escaped and it took only 35 years for the species to spread all over the country. The first den in the wild was found in Reykjavik in 1937. Today they are common all around the coast and near most freshwater habitats.

In the late 1940s, Icelanders began hunting the mink intensively in an attempt to keep the population at a low level, or even to exterminate it. In 1948 alone, over 1200 were killed.

It is still controversial as to how much damage they are actually doing in Iceland. They undoubtedly take some wildfowl in places like Myvatn and have certainly caused large changes in the breeding distribution of ducks there, but the effect on the actual population sizes of the species concerned is open to question. Similarly, mink disturb puffins and black guillemots at their nesting colonies though, again,

whether or not this has an actual reducing effect on the populations is unknown. Around the coast the most important food at all times of year is fish and, inland, fish also feature prominently, especially in winter. Mice, passerine birds and invertebrates are more common food in summer and autumn.

Evidence suggests that the hunting of mink is not having any effect (indeed some populations have been increasing, at least until recently) and they are still a fairly common sight in many areas. They are still farmed in increasing numbers, in 12 different mink farms with about 6,000 females in all. At the time of writing, applications to establish about 20 new farms are being considered. To give some idea of the scale of the operation, in 1983, 24,000 cubs were born and 22,000 pelts auctioned abroad for $600,000.

Arctic Fox

The arctic fox has inhabited Iceland since the end of the last Ice Age, after following the ice-covering from southern Europe as it moved north. It is still fairly common in places (though absent from all inhabited islands), despite continual efforts to reduce its numbers. Man has gassed, trapped, poisoned and shot foxes in Iceland for centuries.

There are two distinct colour forms. The "blue" variety, which comprises about two thirds of the population overall and considerably more on the coast, is chocolate brown in summer and a lighter shade of brown (tinged with a blue sheen) in winter. Some individuals also have white patches on the chest and chin and, occasionally, white toes. The "white" variety is a spectacular pure white colour in winter, moulting to a grey to brownish-grey upper coat and light grey to white underside in summer. Animals of different colours interbreed freely — and the offspring are either "blue" or "white" — there is no intermediate.

Apart from these differences, both varieties have an array of adaptations to cold climates. Arctic foxes are considerably smaller than their red cousins, with a shorter tail and neck and smaller, more rounded ears. Their winter coats are very thick, with plenty of underfur, compared with their comparatively lightweight summer coats. Their broad paws have long fur on the bottom, protecting them from the cold, as well as sharp claws to help keep a footing on icy ground. The foxes also have behavioural adaptations such as digging into the snow for shelter during blizzards. The overall result is that they only begin to shiver when they have been exposed to temperatures of -70°C for almost an hour!

The choice of food for arctic foxes in Iceland is fairly restricted, but they are nevertheless opportunistic predators like red foxes elsewhere. They spend a great deal of time foraging, particularly along the seashore, and eat a lot of carrion. For example, they will feed on seal and reindeer carcasses, various dead seabirds such as guillemots, and fish such as lumpsuckers. Live prey includes eider ducks and various wading birds, ptarmigan and rodents, as well as some invertebrates (notably marine mussels) and the eggs and chicks of small birds. In other countries, they sometimes follow polar bears hundreds of kilometres onto pack-ice and scavenge from the carcasses of seals killed by the bears. This behaviour has never been recorded in Iceland but there is no reason why they should not take advantage of the occasional bear visitors. Arctic foxes from Greenland almost certainly reach Iceland intermittently on board pack ice, too, and they may well bring the technique with them. Indeed, in 1869, one was observed on ice almost exactly midway between the two land masses, though even this does not prove that a Greenland fox has ever set foot in Iceland.

One suspected feeding habit that is very controversial is the belief, dating back to the first century of settlement, that arctic foxes kill sheep and lambs. There is some evidence to this effect, though whether or not the farmers' animals are actually killed by the foxes or eaten after they have died is uncertain.

Nevertheless, the damage caused by

Arctic foxes are so well adapted to the cold that they only begin to shiver when they have been exposed to temperatures of -70° C for almost an hour!

foxes today amounts to only a fraction of the money spent on exterminating them. Since 1295, Icelandic legislation has actually promoted the foxes' extermination with state-subsidised hunting — and they have been heavily persecuted ever since. Special laws prescribe systematic methods aimed at making the arctic fox extinct in Iceland. Hunting by paid hunters (and others) sometimes using snowscooters with rifles and telescopic sights is extensive — so, due to ever-mounting pressure, large tracts of land are now more or less devoid of foxes. In 1939, skin dealers estimated that there were 2—3,000 pairs in Iceland. Other than that, there are no population estimates for the country but it is interesting to note that annual tallies have dropped considerably from over 1500 less than 30 years ago to barely 300 in 1984. These and other estimates do suggest that, since the 1950s, the number of foxes in Iceland has been reduced by at least two thirds.

Foxes have been farmed successfully in Iceland since the end of 1979. Experiments were made before the Second World War but, due to poor marketing conditions and inexperience, these were unsuccessful. Fox farming is now proving immensely popular, as shown by the fact that the number of farms rose from 10 in 1981 to over 120 by the end of 1984. Most of them operate on a fairly small scale, as a sideline to more traditional types of agriculture and husbandry, with an average stock of only 150 animals.

Iceland only accounts for a fraction of world fox fur production, which was three million pelts in 1984, but there are plans to

take a larger share of the market in coming years. In the same year, Iceland's 6,000 vixens produced some 25,000 cubs; and 21,000 pelts were auctioned abroad for $850,000. It is likely that the farms themselves will grow (in size as well as number) and they seem to be becoming more of a full-time occupation as opposed to a sideline, which is normal at the moment. This is an interesting anomaly, because in many other countries in the west there has been a decline in the demand for the more expensive furs such as mink, fox and sable — probably due to a combination of conscience and lack of cash. The Federation of Icelandic Fur Farmers is nevertheless looking towards a figure of 350,000 vixens and 2 million skins a year in the not-too-distant future.

Wild foxes can still be seen in Iceland, with a little patience and a little more luck. They most often occur in the interior of the country, especially on the western plateaux, and in the north and north-west. March is the best time to look for them, when they are both active and vocal while establishing territories. It is rarely possible to approach them closely, though. They are fairly tame in most other parts of their Arctic range, but in Iceland their flight distance from man and their guile at evading hunters is equivalent to that of the red fox elsewhere.

Incidentally, there is no good reason why the red fox could not live in Iceland. A few individuals have escaped from fur farms over the years but do not seem to have survived. Nevertheless, the climate is relatively mild and the habitat is comparable to that in some of the more northerly parts of its range. Its absence is therefore likely to be a consequence of geographical isolation. The same applies to a number of other potential mammalian residents.

Domesticated Mammals

The first settlers in Iceland brought large numbers of livestock with them from their Norwegian homes. For the first 800 years,

The total winter stock of sheep in Iceland is roughly 900,000, though this rises to over two million during lambing.

There are many tales in the old Icelandic literature about bonds of friendship and fidelity which were formed between dogs and people.

until the 17th century, cattle were the principal farm animals, reaching a peak of 120,000 head, which is over double today's number.

But, as a result of over-grazing, cattle stocks diminished and sheep became the principal livestock. But even the hardy sheep had to fight for survival and many great flock losses resulted in starvation and death for Icelanders. Today, the output of meat and dairy products is considerably larger than is needed for domestic consumption, thanks to modernised farming techniques and co-operative efforts. There are 61,000 cattle in Iceland today, 37,000 of which are dairy. Apart from a few calves which found their way from Britain, almost all of them are descendants of the cattle brought by Norwegian settlers 1,100 years ago.

The sheep, too, are an ancient Nordic breed, with short tails and, on most individuals, a white coat. They yield meat, wool and skins, renowned for their high quality throughout the world. A few individuals of foreign stock have been imported on occasion in the past – but they cannot match the Icelandic sheep for their hardiness and longevity.

Icelandic sheep are usually found in the mountains, the unpopulated areas, in summer. They graze there untended, but people ride out in autumn and round them up, driving them down into the settled areas. There they are sorted according to farmers' individual markings. The sheep are then kept in barns on the farms over winter. The total winter stock of sheep is roughly 900,000, though this rises to over two million during lambing. Lambing

takes place from the second week in May until early June and, when the grass is suitable for grazing again, they are moved back to the mountains.

Hay is the basic feed for all Icelandic livestock, in addition to summer grazing, so mixed farming of sheep and cattle is the general rule. Many farmers also own some horses, and a few own pigs or goats — though the income from these is relatively modest.

Together, livestock account for 90% of the income of Iceland's 4,500 farms. The remaining 10% is divided between cultivation of vegetables and other plants in greenhouses, grass, potatoes and turnips, some trout and salmon farming (which is on the increase) and, to a very small extent, mink and fox fur farming. Experimental cultivation of other fur-bearing animals, such as angora rabbits, has also begun.

Two domestic animals are of particular interest: the Icelandic dog and the Iceland horse, or "Viking horse".

Icelandic Dog

In appearance, the Icelandic dog is typically Nordic, with upright ears and a curled tail and thick fur. It is said to have come to Iceland directly from Scandinavia with the settlers in the 9th century. There are many tales, in the old Icelandic literature, about bonds of friendship and fidelity which were formed between dog and man. Lively, gentle, inquisitive and courageous, they have made excellent comrades to the Icelandic people — but they have also made invaluable sheep dogs and watchdogs. They can move very quickly and, while their hunting skills are well-developed, they are not savage; though this is hard to believe after seeing them chase visitors' cars!

An organisation called the Iceland Kennel Club has been operating since 1971 to guard against the ever-present danger of interbreeding with other breeds. It had become considerably mixed with foreign strains in previous years but breeders have been able to successfully restore a pure Icelandic strain.

But, while the animals are encouraged and fairly common in the countryside, there is a bye-law (dating back to 1924) which bans them from Reykjavik on health grounds. The government maintains that, by eating the raw offal from slaughterhouses, roaming dogs can harbour a disease caused by intestinal worms in sheep. The implication is that they pose a threat to the people of Reykjavik. But despite the ban there have always been many dogs being kept as pets in the capital. Every now and then a dog owner was arrested, fined and told to get rid of his pet. Very few did and it has been a subject of heated debate. But an estimated 3,000 illegal tails wagged for joy in the summer of 1984, when Reykjavik city council agreed to allow owners to apply for an exemption and a licence, on fulfilment of a number of strict conditions. These include ensuring that the dogs meet the demands for personal hygiene made upon other recognised citizens of the capital, as well as such things as maintaining satisfactory insurance. The bye-law itself, however, still stands.

Iceland Horse

Horses came with the first settlers to Iceland. In those days they were romantically nicknamed "the most useful servant" — tough, strong animals, they bore the brunt of a long and arduous working day. They brought home hay from distant fields, helped round up sheep in the mountains in autumn, took part in festivals and other public gatherings and were the only means of transport for both people and goods. They were used to travel between remote inland farms, to trading points on the coast (journeys that sometimes took weeks or months), to carry the doctor or mid-wife to sick people and expectant mothers, and to take the dead to their graves. There were no bridges in Iceland until this century and all big and dangerous rivers had to be crossed on horseback. This was always a tricky affair which often proved fatal to both horse and man. Perhaps most of all, they can live without requiring too much attention — and they add colour and life to an otherwise stormy winter landscape.

The Iceland horse has been man's "most faithful servant" ever since the times of the first settlement.

Without the horse, Icelanders would in all probability not have survived in their barren, mountainous and remote island. Not surprisingly, it has been the most common subject for Icelandic poets through the ages. The bond between man and horse is so strong that some horses show a well-known and rather embarrassing trait whereby they tend to run back home when they have been sold or transferred to new and unfamiliar places. They will run for days, weeks or months across mountains, wastelands and dangerous rivers to get back. Some individuals have

even been known to traverse half the country. No-one can explain this homing instinct and keen sense of direction.

There is a law forbidding the import of horses – and any horse leaving Iceland can never return. This means that the present-day Iceland horses are not only the same race as those of the Viking age but are also probably descended from horses used by people such as the legendary brothers Hengist and Horsa when they invaded England in the 5th century. But, above all, their long isolation has preserved some of the peculiarities lost in other European races.

Whereas in other countries horses were bred to become heavier and stronger, to pull carts and carriages, for use in the cavalry, for shows and many other uses, Iceland's animals remained small, all-round family horses. Their average height is only 13 hands, they are hardy and sure-footed, friendly and docile and have a flowing mane. The hair changes according to the season, being shaggy in winter and short in summer.

Icelandic farmers have consistently refused to breed horses in accordance with market demands, but have consciously tried to preserve with the utmost precision and care their original traits. A tradition, dating back to the old sagas, however, is for each farmer to maintain his own particular colour, and this has obviously been selected for over the centuries. As a result, colours are quite varied, though usually restricted to different shades of brown, black and chestnut. The only other forms of selection have been the Icelandic winter – only the strongest strains have survived the rigours of living out in the open – and volcanic eruptions. In the late 18th century, when the greatest volcanic eruption in history anywhere in the world took place in the south of Iceland, 23,400 of the country's 32,000 horses were killed in a 24-year period. Icelandic horses have lived with the elements all their lives.

Perhaps the most extraordinary characteristic is the fifth gait, a running walk, which is not found in many other breeds of horse.

Without the Iceland horse, Icelanders would in all probability not have survived on their barren, mountainous and remote island.

Horses were still the only means of transport in Iceland until comparatively recently. But cars and planes have taken over their role. Today the Iceland horse has only two practical functions, one dwindling and one increasing. Firstly, every September, farmers from each district cooperate in gathering all the sheep from common grazing land in the interior, in order to sort them into individual ownership. Horses are still in use in many areas but jeeps, tractors and even aircraft are gradually taking over.

Secondly, they have enjoyed a steadily growing interest and importance as a source of pleasure. With nearly 60,000 horses in all, and since more than half of them live outside all year round in a semiwild state, they are still a conspicuous part of the Icelandic landscape. There are thousands of regular horseback riders in Iceland, riding clubs in all the main towns and dozens of different riding tours for tourists. And this growing interest in the Iceland horse is by no means limited to Iceland. Even in the 19th century, foreign travellers were full of praise for the animals – and today there are clubs encouraging and cultivating their use all over western and northern Europe. Exporting horses from Iceland is a long-established business; around 150,000 have been sold abroad since the middle of the last century, although the purpose has changed somewhat over the years. Originally used as carthorses and for mine work, they have since been elevated to the status of highly-prized sport and leisure animals.

CHAPTER 5

SURROUNDED BY SEA

Nearly twenty different marine mammal species are regular visitors to Iceland and more than half a dozen others have been recorded at one time or another.

Among the seals, two species breed around the coast: the common or harbour, and the grey. Ringed, harp, bearded and hooded seals, and the Atlantic walrus, all occur as vagrants, most commonly in the north.

Harbour seals are by far the commonest. Parties of them haul out of the water all around the coast (except in the extreme north) particularly around river estuaries, inside fjords where there are plenty of rocks and islets and in shallow waters. In mid-summer, when they are moulting, it is not uncommon to see several hundred on a beach together in the south and west. The Reykjanes peninsula west of Reykjavik is as good a place as any to see them. They often position themselves at their chosen hauling-out place long before low tide and end up perched on some inaccessible rock until the tide reaches them again and they are able to swim off!

The harbour seal in Iceland is, strictly speaking, a sub-species known as the Eastern Atlantic harbour seal, which is also found around the coasts of Britain, Ireland, Scandinavia and Holland. The southern shores of Iceland are thought to support as many as 25—28,000 of them (out of as many as 30—40,000 in the country as a whole) — over half the world total. The best time to see them is towards the end of June or the beginning of July, when they are pupping, or from the middle of August to the middle of September, when the adults are ashore once again to moult.

Grey seals are less abundant than harbour seals, but still with a total population of up to 10,000 — something like 10% of the world population. They are also considerably harder to find, as they move around a great deal. Although records from the north have increased in recent years, they occur mostly along the south and west coasts, from Eystrahorn round to Hunafloi, with the largest numbers breeding on the islands, skerries and islets in Breidafjordur, and on both sides of the West Fjords. Sizeable numbers also occur at Hvalseyjar and Myrar.

Pupping times for grey seals vary considerably, but they do always produce their pups in the colder months of the year, usually any time between the end of August and the beginning of January. About a month before pupping, large numbers of pregnant cows, and bulls of all ages, assemble on or near the breeding beaches. They also spend long periods hauled out (though not at the breeding sites) during February and March, which is when the annual moult takes place.

The remaining five seal species occur in varying numbers from their Arctic homes further north. Their numbers vary considerably from year to year, but they are usually quite numerous offshore. The ringed seal is the commonest of these vagrants. It is commoner than any other seal species in the Arctic, with a total estimated world population of six to seven million. Iceland is at the southern extreme of its range and,

Preceding pages: The great wealth of plankton in Icelandic waters provides optimum conditions for a rich marine life.

The common, or harbour, seal is indeed common in the shallow Icelandic waters, highly visible as they play or rest on off-shore rocks and skerries.

Grey seals are less abundant than common seals — but Iceland still harbours about ten per cent of the world population.

consequently, most sightings are on the north coast. They regularly visit Akureyri in winter and spring, for example. Occasional stragglers move further south, nearly always down the west rather than the east coast. They rarely breed in Iceland, even though they breed along the entire Greenland coast. Most sightings are in the winter, in bays and fjords (very rarely in the open sea) but they can be seen at any time of year.

The harp seal, too, occurs along all coasts of Greenland (except the extreme north) and is a fairly common visitor to Iceland, particularly in the north. Although most occur in late autumn and winter, they can be seen at any time of year.

The bearded seal, a spectacular animal with its great profusion of long, very sensitive, glistening white moustachial whiskers which gives it its name, and the hooded seal, are both rare visitors to the north, again from the Greenland coasts. Hooded seals are frequent but irregular, and the bearded is very rare.

Walruses occasionally put in an appearance around Iceland's coasts, from their main breeding grounds in west Greenland or farther north. The general trend is for them to move north or south with the southern edge of the ice pack. The Greenland ice begins advancing southwards in October and the further south it moves, the more likely an Icelandic sighting becomes. As it resumes its move northwards in summer, the chance of a walrus sighting declines. As a result, most walruses are sighted in winter, along the north and west coasts. The number of recordings has de-

clined dramatically since the beginning of this century. Something between 30 and 40 walruses have been seen in Iceland since 1900.

The most recent record of a walrus was of a young male which spent a couple of months on a beach north of Reykjavik, at Rif in Snaefellsnes, early in 1983. He looked suspiciously like "Wally the Walrus" who had been returned to Greenland the year before, courtesy of Icelandair, NATO and the Iceland Coast Guard, after "holidaying" in Skegness, England!

Considerably less is known about the whale and dolphin species which frequent Icelandic waters. Roughly twenty have been recorded within the 200-mile fishing limits, though very few are seen regularly from the coast. Nevertheless, although many whales go on regular and predictable migrations or have well-known ranges, they have a habit of turning up in the most unexpected places. Iceland is not the best country in the world for watching them (you need to be off the west coast of North America or in the southern hemisphere for that!) but it is in a good position for observing some of these migrations and for seeing stragglers from both the Arctic and from further south.

Most whales begin moving south in autumn, disappearing altogether during the winter. They visit Iceland in spring and summer, when they do most of their feeding, to exploit the rich fishing grounds. They were once so common that a 13th Century Norwegian writer placed them on the top of a list of "items considered most remarkable about Iceland"; the others were ice, volcanoes, hot springs and earthquakes.

The handful of species most likely to be seen today are sperm whale, minke whale, killer whale, longfin pilot whale, fin whale, common porpoise and white-beaked dolphin. Killer whales are not only numerous, but also prefer coastal areas such as shallow bays and estuaries, and so are seen most often. They are found in all of the world's oceans, but are more numerous in the northerly latitudes and particularly around Iceland. They have never been popular with herring fishermen; in 1955 several hundred were killed in one place by the US Navy, at the fishermen's request, with machine guns and depth charges. Killer whales are usually seen in "pods" of 5—20, and are great fun to watch. Their reputation as man-eaters is unwarranted — there isn't one authentic report of a killer whale having harmed a human in any way without provocation.

The table opposite summarises the status and sightings of whales in Icelandic waters: There is some evidence that the grey whale, **Eschrichtius robustus,** existed in the sea around Iceland in the early Middle Ages, and possibly into the 16th Century, but it certainly does not occur now.

It is rare these days to see the larger whales from the coast, but smaller species can still be seen. One of the best, and most accessible, places for observing these is on the Reykjanes peninsula, anywhere along the coast between Hafnir and Grindavik, or at Krisuvikurberg. There are no guarantees — whale watching is a very hit and miss affair at the best of times — but there are plenty of seabirds around to keep you occupied, in case the whales are not forthcoming. Killer and minke whales, porpoises and dolphins are all regularly seen from this point between April and the end of July.

STATUS AND SIGHTINGS OF WHALES IN ICELANDIC WATERS

Right whale

Once widespread but now rare everywhere in the northern hemisphere as a result of extensive hunting. Very occasionally seen near Iceland in summer, though virtually never near the coast.

Bowhead whale

Has never been very common around Iceland. Now virtually exterminated by hunting, but recorded very occasionally.

Fin whale

Population decimated by whaling but still fairly common in Icelandic waters. Occurs all around the country, though usually in deeper water. First appears in March, though main migration arrives end of May or the beginning of June.

Blue whale

Last century was numerous around Iceland's coasts and even in many of the fjords. Still occurs all around the country but now rare (as it is worldwide) and only occasionally seen. Probably begins arriving in April.

Minke whale

Fairly common around Iceland, and sometimes seen close to land, since mostly an inshore species.

Sei whale

Fairly common in Icelandic waters, though numbers fluctuate considerably from year to year. Occasionally seen near the coast, off the south-east and south, usually in late summer.

Humpback whale

Fairly common in Icelandic waters and occasionally seen from ships, particularly off the east and south-east. Occasionally seen close to land.

Northern bottlenose whale

Found all around Iceland in summer and autumn, though by no means common. More often in deep offshore waters (most common in sea between Iceland and Jan Mayen) though occasionally near the coast in July. Some strandings.

Beaked whale

Probably rare visitors from the south. Although characteristically shore-hugging species, and likely to occur, only one (unverified) record around Iceland in recent years. A handful of specimens known from earlier this century, from strandings and incidental catches by whalers.

Narwhal

A rare visitor from the Arctic, occasionally seen in the deeper waters around Iceland, mostly in the north and north-west.

White whale

A rare visitor from the Arctic, rarely seen in shallow water around Iceland.

Sperm whale

Occasionally seen from the coast all around Iceland, particularly in the west. Nearly always remains at edge of the shelf. Most sightings are in the late spring through to early autumn.

Common porpoise

Very common all around Iceland. Particularly off south and south-west coasts in spring, when they pursue capelin visiting coasts for spawning. Often chase herring into bays and fjords in summer. Leave in large numbers in winter, though some remain. Regularly drowned in fishing nets in spring. Fairly easy to spot, being highly vocal and demonstrative, often splashing a great deal at the surface.

Longfin pilot whale

Well known around Iceland and regularly stranded, but mostly seen in deeper waters. Approaches north-west and west shores from August to October, probably in search of squid. In autumn 1983 many hundreds were stranded near a tiny fishing village on the west coast; most of them were kept alive and successfully returned to sea by the villagers. Normally seen August to October in Faxafloi, Breidafjordur and Hunafloi.

Killer whale

Particularly numerous in Icelandic waters and often seen close to land. Most often seen during summer and autumn, when herring move near the coast.

White-beaked dolphin

Very common all around Iceland in summer and occasionally caught accidentally in fishing nets. Often appears in schools of several hundred.

Atlantic whiteside dolphin

Believed to occur around Iceland, but no official records.

Bottlenose dolphin

Very likely occurs around Iceland occasionally but no official records.

Common dolphin

Despite its name, this species is by no means common in Iceland, which is at the northern extreme of its range. There is one possible record from recent years. A handful of proven records earlier this century — mostly from dead specimens washed ashore or caught in nets.

CHAPTER 6

INVISIBLE OR ABSENT?

Visitors to Iceland cannot help but notice the countless birds and flowers. They may even be lucky enough to see an arctic fox, or a seal, or one of the other mammalian residents.

But one thing they never see is a reptile or an amphibian. No amount of searching will find a frog, toad, newt, salamander, lizard or snake — because there aren't any. Iceland, being such an isolated country sitting in the middle of the North Atlantic Ocean far from anywhere, is a difficult place to get to. Birds can fly, seals can swim, plants can send their seeds on the winds and reindeer get taken there by man. Only sea turtles, reptiles which do have access to the coasts via ocean currents, have been recorded; there has been one verified sighting, of a rare leatherback turtle, **Dermochelys coriacea.** Snakes and lizards have had no such means of transport.

But, even more importantly, reptiles and amphibians are primitive animals that would be unable to survive in Iceland's inhospitable arctic interiors and very variable

weather and climate. Whereas birds and mammals are able to maintain more or less constant body temperatures — which allows them to be almost constantly active in a wide range of conditions, even in some of the coldest areas on earth — reptiles and amphibians generally cannot. They have variable body temperatures and are forced to live at those of the surrounding air or water, or to gain heat by basking in the sun. If it is too cold, activity is more or less impossible.

Insects, too, are restricted in numbers for the same reasons. Over 1,100 different species have been recorded, but this is very small compared with other North European countries, as the table below illustrates for one particular group, the lepidoptera.

It seems quite likely that 1,100 or so is an underestimate, as new records are being added to the list all the time. Nevertheless, the climate is hostile to insects and this, together with Iceland's isolation, will inevitably keep numbers down.

Observations on insects go back as far as the old sagas, where several references are made to "rain-worms". But the first accurate recordings were not made until 1608. The Icelandic clergy used to make detailed notes of remarkable events which happened during the year. Usually these were of serious diseases, shipwrecks and other disasters, but they sometimes included weather and farming reports. In 1608 they began referring to the rain-worms, or "grass-larvae" as they were called, which the clergy believed fell with the rain. They were almost certainly antler moths, whose larvae pupate below ground and often appear in enormous numbers during heavy downpours.

Most recordings of insects in Iceland have, however, been made since the Second World War. With stepped-up research activities, the list has almost doubled in the last 35 years. During a twenty-three year period, from 1947 to 1970, a local collector living in Kvisker in the south-east added no fewer than seven species to the Icelandic

LEPIDOPTERA SPECIES: A COMPARISON

	Area (sq kms)	Number of lepidoptera species recorded	Number of resident and visiting species of these countries also known from Iceland
Norway	322,600	1,700	76
Britain	242,600	2,469	77
Orkney	975	282	52
Shetland	1,400	145	41
Faroes	1,400	56	36
Iceland	104,800	82	82
Greenland (ice-free coastal areas only)	342,000	53	13

Preceding pages: The Laxa River in Adaldalur, N. Iceland is one of the best salmon fishing rivers in the country.

Kvisker, in south-east Iceland, where a local collector discovered seven insect species which were new to the Icelandic list.

list on his own. And some of those were of considerable zoogeographical interest. They had never been found before in Iceland and have only infrequently been seen since.

The fact that those seven species have been discovered is due to the initiative of only one person, working in a restricted place in his spare time. It seems highly likely that further additions to the Icelandic fauna will "turn up" if his work is followed up by other residents in different parts of the country and by visitors.

Most of the new "discoveries" have been flies, particularly midges. As in other arctic and sub-arctic countries, flies form the largest and most important group, and dominate the Icelandic scene with 425 species recorded so far. There is no reason to believe that the list will not grow considerably larger, since 5,000 or more species have been recorded in neighbouring countries such as Britain and they are able to exploit a very wide range of food materials and habitats, including those the Arctic has to offer.

Bees and wasps, with about 230 species, come a distant second in the numbers game, but are well adapted to life in Iceland. Along with locusts and some of the larger moths and butterflies, they have designed a system for warming up their flight muscles when outside temperatures are too cold, by a process similar to shivering in man. Perhaps surprisingly, ants, which are closely allied with bees and wasps in the same group known as the hymenoptera, are completely absent.

Beetles come third with about 160 diffe-

rent species and, with a couple of exceptions, most of Iceland's remaining 18 insect orders are represented by only a handful of species. For example, only one species of dragonfly, **Hemianax ephippiger,** has been recorded. Even this normally breeds much further east and occurs in Iceland only as a vagrant.

As research work increases, more insects and other invertebrates are being recorded all the time. For example, the discovery of a new species of water beetle in a single tiny pond a few years ago, is typical. Some scientists had been working at the spout of the glacier Solheimajokull, near Skogar, in south Iceland. In most of the pools they investigated, two species of water beetle, **Agabus solieri** and **Hydroporus nigrita,** were very common. In one particular pond, they discovered four specimens of **Oreodytes sanmarki,** a water beetle new to the country. As far as is known, it occurs nowhere else in Iceland. Other species, too, like **Agabus uliginosus** (another water beetle) in its single pond in Berufjordur, occur in only one place and nowhere else.

But it is the butterflies and moths which are the best known. 82 different species have been recorded – mostly indigenous and, to a lesser extent, migratory moths – but including a few species of migratory butterflies. These occasionally turn up in dramatic numbers but are probably never able to survive the winter.

There is still some controversy over whether there are regularly breeding indigenous butterflies in Iceland or not. Both red admirals and painted ladies regularly appear – and both species have bred – but they are well known migrants and neither seems to be able to survive the Icelandic winter. The painted lady, in particular, is sighted most years and enormous numbers have been known to occur all over Iceland since 1949, following massive invasions of northern Europe. It certainly breeds if it appears early enough in the year and the weather is favourable. Two other butterflies, the peacock and the small tortoise-

shell, have also occurred a handful of times. There are thirteen immigrant species of moth, some of which occur regularly and even breed, others of which are very rare. The table below summarises the status of all Iceland's immigrant lepidoptera.

No endemic moths (other than a subspecies of the Iceland dart) are known to occur in Iceland, but the indigenous species, which are mostly resident in the south and west, have an interesting range of origins and comprise a mixture of European and American species.

The chances are that, before the end of the century, there will be more butterflies and moths on Iceland's list. There are 13 species in particular which would be well suited to Iceland's climate and terrain — and are already found in Orkney, Shetland and the Faroes — so they could be expected to turn up in the future. The two carpet moths **Perizoma didymata** and **Perizoma albulata,** for example, are both extremely plentiful in the Faroes, and the larvae of both species feed on the small yellow rattle, a plant frequent in Iceland — yet they have never occurred. No-one knows why, particularly as there is some evidence to show that insects are being carried to Iceland on the winds.

Other species have appeared with imported fruit, dried vegetable products and other goods from abroad. They wouldn't be present without the help of man. Among these are the Mediterranean flour moth which has been found in bakers' shops and, on a number of occasions, in houses; the cinnabar moth and the blue underwing, which have occurred once each; and the lackey moth which arrived as a cluster of eggs around the twig of an imported fruit tree. Perhaps the most unusual record (which hasn't been accepted as "official") is of a fragment of a wing found in a street in Reykjavik, belonging to the African butterfly **Euphaedra gausape.**

The following table summarises what is currently known about all Iceland's butterflies and moths.

STATUS OF ICELAND'S IMMIGRANT LEPIDOPTERA

Recorded once or twice	Appear regularly, sometimes plentiful	Appear regularly, occasionally breed if early in year and weather favourable
Gem	**Udea ferrugalis**	Diamond-backed moth
Death's head hawk moth	Rush veneer	Red admiral
Small tortoiseshell	Convolvulus hawk moth	Painted lady
Large wainscot	Dark sword grass	Angle shades
Hummingbird hawk moth	Pearly underwing	Silver Y
Peacock		
American wainscot		

LEPIDOPTERA SPECIES RECORDED IN ICELAND

TINEIDAE

1. Clothes Moth (**Nemapogon personellus**)
2. Dark Brindles Clothes Moth (**Monopis rusticella**)
3. Webbing Clothes Moth (**Tineola bisselliella**)

GLYPHIPTERIGIDAE

4. Cocksfoot Moth (**Glyphipterix simplicella**)

YPONOMEUTIDAE

5. Diamond-backed Smudge Moth (**Plutella xylostella**)
6. Smudge (**Plutella senilella**)

COLEOPHORIDAE

7. Case Moth (**Coleophora algidella**)
8. Case Moth (**Coleophora alticolella**)

OECOPHORIDAE

9. White-shouldered House Moth (**Endrosis sarcitrella**)
10. Brown House Moth (**Hofmannophila pseudospretella**)

GELECHIIDAE

11. **Bryotropha similis**
12. **Gnorimoschema valesiellum**
13. Groundling (**Scrobipalpa samadensis**)
14. Orache Groundling (**Scrobipalpa atriplicella**)

TORTRICIDAE

15. **Epinotia caprana**
16. **Epinotia solandriana**
17. Marble (**Lobesia littoralis**)
18. **Apotomis sororculana**
19. Dotted Shade (**Eana osseana**)
20. Marbled Button (**Acleris maccana**)
21. Rusty Button (**Acleris ferrugana**)

COCHYLIDAE

22. **Cochylis dubitana**

PYRALIDAE

23. Grass Moth (**Crambus pascuella**)
24. Pyralid Moth (**Gesneria centuriella**)
25. **Udea ferrugalis**
26. Rush Veneer (**Nomophila noctuella**)
27. **Pyla fusca**

			Occurrence in Iceland of the Indigenous species						Occurrence outside Iceland		
Occ	Imm	Ind	NW	N	E	S	W	Cen	GB	Nor	NA
X									X	X	
X									X	X	X
X									X	X	X
		X					X		X	X	
	X								X	X	X
		X	X	X	X	X	X	X	X	X	
		X	X			X	X			X	
		X		X	X	X	X		X	X	X
X									X	X	X
X									X	X	X
		X	X	X	X	X	X		X	X	X
		X			X	X	X		X		X
		X	X			X	X		X	X	
		X					X		X	X	X
		X					X		X	X	
		X	X	X	X	X	X		X	X	X
		X				X	X		X	X	
		X		X	X	X	X		X	X	
		X	X	X	X	X	X	X	X	X	X
		X		X		X	X		X	X	X
		X	X	X	X	X	X	X	X	X	X
		X				X	X		X	X	
		X	X	X	X	X	X	X	X	X	X
		X				X		X		X	X
	X								X	X	
	X								X	X	X
		X	X	X	X	X	X	X	X	X	X

28. Carob Bean Moth (**Ectomyelois ceratoniae**)

29. Mediterranean Flour Moth (**Ephestia kuehniella**)

30. Indian Meal Moth (**Plodia interpunctella**)

PTEROPHORIDAE

31. Icelandic Plume (**Stenoptilia islandica**)

NYMPHALIDAE

32. Small tortoiseshell (**Aglais urticae**)

33. Red Admiral (**Vanessa atalanta**)

34. Painted Lady (**Vanessa cardui**)

35. Peacock (**Inachis io**)

GEOMETRIDAE

36. Gem (**Orthonama obstipata**)

37. Flame Carpet (**Xanthorhoe designata**)

38. Red Carpet (**Xanthorhoe munitata**)

39. Common Carpet (**Epirrhoe alternata**)

40. Yellow-ringed Carpet (**Entephria flavicinctata**)

41. Grey Mountain Carpet (**Entephria caesiata**)

42. Dark Marble Carpet (**Chloroclysta citrata**)

43. July Highflyer (**Hydriomena furcata**)

44. Argent and Sable (**Rheumaptera hastata**)

45. Winter Moth (**Operophtera brumata**)

46. Pretty Pinion (**Perizoma blandiata**)

47. Small Rivulet (**Perizoma alchemillata**)

48. Lead-coloured Pug (**Eupithecia plumbeolata**)

49. Satyr Pug (**Eupithecia satyrata**)

50. Juniper Pug (**Eupithecia sobrinata**)

51. Narrow-winged Pug (**Eupithecia nanata**)

52. Mottled Umber (**Erannis defoliaria**)

SPHINGIDAE

53. Death's Head Hawk-moth (**Acherontia atropos**)

54. Convolvulus Hawk-moth (**Agrius convolvuli**)

55. Humming-bird Hawk-moth (**Macroglossum stellatarum**)

LYMANTRIIDAE

56. Vapourer (**Orgyia antiqua**)

			Occurrence in Iceland of the Indigenous species						Occurrence outside Iceland		
Occ	Imm	Ind	NW	N	E	S	W	Cen	GB	Nor	NA
X									X		X
X									X	X	X
X									X	X	X
		X		X	X	X	X	X		X	
	X								X	X	
	X								X	X	X
	X								X	X	X
	X								X	X	
	X								X		X
		X	X	X	X	X	X	X	X	X	X
		X	X	X	X	X	X	X	X	X	X
		X	X	X	X	X	X		X	X	X
		X				X			X	X	
		X	X	X	X	X	X	X	X	X	X
		X	X	X	X	X	X		X	X	X
		X	X	X	X	X	X	X	X	X	X
		X	X	X	X	X	X	X	X	X	X
		X				X	X		X	X	X
		X			X	X			X	X	
		X					X		X	X	
		X				X	X		X	X	
		X	X	X	X	X	X		X	X	X
		X	X			X	X		X	X	X
		X		X		X	X		X	X	
		X				X			X	X	X
	X								X	X	
	X								X	X	X
	X								X	X	
		X				X			X	X	X

NOCTUIDAE

57. Iceland Dart (**Euxoa islandica islandica**)
58. Dark Sword Grass (**Agrotis ipsilon**)
59. Northern Rustic (**Standfussiana lucernea**)
60. **Rhyacia quadrangula**
61. Large Yellow Underwing (**Noctua pronuba**)
62. Pearly Underwing (**Peridroma saucia**)
63. Ingrailed Clay (**Diarsia mendica**)
64. Great Brocade (**Eurois occulta**)
65. Broom Moth (**Ceramica pisi**)
66. Antler Moth (**Cerapteryx graminis**)
67. White-speck or American Wainscot (**Mythimna unipuncta**)
68. Red Sword Grass (**Xylena vetusta**)
69. Sword Grass (**Xylena exsoleta**)
70. Dark Brocade (**Blepharita adusta**)
71. Satellite (**Eupsilia transversa**)
72. Blue Underwing (**Catocala fraxini**)
73. Brick (**Agrochola circellaris**)
74. Angle Shades (**Phlogophora meticulosa**)
75. Exile (**Apamea maillardi**)
76. Square-spotted Clay (**Photedes stigmatica**)
77. Large Wainscot (**Rhizedra lutosa**)
78. Pale Mottled Willow (**Caradrina clavipalpis**)
79. Silver Y (**Autographa gamma**)
80. Scarce Silver Y (**Syngrapha interrogationis**)

ARCTIIDAE

81. Cinnabar moth (**Callimorpha jacobaeae**)

LASIOCAMPIDAE

82. Lackey moth (**Malacosoma neustria**)

TOTAL

			Occurrence in Iceland of the Indigenous species						Occurrence outside Iceland		
Occ	Imm	Ind	NW	N	E	S	W	Cen	GB	Nor	NA
		X	X	X	X	X	X	X			
	X								X	X	X
		X				X			X	X	
		X	X	X		X	X	X			X
		X		X	X	X	X		X	X	
	X								X	X	X
		X	X	X	X	X	X	X	X	X	
		X				X	X		X	X	X
		X		X		X	X		X	X	
		X	X	X	X	X	X	X	X	X	X
	X								X		X
		X				X			X	X	X
		X				X			X	X	
		X		X	X	X	X		X	X	X
		X				X			X	X	
X									X	X	
		X				X			X	X	
	X								X	X	
		X	X	X	X	X	X	X	X	X	X
		X		X					X	X	
	X								X	X	
		X	X						X	X	
	X								X	X	X
		X	X	X		X	X		X	X	
X									X	X	
X									X	X	
11	17	54	25	30	26	48	42	17	77	76	46

Key:
Occ = Occurrence depends on presence of man
Imm = Immigrant
Ind = Indigenous
NW = North-west
N = North
E = East
S = South
W = West
Cen = Central
GB = Great Britain
Nor = Norway
NA = North America

Little may be known about the insect fauna of Iceland, but even less is known about other invertebrate species, except that they occur in great variety. On the whole, the invertebrate fauna is composed mostly of boreal and arctic-boreal species, with occasional arctic species and stragglers from the south.

Some of the most interesting ones occur in the sea, including about 225 different polychaete worms, 185 amphipod crustaceans, 170 non-parasitic copepods, 130 different gastropods, 90 species of echinoderms and 95 different bivalve molluscs. One interesting species is a freshwater bivalve, the freshwater pearl mussel (**Margaritifera margaritifera**). A very rare animal threatened with extinction worldwide, it has been extensively exploited for its highly-valued pearls, and its range is being reduced through habitat destruction and pollution. It occurs in Norway as far north as 70°N and it is in no way unlikely that it may also occur in Iceland. But the latest – and still unconfirmed – report was in 1863.

Iceland also has an interesting selection of terrestrial molluscs. There are just over thirty different land snails, mostly preferring the extreme south of the country. They include the common **Cochlicopa lubrica** and relative rarities in Europe such as **Vertigo modesta.**

But, in terms of sheer numbers, fish are probably the "invisible" species in which Iceland most excels itself. Most of these are marine species – and it is typical that most of the freshwater ones really represent marine fish that are gradually establishing themselves in freshwater.

Eels are common in the south and southwest, occur only occasionally in the northwest and west, and are completely absent in the east; and three-spined sticklebacks are very common around the coast and in lowland freshwaters. But the three species occurring in greatest numbers are salmon, arctic charr and trout. They abound in rivers and lakes everywhere. All three are widespread, though particularly common in rivers of the south-west and north. Trout and charr are found in almost all the lakes, but especially Thingvallavatn and Myvatn, where billions of flies, which in midsummer drive people mad, provide an ample supply of food. They guzzle themselves on this rich larval handout by the thousand. Trout fishing permits are easy to obtain.

Members of the Reykjavik Angling Club live in the only city in the world with a first class salmon river virtually running through it.

Iceland's salmon rivers, however, are so good that permits are both rather expensive and often hard to get. Out of 250 rivers in Iceland, 80 of them hold salmon. Pollution is practically non-existent, but many rivers are too cold, particularly in the south-east where they drain from Europe's largest ice-cap, Vatnajokull. Also, because Iceland is so mountainous, most rivers are full of cascades and waterfalls which make many of their courses impassable, even to migrating salmonids. During the past 30 years, about 40 special fish passes have been built over partial and total obstructions in rivers such as these. Other rivers are being improved for salmon by releasing water from impounded lakes in their upper reaches.

Salmon fishing in Iceland is very popular. Resident and foreign fishermen hook an average of 40,000 of the fish per year. There are over 20 different angling clubs in the country, the largest being the Reykjavik Angling Club, which was founded in 1940 and now has a membership of nearly 2,000. Its members live in the only city in the world with a first class salmon river virtually running through it – the Ellidaar river, on the outskirts of Reykjavik.

The salmon fishing season varies from river to river, depending on the temperature of the water, but is specifically 90 days from the day the first fly is cast. It generally

lasts from early June to early September, with July being the best month. Most of the best rivers limit their permits to certain angling societies or are cripplingly expensive. But there are places with both an abundance of fish and freely-available permits, such as Medalfellsvatn, behind Mount Esja (licences are available from Medalfell farm) and Votn in Svinadalur, a few kilometres north of Hvalfjordur (for which licences can be obtained from Geitaberg farm and Ferstikla Gas Station). Overseas anglers wishing to obtain salmon fishing permits for any waters would be advised to contact either the Director of the Institute of Freshwater Fisheries, in Reykjavik, or the Secretary of the Reykjavik Angling Club first. If you plan to take your own fishing gear, bear in mind that there are no fish diseases in Iceland and the authorities require a vet's certificate on entering the country to show that all the gear has been sterilised.

About 40% of the total salmon catch in Iceland, which amounts to some 250 tons a year, is taken by nets in the lower reaches of the largest three glacial rivers. But the majority of rivers are mostly unaffected by netting. Coastal nets account for only about 1% of the total catch these days — and all rod salmon fishing along the coast is banned by law. Indeed, more salmon are probably being put into the sea than taken out of it. A new farming technique called salmon-ranching, which involves large sea-pens holding hundreds of thousands of young salmon, is being developed. Efforts to date look very promising, with something approaching half a million salmon smolts being released throughout Iceland every year.

In recent years, there has also been an increasing interest shown in sea angling. Several international competitions have been held near Reykjavik and Akureyri and sea trips can always be arranged for individuals or groups from any port. The main season is from 1st June to 1st September.

The great wealth of plankton and benthic fauna in Icelandic waters provide optimum conditions for a rich marine fish life. Almost 250 species of marine fish have been recorded — including cod, haddock, herring, whiting, saithe, ling, plaice and lemon sole — but only about 70 of these are known with certainty to propagate in Icelandic waters. The others are migratory visitors or stragglers from oceanic waters, mostly of southern origin. True arctic species are found only off the north and east coasts, for example the Greenland halibut which is known to spawn in these waters.

The rich fishing banks constitute the very foundation of Iceland's economy. Cod is the most important species, in terms of revenue, though capelin catches have been much higher. Other valuable fish include haddock, ocean perch, saithe, catfish, ling and blue ling, halibut, plaice, lemon sole, redfish, tusk and herring. Annual catches of all these species together are in the order of 1.5 million metric tons. On top of that, scallop, shrimp, lobster and over thirty other marine species are involved in the industry.

Iceland has fishing vessels of all shapes and sizes — from tiny one-man craft braving the elements — to stern trawlers with the latest and most advanced equipment. There are about 1,000 vessels in all.

The old traditional processing methods (dating back to the 9th century) of salting and drying are still important today, but since the early 1930s, exports of frozen fish from Iceland to the USA, Britain and the Soviet Union (and, to a lesser extent, to other countries) have been of overriding importance to the Icelandic economy. Japan is the exclusive importer of frozen capelin and capelin-roe. There are over 100 fish freezing plants in operation at the present time.

The only sizeable marine fish likely to be encountered around Iceland is the Greenland shark, which is very common. During spring, adults up to eight metres long can be found in shallow waters around the west, north and east coasts. In the autumn and winter they usually move into deeper waters but occasionally younger sharks come into the shallows following shoals of spawning fish. They are fished from November to May, to provide a meat which is treated as a delicacy in Iceland. It is pressed

Iceland has fishing vessels of all shapes and sizes — from tiny one-man craft, like the "trilla" shown here, to trawlers with the latest and most advanced equipment.

under rocks and then hung in the cool winds to mature, which takes up to three months.

There are no reports of Greenland sharks killing people. They are, however, voracious feeders, taking fish and even seals, whales, seabirds and swimming land mammals such as reindeer. It seems far more likely that it is a lack of opportunity in the cold Icelandic waters rather than generosity that keeps man out of their menu!

Finally, one animal which could be either invisible or absent — no-one knows for sure — is a monster called Lagarfljotsormurinn, or the Lagarfljot serpent. Sightings of this strange creature have been recorded from Lake Lagarfljot in east Iceland since the 14th century. According to the literature, and to eye witnesses still alive, it appears on the lake in very different forms, resembling on different occasions a snake, dragon, skate, seal, horse, a whale blow and even a house!

It has been suggested that methane gas, which was discovered in the lake in 1960, is the main cause, along with misinterpretation of some sea animals. But there are many Icelanders who faithfully have no doubts about the monster's existence.

There are rumours of monsters in some other lakes and rivers of Iceland, though they have never been photographed or caught. The most recent sighting was at Kleifarvatn, in the south-west, in November 1984.

CHAPTER 7

WHERE TO GO

Reykjavik Area

Most journeys to and from Iceland start and finish in Reykjavik, so it is the one place travellers usually manage to get to. The city itself is surprisingly interesting from a natural history point of view — and it makes an excellent base from which to visit other places, by plane, coach or car.

Despite a population of over 90,000, Reykjavik has a fascinating bird fauna and is the only city in the world with a major salmon river running through it.

Lake Tjornin, right in the city centre, is the obvious place to head for, at any time of the year. In summer, it has the world's only colony of arctic terns in a capital city (though only a handful of them are left after drastic population declines in recent years) as well as records of nesting red-necked phalaropes. In winter, there are whooper swans and large numbers of wild ducks sliding around on the ice and being fed by the locals; and there is a small feral population of greylag geese, residents in Reykjavik since 1959. Other birds to look out for on the lake are: eider, Barrow's goldeneye, wigeon, black-headed gull,

lesser black-backed gull, tufted duck, gadwall, scaup and mallard, as well as the less regular passage visitors and vagrants, such as pintail, red-breasted merganser, goosander, pink-footed goose, turnstone and oystercatcher.

In most places around the town centre redpolls, white wagtails and redwings (whose melodious song will follow the visitor in most places throughout the country) are common, and regular nesters. In spring and autumn, there are always small flocks of golden plover on the playing fields and grass verges and, in summer, wheatears are particularly common.

Around the coastal areas of the town meadow pipits, turnstones, dunlin, purple sandpipers (which tend to be very tame), oystercatchers and redshanks are all common. Eider ducks can be seen in flocks of hundreds, particularly in the autumn and winter.

At the height of summer, the harbour is not especially good for birds, though most rare gulls in Iceland tend to be non-breeders "hanging around" at this time of year. But anything can turn up at any time and from October onwards the gull numbers gradually build up towards a population high in mid-winter. It is possible to see more than eight different species here, including Iceland gulls which, surprisingly, do not actually nest in Iceland but fly over from Greenland for the winter. The Iceland wren is not uncommon, especially by the seashore; and snow buntings can often be seen at any time of year — but arrive by the truck load in severe weather — usually with the odd merlin in their wake.

Reykjavik also has a rare luxury in Icelandic terms — more trees than most of the rest of the country — and an interesting, albeit small, botanical garden. Reykjavik Botanical Garden, in Laugardalur (near the stadium) has a good collection of native plants and of certain foreign species that are being grown experimentally. It is open from June to September, weekdays 8.00 am to 10.00 pm and weekends 10.00 am to 10.00 pm.

The Icelandic Museum of Natural History is also worth a visit. Open Sunday, Tuesday, Thursday and Saturday from 1.30 pm to 4.00 pm all year round and daily from 1.30 pm to 4.00 pm in the summer, it has samples of rock formations, most higher plants found in the country, and mounted birds and mammals.

There are several other places within very easy reach. Near the golf course at Seltjarnarnes, to the west of Reykjavik, is a very good spot for shore birds in spring and autumn. Ringed plover, dunlin, purple sandpiper, knot, turnstone and sanderling are the most common. Summering non-breeders in the area include turnstone, purple sandpiper, glaucous gull and red-necked phalarope. There is also a sizeable colony of arctic terns that is a major handicap for the golfers.

Again not too far from Reykjavik, on the Reykjanes Peninsula, are two spectacular bird cliffs: Hafnaberg and Krisuvikurberg. Shag, herring and glaucous gulls, kittiwake, razorbill, puffin, common guillemot, and Brunnich's and black guillemots are all common. Grey phalaropes may still nest nearby (they used to in some numbers until a few years ago), and purple sandpipers and snow buntings also breed on the barren plains behind.

For rare birds, the Reykjanes peninsula is also excellent for vagrants during the autumn — particularly along the coast north of Keflavik Airport — in the "toe" of the "boot", as it appears on a map. This is the region, between Keflavik and Skagaflos and on to Hvalsnes, where local birders go in late August and September for vagrant American waders and, in September, October and early November, for vagrant American passerines.

There are also plenty of day trips from Reykjavik and, while the general rule of thumb for the naturalist should always be the longer you stay the more you will see, a fleeting visit is always better than none at all. Many of the "top 10" sites mentioned in this chapter can be visited on a day trip from Reykjavik, if you are pushed for time. For those who can afford it, day trips from Reykjavik are also available to Kulusuk Island, on Greenland's east coast, or to Angmagssalik or Narssarssuaq for longer stays.

Preceding pages: Lake Tjornin, right in the centre of Reykjavik, offers some excellent bird watching opportunities.

The first party of tourists flew from Iceland to Greenland in 1960. It was a land previously visited only by adventurous scientists and hunters — it scarcely occurred to ordinary travellers to try to negotiate the icebergs of the Greenland fjords. But today there are several direct flights, taking two hours each way, from Reykjavik to Kap Dan on Kulusuk Island. The day trip, organised by Icelandair and Reykjavik Excursions, takes about 12 hours altogether.

Kap Dan is a small isolated eskimo settlement of about 450 people. In fact, it is so remote that it was unknown to the rest of the world until the late 19th century. The inhabitants live mainly by fishing and sealing, and still use the original hand-made kayaks. It is one of the few remaining eskimo settlements that has — as yet — resisted wholesale westernization. But occasional visits by small parties of tourists during the summer are already having a considerable effect on the eskimos, prompting them to do dancing displays, make and sell souvenirs and so on.

The weather in the height of summer is not too cold, the sun is usually shining, the sky clear and the atmosphere crisp and fresh. That is fairly normal for a southern Greenland summer. Visibility is usually excellent and the magnificent mountainous landscape, fjords, glaciers and alpine peaks offer indescribably good views. Even in summer, there are huge floating icebergs off the coast and thousands of pieces of floating ice to add to the scene. One of the other striking things about the place is the silence, which has to be "heard" to be believed.

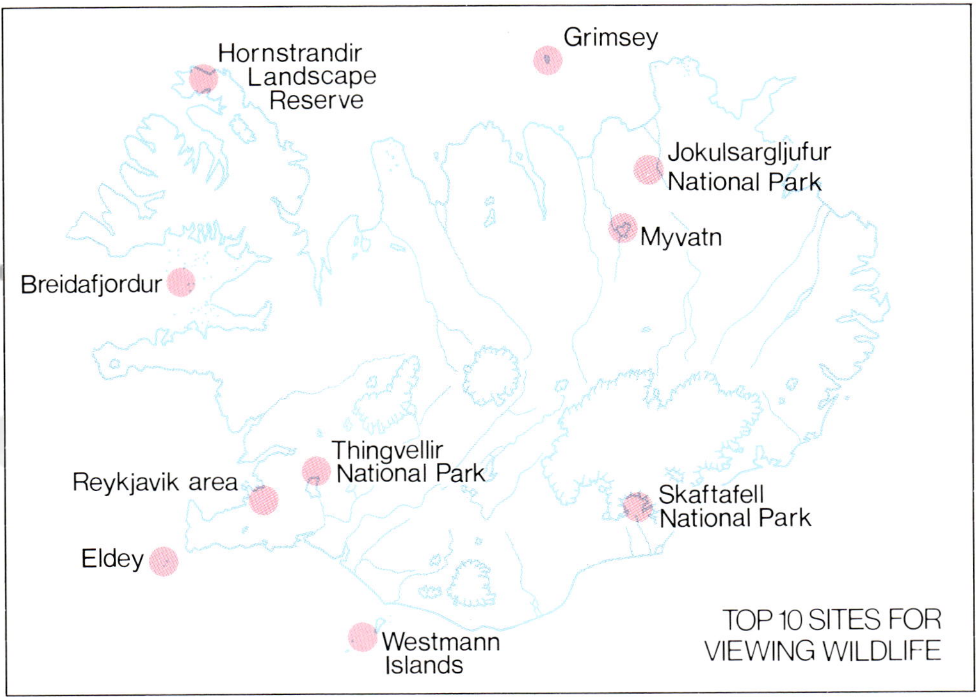

Eldey rises spectacularly from the sea to a height of nearly 80 metres, with precipitous cliffs on all sides.

But be warned. The weather is very changeable – not only may your flight out there be delayed or cancelled – but so may the flight back. It is not unknown for "day-trippers" to find themselves stranded on Kap Dan for several weeks.

Kulusuk Island offers a fascinating array of hardy plants, spectacular tundra landscapes, the odd polar bear in spring, some seals and walruses, interesting birds and plenty of huskies. If you go just for the day, all you can be sure of seeing will be the huskies. After flight delays, a forty minute walk from the airstrip to the village, and so on, there is really very little time to do much more than wander round the village for a while. Go prepared with some Danish krona (it takes ages to change foreign currency at the "bank") and treat any wildlife you see as a bonus.

Eldey

Don't get too excited about Eldey, or Fire Island as it is otherwise known, because you can't actually go there. It is totally protected and also inaccessible, because of its high cliff walls. The only way to see it would be to charter a boat, to sail around the island, which is well worthwhile if you can face the cost.

However, it is home to the world's third largest gannet colony – and so worthy of a mention here, even though it is out-of-bounds to most of us. The island, lying a little over 14 kilometres south-west of the Reykjanes peninsula in the south-west of the country, rises spectacularly from the sea to a height of nearly 80 metres, with precipitous cliffs on all sides. The top is only 100 metres long and 80 metres wide. In absolutely jam-packed conditions, at least 16,000 pairs of gannets nest every year and nearly 50,000 of them can be seen sitting there towards the end of the nesting season. Their droppings completely blanket the top and are so thick and caustic that not so much as a blade of grass is able to grow there – and the stench is overpowering.

The first person to scale Eldey's dangerous cliffs did so before 1750. Regular attempts followed, to collect the birds and their eggs, prompting the authorities to place the islet under total protection in 1940. The last gannet hunting trip was made on 26th August 1939. But it was too late for the world's last breeding pair of great auks, which also lived on the islet. They were killed by a hunting party in 1844. These days, only one scientific expedition is allowed to visit Eldey. The gannets are managing to keep up good numbers by utilizing the ledges and the rocky ridges as well as the top!

Thingvellir National Park

Such a mixture of people and cultures settling in Iceland could easily have led to social problems. The Icelanders recognised that rules and laws were needed, together with some sort of establishment to enforce them, and picked two men to sort it out. One man was sent to Norway to study laws there and the other was sent around Iceland to tell people what was happening and also to find a suitable place for the proposed assembly. The site he chose was Thingvellir, or "Parliament Plains".

Lying 50 kilometres east of Reykjavik, with the largest lake in Iceland and an attractive volcanic landscape of mountains and lava flows, Thingvellir National Park has been in existence since 1930. It was the first National Park to be established in the country.

The original idea behind the creation of the park was to protect this historic spot and, being easily accessible, it is now a great tourist attraction.

The lake itself (of which only the northern part is within the park itself) is of inter-

Thingvellir National Park lies only 50 kilometres east of Reykjavik and contains part of the largest natural lake in Iceland.

est to bird watchers. It is locally acknowledged as one of the best areas in Iceland for gyrfalcons, which are regularly seen there and sometimes breed. It is also Iceland's most northerly breeding site for black-tailed godwits. Waterfowl populations are fairly small, at least compared with Lake Myvatn, probably because of disturbance from holidaymakers in their summer cottages and because of the lake's depth. In most places it is too deep for diving ducks to find food. Some species, such as teal, wigeon, slavonian grebe and water rail, have disappeared in recent years as breeding birds. On the other hand, species such as tufted duck and lesser black-backed gull have started to breed in the area fairly recently. There are also one or two breeding pairs of great northern divers (and flocks of over a dozen all over the lake in autumn); Barrow's goldeneye does not breed but is also seen in small flocks, during autumn and spring; harlequin ducks breed in small numbers by the River Oxara; long-tailed ducks are regularly seen; and there are many ptarmigan, red-necked phalaropes, arctic terns and snow buntings.

There is only one common fish, the arctic charr. The brown trout has declined considerably following the construction of a hydroelectric station locally.

Thingvallavatn is in regular daily contact by bus with Reykjavik. Alternatively, it is possible to drive around its entire perimeter in good weather, though the road is mostly in very poor condition and can be particularly marshy in parts after heavy rain. There is unlimited access and marked hiking trails within the park.

Westmann Islands

The Westmann Islands group, sitting within sight of Iceland's south-west coast, consists of some 15 islands and 30 reefs and rock-pillars. Thought to have been created entirely by volcanic activities towards the end of and after the last glaciation, it constitutes one of the most important seabird haunts in Europe.

The islands are the only Icelandic breeding stronghold for manx shearwater, Leach's petrel and storm petrel, though the nocturnal habits of all three make bird watching difficult. In 1977, however, both petrel species were discovered nesting at Ingolfshofdi, and there are unconfirmed reports from Reynisfjall. The area is teeming with gannets, which can be seen everywhere but breed specifically on four of the smaller, outlying islands. There are also myriads of cliff-nesting birds and, in particular, five species of auk breed in the group. By far the most common are puffins (with hundreds of thousands nesting) but there are also large numbers of common guillemots, and a few Brunnich's and black guillemots. A great variety of other species also breed, including fulmars and glaucous gulls. Indeed, more species of seabirds nest in the Westmann Islands than any other locality in Iceland. There are 15 species there altogether. Many others birds use the Westmann Islands as an important staging post on their migrations.

Because the soil is especially fertile, largely due to the seabird droppings, and thanks to the damp climate, conditions are particularly favourable for a rich vegetation. In-

Scientists are closely following the colonization of Surtsey, recording all new species of animals and plants as they arrive on the new volcanic island.

deed, plant life, particularly on the outer Westmann Islands, is prolific albeit scanty in species. About forty different flowers occur on the islands, including common yarrow, common orach, sea rocket and procumbent pearlwort.

There are two islands of particular interest to the casual visitor: Heimaey, because of its accessibility, and Surtsey, although inaccessible to most people, because of its tremendous interest to evolutionary biologists.

Surtsey

Surtsey is the most recent addition to the group. It was spectacularly created by a submarine eruption lasting over three years during the period 1963–67.

Eruptions actually began on 14th November 1963. They originated in a submarine mountain chain, the Mid-Atlantic Ridge, which takes a zig-zag path from north to south along the floor of the Atlantic Ocean. As the hot lava came into contact with the cold sea water, it cooled to form an accumulation of porous, ashy material and "pillow" lavas. This formed a table-shaped platform of debris, on which Surtsey now rests. More resistant "fluid" lava was piled up over the ash and cinder deposits, making Surtsey a permanent island.

The eruptions lasted until 4th June 1967. A new island had been formed, 10 kilometres off the southern coast of Iceland. Named in honour of Surtr, the god of fire in Norse mythology, it ultimately rose to a height of 173 metres above the sea. Two other islands were built up at the same time, but they were washed away.

In the months and years after its eruptive force had been spent, scientists from all over the world have come to study the birth of this newest volcanic island, measuring a mere 2.6 square kilometres in area. It was much like a reduced picture of Iceland itself, as it must have been when it emerged from under the glacial sheet of the Ice Age.

At first the island was completely devoid of life. The hot lava which had covered Surtsey like the icing on a cake was over 1000°C when it flowed, so its surface was sterilized from the start. And it was repeatedly sterilized by the constant fall of ash from nearby craters in the sea. Nothing could withstand the heat and the continual ash fall.

The sequence of events the world saw was not rapid. But when things quietened down a little, even before the eruptions had finished, seabirds began to settle on the island and micro-organisms and plants were carried there by the air and ocean currents.

The first terrestrial invertebrate to appear on Surtsey was a dipteran fly, which was discovered on 14th May 1964. The following year there were 6 species of flies and midges, 2 species of moths and 1 species of mite. Most of them were already common on neighbouring islands. Many species of butterflies and moths have now been recorded, including the silver Y moth, which is not native to Iceland but migrates from Britain and elsewhere in Europe.

The first seeds and sprouting plants were also discovered fairly early on, either carried in on the wind or else dropped by birds. Once, a shower of small fruits of the groundsel came drifting in on the air like an invasion of parachutists.

But it was not until the summer of 1965 that the first of the higher plant species managed to grow there, the sea rocket. By 1967, four species of coastal plants were resident and the sea rocket had become a flourishing permanent colonizer, blooming and producing large numbers of seeds.

Inland, plants were slower to appear. There was no ocean carrier to help, the substrate was still sterile, the salinity high and the moisture content low. But after a few years the first mosses began to get a foothold near the old craters and, together with a few algal species, quickly took advantage of the warm and hot vapours still being ejected, which provided both heat and moisture.

Only these few species could survive on Surtsey as pioneers — most plants can colonize an area only if others have carefully prepared the ground before them. These days, it is reckoned that at the very least an average of one new species of vascular plant is added to the island's flora every year.

The seas around the Westmann Islands have always been extremely rich in marine life. During the explosions, lava and ash flowed down the sides of the new island and covered and destroyed all the organisms on the sea floor. But recolonization of the benthic plants and animals soon began. Barnacles quickly settled on the young rocks within a few years and even seals returned to their favourite but somewhat changed fishing grounds, and made use of the new beaches provided for them to rest on.

It is the birds, however, that have always been the most evident around Surtsey, particularly gulls and waders taking advantage of the rich marine life around the other islands as a source of food. Many were present from the beginning, but they were relying completely on energy sources obtained from outside the boundaries of Surtsey. Indeed, most of them still are.

60 species of birds have so far visited Surtsey, but with every passing year the list grows and grows. To date, the visitors have included: redwing, snow bunting, dunlin, oystercatcher, kittiwake, great black-backed gull, herring gull, glaucous gull, arctic tern, red-necked phalarope, turtle dove, common guillemot, raven, merlin, long-eared owl, wheatear, pink-footed goose, red-breasted merganser, squacco heron, short-eared owl, European robin, corncrake, willow warbler and redstart.

Most of them have just been passing through or vagrants. Surtsey lies on the major migratory path for birds travelling between Iceland, and Greenland and Can-

Heimaey is world famous for a fateful volcanic eruption which began there on 23rd January 1973. These days, life on the island is back to normal.

ada and, inevitably, being the southernmost territory of Iceland, has become the first landing place for migratory birds arriving in spring from other European countries.

But while many of them are unusual rarities with only a very small part to play in the island's ecosystem, others have stayed. The merlin, for example, is nearly always present and can be seen feeding on the visiting wheatears, while the kittiwake (which even alighted on the island during intervals between the worst eruptions) could almost be described as common. And most species unknowingly bring some kind of plant or invertebrate with them, or provide excreta fertilisers containing essential minerals and organic matter. Snow buntings from Britain that have alighted on Surtsey have been found to have viable seeds (that are able to germinate) in their gizzards and droppings, thereby playing their part in long-distance dispersal. Mineralogists were able to identify grains of sand found with the seeds as originating from the moors of Scotland.

The first birds actually began nesting in the summer of 1970. One pair each of black guillemot and fulmar, seabirds common to the Westmann Islands, were the first — and they now nest every year and are slowly building up their numbers. Several pairs of great black-backed gulls have laid their eggs and raised their young on Surtsey in recent years, and kittiwakes and herring gulls have also nested.

So a few living organisms have found their stay tolerable, gained a foothold and even increased. These pioneers make it easier for others, such as birds, to follow in their wake. Bird droppings act as fertilisers that augment the vegetation and this, in turn, makes the spot a better habitat for the birds themselves. Decomposing plants and other refuse also become food for insects and various bacteria. All parties derive some benefit from the co-existence — the first few links of a food chain are formed — and it is the beginning of an ecosystem. But still the lack of food sources hinders the real colonization of most **terrestrial** birds.

Today Surtsey is a protected area and has been made a scientific research station. Scientists are closely following its colonization, recording all new species of animals and plants as they arrive — and watching constantly for any signs of renewed activity! The birth of Surtsey was itself an interesting geological phenomenon, but the island has become an almost unique biological laboratory, providing a natural lesson on how species manage to disperse across the oceans to remote islands and how they colonize such barren, hostile habitats.

Visits by outsiders are understandably severely restricted. One chance factor in the immigration of a living organism may have a great effect on the future development of the island community. It is possible to obtain special permission to land there, but it is very rarely granted. Alternatively, it is possible to view the island from the air, and there are several excursions of this kind from Reykjavik to choose from.

Heimaey

Surtsey is second only in size to Heimaey, at 5 kilometres long the largest and most accessible of the Westmann Islands. It is also the only inhabited island in the group.

Heimaey, too, has a dramatic volcanic history (it was itself formed by volcanic eruptions at the end of the last Ice Age) and is world famous for a fateful volcanic eruption which began there on 23rd January 1973. During that tragic night, a sudden eruption began right next to the town. In a miraculous operation the entire population of 5,300 was moved by boat and plane, in the dead of night, to the mainland in a matter of a few hours and without a single accident. The eruption lasted until May and, when the islanders gradually began to return to their homes, they found half the town completely submerged in lava. The rest was blanketed with thick layers of ash.

The harbour and the main fish-processing plants (Heimaey is the most important fishing centre of Iceland and most people on the island are engaged in fishing) were saved by cooling the onmoving lava flow with sea water and eventually stopping it. But there was a great deal of damage elsewhere and the islanders had to set about the long task of reconstruction and restoration of the town. Gradually they returned to their much altered island home. Though many buildings had disappeared, the island itself had been considerably enlarged (by an estimated 200 million tons of lava) and the harbour had been greatly improved thanks to some volcanic infilling in the right places. The islanders have also managed to harness the heat in the lava to heat their houses!

These days, life on the island is back to normal and the events of 1973 are almost, but not quite, forgotten. The eruption is now often spoken of as a turning point — events are said to have occurred before or after the eruption. Not everyone has returned, though, and the population now stands at about 5,000. Most of the grass you can see in the area has been planted by the islanders, after putting soil down first, with the result that it is now almost as green as it once was.

Heimaey is rich in plant and animal life. The only exception to the rule is the fact that it has a grand total of only one tree, the pride and joy of the islanders and a feature of all the "island tours". But seabirds are everywhere and the island has some of the most spectacular bird cliffs in Europe. As chapter 8 explains, egg-gathering and bird-catching once played a major role in the life of the islanders. Puffin catching is still a popular sport and, even these days, some 100,000 puffins are taken every year with no obvious harmful effects on the population.

The main season is July—August, when puffin-catchers (who sleep overnight in the white huts, which are erected specially for these hunting trips and are clearly visible on all the outlying islands) sit out of sight on the cliffs and catch them with special nets as the birds fly alongside, or trap them in their nesting burrows. One man has been known to catch more than 1,300 in a single day. These days, 700—900 is considered good. Smoked puffin is eaten on Heimaey and also sold to the mainland.

Fulmars, too, are taken in moderate numbers. The locals scale the cliffs and stun the young birds with sticks, then throw them down to be picked up at the bottom. Eggs are also taken, from guillemots and fulmars, by lowering one another over the clifftops on ropes.

A spectacular sight not to be missed is the large numbers of shearwaters which can be seen gathering off Heimaey's coast in the evenings in early summer.

It is possible to visit Heimaey for the day from Reykjavik, or to go for a longer stay. There is an airport (the same runway which was used for the rescue operations) with daily air connections with the capital, as

Young puffins are often disorientated by the lights of Heimaey, soon after leaving their burrows, and are safely returned to the sea by the children of the town.

well as ferryboat connections with Thorlakshofn. There is a guesthouse, a first class hotel, camp site, several cafes, a bank, a hospital and all other facilities.

But a few words of warning. The flight normally takes only 25 minutes — but don't hold out too much confidence in arriving on time. Varying weather conditions make it a very irregular and unreliable service. You can sometimes wait days to get there and even then, after a bumpy flight you will never forget, take days to get back. But take heart — Icelandair's pilots on the route are reputed to be among the best in the world. And they certainly need to be! As conditions do change all the time, it is well worth taking overnight gear — even if you don't intend to stay! But on a clear day, if you are lucky, you can be rewarded with fabulous views of Hekla and Surtsey from the air.

The ferry takes a long time anyway, involving an hour's coach ride from Reykjavik to Thorlakshofn on the south coast, and then a three hour boat trip to Heimaey. It can be very rough at times but provides some fantastic views of the seabird colonies and of Surtsey.

Finally, beware of the Summer Festival which takes place during the first week in August, because scores of Icelanders come over from the mainland and consequently there is rarely any available accommodation.

Skaftafell National Park

As well as containing the biggest ice-cap, the widest expanse of sandplain in Iceland, and being within a stone's throw of the highest peak, Skaftafell is also one of the best places in the country for wildlife.

Although it did not officially become a national park until 15th September 1967 (the second to be established in Iceland) the region has been famous for centuries for its scenery and natural beauty — splendid waterfalls, impressive ravines, a luxuriant and varied vegetation and enormous colonies of breeding birds.

The landscape is deeply dissected by glacial and fluvial erosion, and the whole area is very characteristic of an alpine region even though the highest point of the surrounding mountains is only 1430 metres above sea level. Three glaciers lie partly or completely within Skaftafell's boundaries: Skeidararjokull, Morsarjokull and Skaftafellsjokull. The first of these is the largest valley glacier in Europe at about 1600 square kilometres. The glacier rivers are also partly or fully within the park, the Skeidara being by far the biggest and a major obstacle to travellers until it was bridged in 1974.

Go to Skaftafell and you cannot fail to see Vatnajokull, or the "Water Glacier". The greatest ice-cap in Europe, it towers above the narrow coastal plain of south-east Iceland. Glacier tongues slide down between the high mountains and innumerable glacial rivers make their winding and unpredictable way to the Atlantic Ocean. Under its ice-cap are fast-flowing rivers, laden with mud and silt. The deposits in these glacial rivers are continually piling up, thus forcing them to change course frequently and form a bewildering pattern between the mountains and the coast.

About 210 species of flowering plants have been recorded in Skaftafell and, below about 700 metres, the vegetation is generally rich. Even some dry river beds and glacial moraines are now covered by a variety of species, even birch shrub in some parts. In the main, the lower slopes of the park are covered with shrubby birch, the tallest of the trees being only 10 metres high. Above the shrub limit, there are heaths, moorland, bogs and sparsely vegetated gravel flats, with scattered birches between 260 metres and about 600 metres. The ground vegetation consists mostly of wood cranesbill, harebell (which must be the most characteristic plant of the region and is typical of East Iceland), lady's bedstraw, angelica, sweet vernalgrass, and common bentgrass.

Two other species characteristic of East Iceland, and more conspicuous in Skaftafell than in most other parts of the country, are the yellow mountain saxifrage, found on stony ground, and the pyramidal saxifrage, on ledges and cracks in the cliffs. A number of other species, rare elsewhere in

Iceland, also grow in Skaftafell, including twayblade, maidenhair spleenwort, and common valerian.

Skaftafell is also good for insects, with a great diversity of species compared with other parts of the country and a surprisingly high proportion of species of southern origin. Since there are no real lakes and few suitable rivers there are few salmon or trout.

The predominant breeding birds of the area — they seem to be all over the place — are great skuas, arctic skuas and great black-backed gulls. About 3000 pairs of skuas nest just outside the Park itself on the Skeidararsandur sand plain, one of the most important breeding sites for these birds in the northern hemisphere. It is a spectacular sight and a thrilling experience for the bird watcher in late May and early June.

Redwings are also common birds, nesting in the birch woodlands and scrubland, and there are snipe, meadow pipits and bramblings (a recent new addition, known mainly as an irregular autumn and winter visitor elsewhere in Iceland). Red-throated divers have also recently been recorded breeding on the moraine ponds in the area and there are a few red-necked phalaropes. The Icelandic wren, a larger, separate subspecies found only in Iceland, is more numerous in the park (particularly amongst the birch scrub) than in any other part of the country. Ptarmigan, also, are particularly common, and often wander among the cars and tents near the park's headquarters.

There are few mammals in the Skaftafell

Go to Skaftafell and you cannot fail to see Vatnajokull, or the "Water Glacier". The greatest ice-cap in Europe, it towers above the narrow coastal plain of south-east Iceland.

area. The arctic fox did occur but, as a result of hunting, is very rarely seen and may even be extinct in this area. Nevertheless, until recently it was probably the only wild mammal likely to be encountered. When one was spotted, more often than not it was in the campsite area. Until recently, Skaftafell was unique in that no rodents were found there, supposedly because they had difficulty in getting access because of its isolation. Until the road circling Iceland was completed, the glacial rivers remained the last obstacle to animals as well as to man. The long-tailed field mouse was first recorded in the area in about 1964 and seems to be doing well. House mice, too, are thought to be establishing themselves after reaching the park via the recently-built bridges across the rivers. Polar bears are said to have made an occasional appearance in the area on drifting ice flows in very severe winters many centuries ago. But the last reported sighting was in 1748 — so there is not a good chance of seeing one! But harbour and grey seals are regularly seen in large numbers on the seashore below Skaftafell to make up for it.

Access to Skaftafell is easy by road from Reykjavik, though it was little more than a decade ago that many of the glacial rivers still had not been bridged and the round-about motoring distance was about 1,100 kilometres. Thanks to the new direct and bridged route, it has dropped to 340 kilometres today. The Park is open from June 1st to September 15th. Outside these dates, visitors are allowed (weather permitting) but permission is required to stay overnight. There are virtually no roads for cars beyond the parking area next to the camp site at Skaftafell itself. However, there are plenty of interesting — and marked — walks from this area, ranging from about one hour in duration to a very full day, to view the various glaciers, waterfalls and wildlife.

The camping grounds are excellent and spacious, with all mod cons and facilities, including a shop and a cafeteria. The setting is magnificent. If you do wish to camp elsewhere special permission from the park warden is needed.

Jokulsargljufur National Park

Established in 1973, Jokulsargljufur National Park comprises a spectacular canyon in north-east Iceland, some 25 kilometres long, about half a kilometre wide and over 100 metres deep. The park itself extends a further 30 kilometres northwards from the Dettifoss waterfall, covering about 150 square kilometres altogether.

The Jokulsa Canyon is the largest canyon in Iceland and downstream there is a unique series of three waterfalls: Selfoss, Dettifoss and Hafragilsfoss. In the central part of the canyon, the valley is broader with a luxuriant vegetation and many spring-fed streams and rivers. Vigabjargsfoss, once one of the most notable of all the waterfalls, is found in this section, but virtually disappeared in 1940 when the river shifted its course. Up in the north, the canyon becomes known as Vesturdalur valley, a spectacular combination of old basalt columns of varying size and shape, sheer cliff walls and grassy plains, ponds and caves. There are plenty of interesting — and marked — walks here, ranging from about an hour in duration to a very full day. These take you to see the Jokulsa river, waterfalls, cliffs and caves, vegetation, historical ruins and birds.

Jokulsa Canyon has a climate of its own, rather more continental than most parts of Iceland outside the north-east. It has a relatively low rainfall and long winters and frosts can occur at almost any time of year; indeed, much the same as at Myvatn.

But, apart from the magnificent scenery, the birdlife of Jokulsargljufur National Park alone makes it worth visiting. As in most areas of Iceland, birds are better represented than other animals. The only common mammal is the long-tailed field mouse. Arctic foxes and mink are seen very occasionally, though the former have declined considerably in recent years and the latter never have had a strong foothold. Reindeer were present in the 19th century, but had disappeared entirely by 1930.

Moorland birds are the most common, notably ptarmigan, snow bunting, meadow pipit, redwing, golden plover, wheatear, wren and snipe. Gyrfalcons and merlins nest in small numbers on the cliffs, as do much larger numbers of ravens. Redshank, red-necked phalaropes and a few species of ducks and geese (which are particularly conspicuous in late summer when they travel downriver with their families) are found near the lakes and ponds.

Jokulsargljufur is the only area in the north of the country where great skuas nest, choosing the sandy stretches near the sea just to the north of the Park. Fulmars have recently established themselves at Asbyrgi, a huge area in the north ringed by sheer cliffs and formed by floods several thousand years ago.

Migratory charr enter the Jokulsa river in late summer, along with very small numbers of salmon. The small lake Astjorn, in the north of the Park, teems with stickleback and has recently had charr introduced.

Altogether, some 220 species of vascular plants are known to grow in the canyon area. The most prominent plant communities are brushwood and heath. There are still some stands of birch and willow woodland, particularly in sheltered places along the river gorge, and rowan occurs on cliffs and scree slopes. The heaths are covered with various types of dwarf shrubs, willows, dwarf birch and juniper, as well as bearberry on the hummocks.

Lichens are common (particularly the bright-yellow **Alectoria ochroleuca**). The bottle sedge is the dominant species in wet bogs and often forms reed beds around ponds. Other common species include: wood cranesbill in sheltered hollows; an-

Jokulsargljufur National Park comprises a spectacular canyon in north-east Iceland, where the sun never sets in summer. This photograph was taken, in mid-June, at 2.00 am.

gelica around the springs; wood millet in woodlands and rocky tracts; willow herb along the river; and serrated wintergreen almost anywhere. The harebell (found in Vesturdalur valley) and Faeroeic lady's mantle (in Asbyrgi) are both present, marking the western boundary of these two East-Iceland species.

Rarities found in Jokulsargljufur include herb paris, rosebay willowherb and meadow vetchling at As in the extreme north, and interrupted clubmoss at Holmatungur on the west side of the canyon in the central section. In the late summer, wooded tracts are often teeming with mushrooms, especially the edible **Boletus scaber,** though also a poisonous species, the fly agaric **Amanita muscaria** — called berserkjasveppur, the berserk mushroom, in Icelandic.

The Jokulsa Canyon is best explored on foot — indeed, many areas are only accessible in this way. Access is from the highway through Kelduhverfi as far as Dettifoss, and from there via a track suitable only for 4-wheel-drive vehicles to the road between Grimsstadir and Myvatn. There are camp sites at Asbyrgi and Vesturdalur, both with wardens who are able to provide information for visitors and occasionally give guided tours on foot during the open season 15th June to 1st September.

Lake Myvatn

Lake Myvatn, in north-east Iceland, is a strange meeting place of the world's temperate and arctic zones, and of the birds and flowers from east and west. Dotted with green islets and set in a lunar landscape of lava flows and volcanoes, it is the fourth largest lake in Iceland. It is a true oasis of life on the edge of a desert.

Myvatn and its associated river, the Laxa, which flows 55 kilometres north to the Arctic Ocean, is renowned throughout the ornithological world for its waterfowl. The area supports Europe's and, arguably, the world's largest concentration of breeding ducks, with as many as 50,000 breeding pairs on the lake and its surrounding area some years. These include anything between a few and 5,000 pairs of each of all fifteen species which nest in Iceland.

It is also the most interesting part of the country from a volcanological and geomorphological point of view. Indeed, nowhere else in Europe offers such a wide variety of natural wonders. The region is littered with a range of pseudo-craters, volcanoes of a multitude of types and shapes (it is near where the Americans trained their astronauts in preparation for landing on the moon) and hundreds of incredibly colourful muddy sulphur pools, or solfataras. And, since Myvatn lies on the western edge of the volcanic belt that runs from north to south, all the geological formations are very recent.

Sulphur is characteristic of the area as a whole and, a few centuries ago, the locals profited considerably from the extraction of it from the sulphur mines at Namafjall. The only time in history when a Swedish king considered a plan for conquering Iceland was when Erik XIV in 1567 had become short of gunpowder and wanted the Icelandic sulphur mines! The plan was abandoned but the extraction of sulphur in the area ceased a long time ago.

Although about 37 square kilometres in area, Myvatn is incredibly indented and irregular in shape, making long-distance views across the water almost unattainable. There are also many mountains around its edges, formed by eruptions under the ice sheet in the glacial periods of the Ice Age. It is a very shallow lake, with an average depth of only about two metres and a maximum of just over four.

Just south of the Arctic Circle, at 63° 35' North, and 278 metres above sea level, Myvatn is covered with ice for nearly seven months of the year. There are regular night frosts and there is a large range in daily temperatures, which together result in considerable wildlife population fluctuations. However, the climate is more continental than in most places in Iceland and the area boasts a relatively large number of days with sun — as well as less rain than anywhere else in the country, thanks to the shadowing effect of the Vatnajokull glacier. In many years, there is less rain at Myvatn

Above: Lake Myvatn is the most interesting part of Iceland from a volcanological and geomorphological point of view.

Below: Lake Myvatn area supports Europe's and, arguably, the world's largest concentration of breeding ducks.

by a factor of ten compared with some areas in the south! But don't discard all hats and umbrellas — small but disagreeable mountain showers are frequent, more often on the east side of the lake than the west!

The area around Lake Myvatn has been settled by farmers for many centuries. It is unique in the country in that it has probably been managed as a kind of nature conservation area since before the eighteenth century. Official status followed a scientific survey in the late 1960s and early 1970s, after which the Icelandic government agreed in 1974 to grant, by a special Act of Parliament, nature reserve status to no less than 440,000 hectares of the area.

Myvatn has an extremely varied and luxuriant flora, even though many areas, notably those with the youngest lava, are frequently almost bare. In spring and early summer flowers grow everywhere — particularly on the route to Akureyri. Common vascular plants in the vicinity include butterwort, field and small gentians, alpine mouse-ear, hairy stonecrop, woody willow, water and mountain avens, ladies' bedstraw, sorrel, boreal fleabane and yarrow.

In general terms, the south and west (which has the majority of arctic and alpine plants) have most of the bogs (dominated by sedges) and moors, while the northern and eastern sides of the lake are primarily covered with birch. Some islands and islets of the ponds are also luxuriantly covered with birch, as well as willow, angelica and meadow buttercup. This is also the place to find the hawkweedleaved treaclemustard (popularly known locally as the "Queen of Myvatn") which is a tall member of the cabbage family and one of the characteristic plants of the district. Bottle sedge forms reedbeds around the ponds.

The islets in the river Laxa are dominated by tea-leaved willow, angelica, marsh marigold, meadow buttercup and wood cranesbill. While the youngest lava is bare, older lava areas which have escaped the devastating effects of wind erosion are covered with many kinds of mosses, at least in areas where shrubs and small birch trees have not yet got a foothold. The commonest mosses, particularly luxuriant amongst the coppices, are **Rhacomitrium canescens** and, to a lesser extent, **R. lanuginosum.** Lichens are also very prominent, in particular the bright orange **Xanthoria elegans** and **X. candelaria,** and the almost white **Cetraria nivalis** and **C. cucullata.** The greenish-yellow **Alectoria ochroleuca** colours the tops of many pseudocraters.

Since the lake is so shallow, solar radiation is able to reach the bottom and there is teeming phytoplankton and other vegetation in the water itself. This is also partly due to spring water rich in nutrients, which drains into Myvatn from the east shore. As a result, at the height of the season (in July) the lake often becomes quite opaque from the profusion of the plankton and algae, particularly blue-green algae. These are the dominant plants in the lake itself, comprised mainly of **Anabaena flos-aquae,** which causes an "algal bloom" in the lake almost every summer, **Fragilaria construens** and **Cladophora aegagropila,** which covers the bottom in extensive mats. Other vegetation in the lake includes spiked watermilfoil, the three-leaved water crowfoot and slender-leaved pondweed.

Since Myvatn is overflowing with nutrients encouraging such a rich plant growth, there is plenty of organic matter for animal life. This has been exploited by enormous swarms of midges and blackflies, which gather on the shores of the lake in calm weather during summer and autumn, and are certainly the most noticeable of the lake's invertebrates. This is where the name "Myvatn" was derived — "my" is Icelandic for "midge" — so "Myvatn" actually means "Lake of the Midges"!

These insects are useful because they

serve to fertilize fields surrounding the lake and, since their larvae live on the bottom, at the same time form an important food source for the fish and ducks. Dark lines can be seen on the bottom, where diving ducks have scraped away for the hidden larvae. The midges make their home in the lake and the blackfly larvae, which form the staple diet of Barrow's goldeneye, harlequin duck and trout, are found only in the River Laxa. The surplus fly production at Myvatn also accounts for the biggest Atlantic salmon in Iceland!

Uncountable billions of several species of midge emerge from the lake at specific times during the summer — and these are, without a doubt, times to avoid. Although the midges don't bite, the swarms (which, incidentally, are formed by "dancing" males trying to attract females) can be unbelievably enormous, particularly at the outlet of Myvatn into the Laxa. But the blackflies can be unbearable because, although they are not so numerous, the females do bite, especially in damp and calm weather. Emergences are usually in June and August, other months being relatively free of the little beasts.

Enormous numbers of other invertebrates also live in both the lake and the river. Notable amongst these are the astronomical numbers of minute crustaceans of various kinds. Indeed, half the known freshwater invertebrates of Iceland, (nearly 250 species out of a total of some 500) can be found here. Important macro-invertebrates among these include **Daphnia longispina** and **Eurycercus lamellatus,** both water fleas; **Chironomus islandicus** and **Tanytarsus gracilentus,** both midges; **Simulium vittatum,** a blackfly; **Lymnaea pereger,** a freshwater snail; and **Tubifex tubifex,** a kind of earthworm.

Four species of fish are found in the region. Most important is the resident population of arctic charr. There are two particularly interesting local varieties, one of which is found only around the submerged springs (which "feed" Myvatn) on the eastern side of the lake, and the other, a smaller version, which lives in caves and fissures in the lava close to the lake. Thousands of these fish are taken from the lake annually.

Trout migrate from the Laxa to spawn near the eastern springs and salmon migrate up the river in spring. The upper part of the Laxa is popular with trout fishermen and the lower section is outstanding for salmon fishing and one of the best salmon rivers in Iceland. A "salmon ladder" has been built to help the fish reach the upper part of the river but, so far, this has not been very successful. Fishing permits are sold at Arnarvatn. Fishing for the charr is also allowed in Lake Myvatn and permits for this are sold at the Elda Lodge in Reykjahlid. Three-spined sticklebacks are very common — though, unlike the other three, of no commercial value.

It is difficult to know where to begin to describe the birds of this birder's paradise. Myvatn's ducks are world famous and there are many other exciting specialities guaranteed to raise the bird watcher's blood pressure. In fact, it is possible to find most Icelandic species at Myvatn (with the exception of cliff-dwelling seabirds) and some of them are rarely seen in other parts of the country.

It would be difficult to find a more crowded and diverse waterfowl breeding ground anywhere in the world thanks largely to the exceptionally rich food supply but also to a wide variety of nesting habitats: there are no fewer than 50 islands and islets. 15 species of duck nest in the area, with up to 100,000 present at any one time.

With about 800 pairs on the lake (virtually the entire European population) Barrow's goldeneye is an abundant species here, even though it doesn't breed anywhere else in the country. Harlequin ducks (which breed nowhere else in Europe) are common on the river, and the great northern diver is frequently noted amongst the throng. All three species are American and breed in no other country in Europe. Furthermore, the American wigeon is now seen every summer but has not yet bred.

The commonest species in the area is scaup, with tufted duck and wigeon not far behind. Common scoter, which rarely breed elsewhere in Iceland, are also numerous and there are a number of red-breasted mergansers, long-tailed ducks, mallard and teal. Less common, but regular, are gadwall (a very rare species anywhere else in Iceland), pintail, shoveler and goosander. Large numbers of eider breed along the lower stretches of the Laxa and are often seen on the lake. Pochard have bred, but only on rare occasions. The common goldeneye is often spotted, though there are no confirmed records of it breeding; and there are about 600 non-breeding whooper swans present in late summer and winter. They normally segregate into well-defined groups to moult in the area, though a few pairs do sometimes stay over to breed.

The exceptionally rich waterfowl populations of Myvatn have been exploited for a very long time, although records have been kept only since 1712. Since then, the birds themselves have been completely protected from shooting or trapping but the exploitation of their eggs has been fair game for the local land-owners, who maintain that duck eggs are still of great importance to their livelihood.

Despite the fact that tradition and law have always demanded that at least four eggs be left in each nest, egg collecting has reached a peak of 40,000 or more a year in the past. The birds still seem to be thriving, however, and egg collections have now dropped to 2-5,000 a year.

There are two species of goose breeding in the area: greylag and pink-footed. White-fronted, brent and barnacle geese are occasionally seen but rarely, if ever, breed.

Other species to look out for, in no particular order, are: slavonian grebe (about 250 pairs nest around Myvatn — nowhere in Iceland is it more numerous); red-necked phalarope, which is surprisingly abundant; arctic and great skuas; and merlin, ptarmigan, whimbrel, raven, snow bunting, redwing, wheatear and red-throated diver. There are hundreds, if not thousands, of nesting arctic terns and just a few pairs of gyrfalcons, nicknamed the King of Myvatn and sometimes seen gliding over the lake.

Arctic foxes are probably the most interesting mammals likely to be seen. But, although once common, their numbers have declined dramatically in the last two centuries, due to hunting. There were twenty dens in the Myvatn area in the 1920s, but only half a dozen active ones are known today.

Mink were first seen in the area in the early fifties, have increased in numbers and are fairly common nowadays. The only other mammal known to occur is the long-tailed field mouse, which is particularly abundant.

Overall, **the** place to head for — without a doubt — is a bridge over the Laxa, in the south-west corner of Myvatn, near where the river joins the lake. This is where the tumbling water forces its way in foaming rapids and eddies between rich banks and numerous small lava islands with luxuriant vegetation of willows and angelica. About 340 small islands dot its channel. Goosander and harlequin ducks are almost exclusively river ducks — and virtually never seen on the lake — so this is the best place to see them. The harlequins here are fairly used to excited bird watchers and consequently make understanding subjects for photographers. There are also good chances of Barrow's goldeneye, long-tailed duck, red-necked phalarope and arctic skuas. Don't forget to walk **upstream** — then the ducks are more likely to come towards you — as the water is so fast-flowing.

Dimmuborgir, half-way down the east side of the lake, is an area of grotesque — but spectacular — lava architecture which is also worth a visit. Lava pillars and walls, 15—20 metres high, tower above a labyrinth of lava canyons, caves and tunnels, through which the old lava rivers once flowed. The most famous cave is called Kirkjan (the Church) which has a large Gothic-style vault. It is reputed to be the best place to see gyrfalcons but, in practice, one's chances are slim. By way of consolation, it is a superb area for volcanists, so a journey would not be wasted. Do make a note of landmarks in the area, because it is easy to get lost. If you do lose your way, keep walking in a straight line until you hit a fence and then follow it in either direction until you come to the only gate!

The road around the lake, only 38 kilometres in length, is always worth a drive or ride, providing close views of its shores all the way round. Remember to leave more time for the eastern side, which tends to be most productive.

And pay a visit to Sandvatn, a small lake to the north-west, which has birch scrub (the only trees for miles) and plenty of ducks. There is more likelihood of seeing gyrfalcon here than at Myvatn proper, as well as passerines characteristic of the area. This is certainly the place for early risers, if you want to get the most out of it. Access is rather difficult, though, and only possible from the south.

Finally, sightseers should not miss the Namafjall sulphur hills with their bubbling muddy sulphur pools and steam vents, just five kilometres east of Myvatn. From the top is an excellent view of the Myvatn area. Godafoss (otherwise known as the Waterfall of the Gods and spectacularly set at the head of a canyon eroded into a lava flow by the river Skjalfandafljot) and Dettifoss, at 44 metres high the most powerful waterfall in Europe, are also essential places to visit.

Access to Myvatn is easy. It is open all year round, except during the period May 15th to July 20th, when the north-west shore and all islands in the lake are out of bounds to safeguard nesting birds. Akureyri, nearby, is in direct contact with Reykjavik by both plane and bus several times each day. The plane ride only takes about an hour and, if you are very luckily blessed with a clear day, provides some spectacular aerial sightseeing as an added bonus. The bus journey is cheaper, but takes about eight hours. If there is a choice, opt for a route which takes you straight through the central highlands and the largest desert in the country, rather than the less spectacular (and more accessible) coastal route.

Myvatn itself is in direct contact with Akureyri by bus, with a regular service from mid-June to the end of August. If you have a car, an approach from the east (the opposite direction) is quite unforgettable for the last couple of hundred kilometres, taking you through an amazing lunar landscape.

Once you are in the area, there is no problem in hiring boats, bicycles, lightweight motorcycles and cars (which tend to be very expensive) in Reykjahlid.

Despite the fact that only about 600 Icelanders live in the entire Myvatn area, there is a great variety of accommodation available to visitors, mostly in the north-east. There are two excellent hotels, a youth hostel, a farmhouse, private homes, a selection of sleeping bag accommodation and even a few beds in one of the post offices. There are also campsites at Reykjahlid and Skutustadir, both with lavatories, hot and cold running water and shops. However you intend to stay, though, it is always worth booking in advance, even if only a few days ahead, since it is an extremely popular destination. Most visitors to Iceland converge on Myvatn at some time or other during their stay.

Grimsey

Grimsey is the most northerly point of Iceland, lying exactly on the Arctic Circle and 40 kilometres from the mainland. Less than four kilometres long and half as wide, it is the permanent home of a hardy breed of sheep farmers, fishermen and, until recently, professional bird-catchers.

The east side of the island is mostly steep cliffs, rising to about 100 metres high, and inclining gradually towards sea level on the western side. There are some spectacular and beautiful views across the sea and towards the mainland in summer. To the visitor, Grimsey also offers well over 100 species of flowering plants, 36 different nesting birds (including 11 different seabirds) and a magnificent feeling of isolation.

Bird life is abundant on the island, especially with regard to cliff-nesters. All six species of auk nest on the island and there are still little auks there — the last of Iceland's remnant population — which have survived a dramatic population decline all over the country. Its extreme rarity probably has a lot to do with climate, since it has never been very common, but there are

Less than four kilometres long and half as wide, Grimsey is split in two by the Arctic Circle.

nevertheless strict legal measures to protect the species. It is already down to only two or three pairs, and yet is incredibly numerous at Jan Mayen and other nearby Arctic strongholds. The dive for extinction seems to be a national phenomenon peculiar to Iceland, almost certainly because it is a peripheral population on the southern boundary of its range.

Also around the coast, there are vast colonies of Brunnich's guillemots and puffins and a few breeders of the rare blue phase of the fulmar. The fulmar colony here is the oldest known in the world, dating back to 1640. Gannets used to breed but don't any more.

Inland, there are plenty of red-necked phalaropes on the pools and snow buntings are abundant. But, apart from a few unconfirmed sightings of arctic foxes, there are no terrestrial mammals – the most recent one recorded was a visiting polar bear in 1973, which was promptly shot. A very small number of common seals breed around the coast most years; the four arctic species of seal which occur in Iceland (ringed, harp, hooded and bearded) occur around Grimsey most winters, sometimes in large numbers.

Access is by a regular boat service or by air from Akureyri, which has regular connections by both plane and bus with Reykjavik. Camping is allowed (there are facilities in the community house) and it is possible to arrange accommodation in private houses from Akureyri. Alternatively, a day trip is quite feasible but frustratingly short!

Further south, the island of Hrisey is also

worth a visit given the time. Also inhabited, and accessible by boat and plane from Akureyri, it offers exceptionally large numbers of nesting ptarmigan, whimbrel and arctic terns.

Hornstrandir is one of the most beautiful — and most remote — parts of Iceland. It is impossible to get to except by sea or foot.

Hornstrandir Landscape Reserve

Facing the Arctic Ocean, on the rocky extreme north-west coast of Iceland, is Hornstrandir. It is an incredibly beautiful and rugged area of 580 square kilometres — and one of the most remote districts in the country. It is also one of the most difficult places to visit, impossible to get to except by sea or foot.

There are no roads or paths and, apart from the keeper's dwelling at Hornbjarg lighthouse in the north-eastern corner, there have been no inhabitants since the last hardy farmer gave up in 1952. Some of the old farmhouses are used as summer homes by their owners but the majority of them — more than forty in all — have been abandoned. Even the weather is usually worse than in most other parts of Iceland. The winters are longer, with heavy snowfall remaining on the ground for many months, and drift ice is often packed in close to the coast in the early part of the year. Worse still, a mild summer drizzle may quickly switch to snow and freezing cold, since weather changes can be incredibly sudden.

All this may frighten off city dwellers who fail to understand and value the reception of dampness, fog and rain, and the need for a long, hard trek. But Hornstrandir's magnificent, awe-inspiring scenery and rich wildlife make all the hardships worthwhile.

Hornstrandir is one of the oldest parts of the country; even the most recent strata of lava is about three million years old — which really does make it old by Icelandic standards. Between the layers of lava beneath, geologists regularly find thick tree trunks — where sheets of lava once flowed over luxuriant forests. Today, there are no great forests but the flora is incredibly rich and lush. Wild flowers can be seen everywhere, from the shoreline to the mountain slopes, living in places which have remained untouched by grazing for many years. Especially common amongst them are buttercups, wood cranesbill, angelica and, in old farmyards, dandelions. It is worth enduring an exhausting hike for such a colourful sight.

Among the diverse features of its landscape, Hornstrandir also has impressive cliffs and ravines full of nesting seabirds during spring and early summer. Two of Iceland's greatest bird cliffs, Hornbjarg and Haelavikurbjarg, stand virtually side-by-side on its northern coast. Rising 500 metres or more above sea level, they remain a good area for gyrfalcon and white-tailed sea eagle, thanks largely to the area's inhospitability and inaccessibility. Even so, you still have to be fairly lucky to see either species there.

In contrast, the ledges are jam-packed with seabirds' nests — the cliffs are teeming with common guillemots, Brunnich's guillemots, puffins, razorbills, kittiwakes, fulmars and great black-backed gulls at the right time of year. Glaucous gulls and eiders are fairly common on beaches all around Hornstrandir and there are even, very occasionally, a few non-breeding little auks. Inland, great northern divers, whooper swans, and, particularly around the river deltas, red-necked phalaropes are all common sights. Ptarmigan and arctic skuas are also abundant. There are nearly 40 species of breeding birds in the area altogether.

Finally, arctic foxes are much in evidence, even though they are continually molested by visiting hunters. Pods of killer whales and several other cetacean species are often spotted offshore.

Hornstrandir is truly "expedition country". It is best explored by boat from Isafjordur (where expert guides are available) but access thereafter is on foot along centuries-old mountain trails or virgin rough ground. There are several guesthouses, hotels and private homes to stay overnight in Isafjordur, but you need a sturdy windproof tent and adequate provisions to stay in Hornstrandir itself. One or two of the abandoned farmhouses have radio transmitters in case it is necessary to call for help. There are also houses designed as lifesaving huts for shipwrecked seamen and these are not intended for use by travellers except in dire emergency.

Breidafjordur

Breidafjordur is an enormous bay, some 270,000 hectares in area, on the west coast of Iceland. Reykjavik is no more than 100 kilometres away at its nearest point. It is a spectacular landscape of shallow sea and smaller bays, dotted with over 2,000 small islands and islets.

It is home to a substantial proportion of Iceland's seabird population, most of the country's grey seals and a considerable number of harbour seals. Hooded and ringed seals are also fairly frequent visitors.

Between 80,000 and 100,000 eiders breed in the area, which is also one of the main strongholds of the small Icelandic population of white-tailed eagles. The abundance of eel-grass is of great importance for the large numbers of brent geese which appear

Breidafjordur, an enormous bay dotted with over 2,000 small islands and islets, is home to enormous numbers of seabirds and seals.

in the area on spring migration, and the intertidal zone is used by tens of thousands of migrating knot and other waders.

The best known of the islands in Breidafjordur is Flatey, which sits right in the centre of the bay. It is one of the few which are inhabited and, even though it is only half a square kilometre in size, is also one of the largest.

Nearly thirty different bird species have been recorded breeding on Flatey itself, or on the surrounding islets. The commonest waders are redshank (with a spectacular average density of 80 pairs per square kilometre) and snipe (90 pairs per square kilometre). The snipe, for some reason, is very rare on islands and islets elsewhere in the bay. A few pairs each of oystercatcher, grey and red-necked phalaropes, dunlin and ringed plover also nest.

Among the seabirds, arctic terns are the most numerous. Black guillemots have increased noticeably in recent years, particularly in the eastern half of the island. They previously suffered considerably from predation by brown rats (they have been absent since 1971) and large numbers have recently moved to Flatey from nearby Bardastrandarsysla, on the mainland, where mink have been exploding in numbers since the mid-1960s. Very small numbers of lesser black-backed gulls, black-headed gulls, kittiwakes, fulmars and puffins also nest on and around Flatey — although puffins are the most widespread and common seabirds elsewhere in Breidafjordur. Mallard and teal also nest in small numbers and, while greylag goose, arctic skua and great black-backed gull have nested in the past, they have not done so in recent years.

Among the passerines, snow buntings are common (the population on Flatey is among the densest known for Iceland) and white wagtails and meadow pipits breed over the whole of the island. Redwings and wheatears, which are steadily declining in numbers, are rare breeders. Although uncommon nesters, ravens frequent the islands in search of eggs.

Breidafjordur as a whole is best explored by boat. There are regular tours from Stykkisholmur to Brjanslaekur (on the north-west peninsula) four or five times a week. These stop off at Flatey and, on some days, make a detour to sail among other islands and islets nearby. Contact the shipping company Floabaturinn Baldur, at either Stykkisholmur or Brjanslaekur, for further information. Other tours, mainly among islands in the south of the bay, are available from Stykkisholmur.

Snaefellsnes, the peninsula forming the southern boundary of Breidafjordur, is also rich in birdlife. Altogether, about 60 breeding species are known, and there are records of four more — shoveler, long-tailed duck, grey phalarope and short-eared owl — which are as yet unconfirmed. The great northern diver is fairly common where there are suitable lakes, though very seldom is there more than one pair at a lake because they are very territorial in the breeding season.

Red-throated divers are very common and they have even taken to colonial nesting at Glamsfloi. Iceland's few breeding pairs of barnacle geese also nest in this area, on one of the many islands of the northern coast. Brent and white-fronted geese, turnstone, knot and sanderling are all regular passage migrants.

CHAPTER 8

HOW LONG WILL IT LAST?

Like many other countries, Iceland has not been too successful at ensuring the long-term survival of its natural resources. Perhaps due to the size of the country in comparison with its population, and aspects of its economic and social structure, its history and culture, environmental issues have proved to be very difficult to approach and bring to a workable solution.

Although one of the first written references to conservation in Iceland was in 1907, it was not until at least twenty years later that any positive recommendations were made. Olafur Fridriksson, the author of an article on the subject, reported that in many foreign countries vast areas had been protected from disturbance and destruction. Fridriksson believed that such action would not be relevant in Iceland because the land had already lost its virgin woodland. He warned that too many features had already been destroyed.

But he did like the idea of a national park at Thingvellir and got carried away suggesting the planting of conifers all over the lava, and importing capercaillie and black grouse to see if they could live there. Although no steps were taken for importing capercaillie and black grouse, in 1928 an Act of Parliament for the conservation of Thingvellir was passed. It was Iceland's first national park.

At around the same time, in 1928–30, the Icelandic Forestry Service began extensive efforts to protect what little natural woodland there was left after centuries of woodcutting and conifer planting. Many of these woodlands are important conservation sites today.

But, despite these early beginnings, the level of conservation awareness in Iceland is still fairly low. Perhaps it is because the need for conservation has not, at least until recently, been as obvious as in other European countries. Iceland did not really experience the industrial revolution and urbanization did not take root until well into this century. For a long time, Icelanders have been spread over the coastline and lowlands, earning their living as fishermen and farmers. As with urbanization, tourism also made a sudden appearance. In the late 1920s, farmers were still offering strangers food and accommodation without expecting payment.

Other eminent naturalists, including Steindor Steindorsson and Sigurdur Thorarinsson, saw what was happening in the late 1930s. Reykjavik had changed from a village to a town; tourism was increasing dramatically; and land transportation was

Preceding pages: These false craters in West Skaftafellssysla, South Iceland, are relatively safe from the problems of urbanisation, tourism and overgrazing common in other parts of the country.

Iceland's hydro power resources are both immense and dramatically under-exploited. This HEP station is at Sog, adjacent to Thingvallavatn.

There are seven major Acts of Parliament concerning conservation-related subjects in Iceland.

being improved. Long-term proposals were put forward for nature conservation in Iceland. An Act was eventually passed in 1956 – and many parts of it have remained unaltered to this day. By then, however, airports, roads and bridges had been built; towns had grown out of tiny villages; four-wheel drive vehicles had been introduced; and individual wealth and leisure time had increased. The result was that vast, largely untouched, tracts of land suddenly became accessible.

In recent years, as well, a new threat has become prominent in Iceland. That is the harnessing of the country's numerous waterfalls. Iceland's hydro power resources are both immense and dramatically under-exploited. Although still only a small part (less than 10%) of the potential water-power in the country has been harnessed, including waterfalls and rivers, there is a trend to favour as much hydro-electric development as possible. Most districts are now striving for a power-plant in their region. The Icelanders themselves do not need all this energy, and it cannot be packed in barrels and exploited, so it is sold to multinational corporations that build heavy industrial plants in the country. In recent years, this has resulted in the introduction of an aluminium smelter, a ferrosilicon plant, and other energy-demanding processes. But there are plans for new major energy developments for a variety of Icelandic processing industries in the future. Some experts expect the income derived from such energy-based projects to exceed that from the traditional fishing industry.

Any conservation policy of the future will rely on economics of this kind more than aesthetic and moral values. As a food-producing nation, special emphasis is likely to be on habitat protection and on managing fish and other wildlife populations for human use. This is illustrated by the fact that two recent Bills on conservation and environmental affairs have been before the Althing for several years – but they have received little attention. Icelanders are increasingly appreciating the quality of a diversified environment, but they are likely to continue to regard wildlife and the natural environment as resources which should be exploited. The only answer is to exploit them within controlled limits.

Environmental issues in general are nearly fully dependent on public interest, which has been noticeably lacking until quite recently. There are few active voluntary environmental organisations and most have the tendency to dissolve almost as quickly as they are formed. Government bodies such as the Nature Conservation Council are terribly under-staffed – and active only thanks to the quiet persistence of a few dedicated individuals.

But there is great potential in terms of public education and conservation information. Iceland has only one teacher training college, one university and two colleges for farmers – so the most influential groups of young people can be easily reached. The few newspapers are frequently read by a large proportion of the population and the radio stations and TV channel are readily accessible to outside presenters.

The British Trust for Conservation Volunteers began an effort with the Icelandic NCC in August 1983, to launch practical conservation projects for volunteers in Iceland. This has been highly successful and it is anticipated that it may lead to the setting up of a similar movement within Iceland, to build and maintain footpaths, help with soil conservation work, do wildlife censusing and so on. Efforts have already begun with the establishment of a centre for conservation volunteers in Skaftafell National Park. So the outlook is more promising. Public education about conservation issues is clearly where the answer to safeguarding Iceland's natural heritage lies.

Legislation

There are seven major Acts of Parliament concerning conservation-related subjects in Iceland:

1 No 59, 1928, on the conservation of Thingvellir.

2 No 36, 1974, on the conservation of Myvatn-Laxa.

3 No 48, 1956, entitled "Act on Nature Conservation". This was reviewed and replaced in 1971.
No 47, 1971, entitled "Nature Conservation Act".

4 No 76, 1970, entitled "Freshwater Fisheries Law" and replacing a similar law of 1932.

5 No 33, 1966, entitled "Act on Bird Hunting and Bird Preservation".

6 No 3, 1955, on Forestry.

7 No 17, 1969, on Soil Conservation.

1971 Nature Conservation Act

The aim of this act is to: "encourage the intercourse of Man and Nature in such a way that life on land be not needlessly wasted, nor sea, freshwater or air polluted".

It covers an enormous range of subjects, from refuse tips and abandoned farm buildings to providing sanitary facilities in public parks and establishing and managing protected areas. The Ministry of Culture and Education is in charge of implementing the Act – indeed, of all matters regarding the conservation of nature – while the Nature Conservation Council (NCC) actually executes the measures necessary.

The NCC relies greatly on small nature conservation committees, of three to seven members, which are dotted around the country, in each county and town. The role of these committees is to further nature conservation in their districts, by means of advice and proposals to the local authorities, the Nature Conservation Council and the Nature Conservation Convention. The Convention assembles every third year to discuss conservation proposals and decide priorities for the most urgent conservation matters to be resolved. It is organised by the NCC and attended by approximately 100 delegates from a wide range of interested organisations.

The NCC can declare the protection of unusual natural phenomena, known as natural monuments, and including waterfalls, volcanic sites, rock formations (all stalactites in lava caves are protected, for example) and localities where fossils and rare stones are found. They are protected if it is considered important to preserve them for their scientific value, beauty or uniqueness.

It can also declare the protection of scientifically or culturally important plants or animals, in order to prevent their disturbance, decline or extinction. Protection can be applied either locally or to the whole country. In theory it may also ban proposed development or extraction projects which may disrupt the natural environment or threaten individual species.

Finally, it can declare the protection of entire areas, if considered important because of an exceptional landscape, vegetation or animal life, or for an historical significance. National Parks in Iceland can only be declared when the NCC is in a position to organise state-purchase of the

Svartifoss, in Skaftafell National Park, is a popular destination for tourists.

land outright for the nation and is in a position to administer them satisfactorily. Nature reserves, on the other hand, can be declared without being purchased.

Any decision of the NCC concerning protection does not, however, come into force until approved by the Ministry of Culture and Education.

Protected Areas in Iceland

Listed overleaf are all areas and sites which had been designated as protected up to July 1984. In addition, there are a further 200 or more sites which the Nature Conservation Council has declared worthy of being protected, as a plan for extending the system of protected areas. These have no formal protection, but the NCC has a priority right to buy land which is registered in this way on behalf of the state. Landowners and those responsible for development are encouraged to respect the importance of each registered area, though the intention is to gradually extend the system of legal protection by adding these sites to the main list. Together, they form the Inventory of Icelandic Sites of Conservation Interest. The aim is to make an Inventory of all natural areas of national and international importance, mainly of scenic, educational, scientific and recreational interest. Special attention is, however, given to the Reykjavik area where more than half of the population lives, and where intense urban development demands high priority for conservation.

PROTECTED AREAS IN ICELAND (as of July 1984)

A Designated by special law

		Year (revised)		Size approx in ha
1	Myvatn-Laxa	1974		440,000
2	Thingvellir	1930		4,200

B Designated under the 1971 Nature Conservation Act

National Parks

(State-owned; have two main functions: to protect outstanding natural areas and to enable the public to enjoy the area within the limitations required for its protection. No grazing is allowed)

		Year	(revised)	Size approx in ha
3	Skaftafell	1968		50,000
4	Jokulsargljufur	1973		15,100

Nature Reserves

(Grazing is allowed, but special instructions declare amount of disruption, by owner, tenant or others, which is allowed)

		Year	(revised)	Size approx in ha
5	Hvannalindir in Kepputunga	1973		4,300
6	Herdubreid	1974		17,000
7	Hornstrandir	1975		58,000
8	Vatnsfjordur	1975		20,000
9	Lonsoraefi	1977		32,000
10	Dyrholaey	1978		510
11	Esjufjoll	1978		27,000
12	Gullfoss	1979		160
13	The beach at Stapi and Hellnar	1979		75
14	Fjallabak	1979		47,000
15	Eldey	1940	(1974)	2
16	Melrakkaey	1971	(1974)	9
17	Svarfadardalur	1972	(1980)	540
18	Grotta	1974		5
19	Husafellsskogur	1974		440
20	Ingolfshofdi	1974	(1978)	90
21	Surtsey	1965	(1974)	270
22	Flatey (Breidafjordur)	1975		100
23	Kringilsarrani	1975		8,500
24	Salthofdi	1977		220
25	Vestmannsvatn	1977		600
26	Miklavatn in Skagafjordur	1977		1,550
27	Budahraun	1977	(1979)	915

		Year (revised)		Size approx in ha
28	Hrisey in Bardastrandarsysla	1977		40
29	Astjorn by Hafnarfjordur	1978		25
30	Varmarosar in Leiruvogur	1980		10
31	Thjorsarver	1981		37,500

Natural Monuments

(Grazing is allowed, but no destruction or changes allowed without approval of NCC)

32	Geysir in Haukadalur	1953		15
33	Hveravellir on Kjolur	1960	(1975)	170
34	Grabrokargigar	1962	(1975)	34
35	Eldborg in Blafjoll	1971	(1974)	50
36	Lakagigar	1971	(1975)	16,000
37	Skutustadagigar	1973		28
38	Stedji (Staupasteinn)	1974		7
39	Eldborg in Hnappadalur	1974		150
40	Surtarbrandsgil	1975		150
41	Alftaversgigar	1975		3,650
42	Kattarauga in Vatnsdalur	1975		1
43	Helgustadanama	1975		1
44	Teigarhorn	1975		120
45	Dima in Lon	1975		8
46	Haalda in Oraefi	1975		5
47	Askja in Dyngjufjoll	1978		5,000
48	Bardarlaug on Snaefellsnes	1980		50
49	Fjallfoss in Dynjandisvogur	1981	(1981)	700
50	Borgir in Kopavogur	1981		3
51	Laugaras in Reykjavik	1982		1
52	Trollaborn in Laekjarbotnar	1983		5
53	Haubakkar by Ellidaarvogur	1983		2
54	Vigholar in Kopavogur	1983		1

Municipal parks and recreation areas

55	Raudholar in Reykjavik	1961	(1974)	45
56	Folkvangur, Neskaupstadur	1972		300
57	Blafjoll	1973	(1975)	8,400
58	Holmanes	1973		260
59	Hrutey in Blanda	1975		10
60	Reykjanesfolkvangur	1975		30,000
61	Alfaborg in Borgarfjordur (East)	1977		10
62	Spakonufellshofdi	1980		30
63	Osland in Hornafjordur	1982		15

Protected Species

The following species are protected by law in Iceland:

A) Plants

1 Bedstraw, marsh
2 Bugle, pyramidal
3 Eyebright
4 Fern, parsley
5 Filmfern
6 Garlic, field
7 Grapefern, glossy
8 Hardfern
9 Heathgrass
10 Knotweed, amphibious
11 Moss, stag's horn
12 Paris, herb
13 Pigmyweed
14 Poppy, Stefanssons Icelandic
15 Primrose, Greenland
16 Rose, prickly
17 Rose, Taeckholm's
18 Rush, mud
19 Saxifrage, foliolose
20 Sedge, hudsonbay
21 Sedge, large yellow
22 Spleenwort, forked
23 Spleenwort, green
24 Spleenwort, maidenhair
25 Spurrey, cliff
26 Starwort, peduncled
27 Stitchwort, northern
28 Tormentil
29 Twayblade
30 Violet, common
31 Woodsorrel

B) Birds

Birds in Iceland are protected by law under Act No 33 of 1966 (although heavier fines were introduced by special law in 1982), which can be summarised as follows:

1 Only the landowner (or someone with his permission) has the right to hunt birds within the boundaries of his property. Anyone can hunt on land outside the boundaries of private properties. Similarly, anyone can hunt within Icelandic territorial waters, but only outside the 115 metre "netting zone" (in private ownership).

2 All wild birds, their eggs and nests are fully protected throughout the year, with the following exceptions:
a) throughout the year: arctic skua, great black-backed gull, lesser black-backed gull, herring gull and raven.
b) 20th August to 15th March: cormorant, shag, greylag goose, pink-footed goose, white-fronted goose and barnacle goose. Eggs of the greylag goose may be taken at any time.
c) 1st September to 31st March: red-throated diver, fulmar, gannet, mallard, teal, wigeon, pintail, scaup, tufted duck, long-tailed duck, red-breasted merganser, great skua, glaucous gull, Iceland gull, black-headed gull and kittiwake. In certain restricted areas, where ducks breed in great numbers, duck eggs may be taken during this period (if at least four eggs are left in each nest) with the exception of the shoveler, pochard and harlequin. Eggs of the black-headed gull may be taken at any time, but only from the first laying. Eggs of arctic terns may be taken legally, but only from the first laying.
d) 1st September to 19th May: razorbill, common guillemot, Brunnich's guillemot, black guillemot and puffin. In certain restricted areas, all seabirds, their eggs and young, listed in (b), (c) and (d) may be taken where such hunting is considered to be a contributory source of the means of livelihood of the local population. It is, however, illegal to shoot these species during the protection period — and birds on bird cliffs may never be shot.
e) 15th October to 22nd December: ptarmigan.

3 The Act also covers special licencing to collect specimens for the museum collection in Reykjavik; for hunting protected birds which are causing substantial damage to cultivated land, fish hatcheries and the like; and for scientific purposes.

4 Illegal hunting techniques are specified, including the use of nets (except hand-

Seabirds have been caught, and their eggs collected, in Iceland since the settlement in 874. At one time, seabirds formed one of the most important sources of food for the islanders.

nets for puffins and other cliff-nesting seabirds); any fixed-hunting devices such as snare-rafts; the use of gaffs, hooks and artificial lights; any form of poison (except under licence for specific species, such as great black-backed gull, raven and arctic skua).

5 Other provisions include licences for photographing nesting eagles, gyrfalcons, snowy owls and little auks; the prohibition of firearms within two kilometres of protected breeding colonies of eider duck from 15th April to 14th July; and various import and export regulations (without a licence, it is unlawful to export any birds, eggs, eggshells or nests from Iceland).

There have been several, as yet unsuccessful, attempts to update this Act.

C) Mammals

The only land mammal with any form of protection in Iceland is the reindeer. Limited hunting is allowed, but only under official supervision and from 1st August to 15th September. Whaling and sealing are both discussed separately in this chapter.

D) Fish

The various fishing seasons and regulations are discussed in Chapter 6 and later in this chapter.

Collecting Seabirds and their Eggs

The influence of man on seabirds can be diverse. On a world scale, the most dramatic and disastrous is undoubtedly caused by

oil spills, when thousands or even hundreds of thousands of birds are killed in a short time.

In Iceland, the extent to which man affects the country's seabird populations is not accurately known. Overfishing is thought to be one of the reasons for puffins and several other species sometimes having difficulties in adequately feeding their chicks. The fishing nets themselves can also kill large numbers — several seabird species are susceptible to getting entangled and drowning. Auks are by far the worst hit, though the extent of the damage varies very much according to the time of year and the locality. There are examples of a single small fishing boat getting about 3,000 auks in 24 hours. In Breidafjordur, fishing nets are believed to account for up to half the average monthly mortality of adult black guillemots in summer.

The deliberate catching of seabirds and collection of their eggs involves even greater numbers. This has been practised in Iceland since the Settlement in 874, when seabirds formed one of the most important sources of food for the islanders. People came to the coastal colonies from all over the country to get cheap food, arming themselves with fresh meat and eggs which lasted for most of the year.

The importance of different species has, of course, varied greatly over the years and in different parts of the country. Manx shearwater, little auk, Leach's petrel and storm petrel are the only ones which have escaped heavy utilisation — they are all either rather small or relatively rare — hence hardly worth taking.

The most badly affected was the penguin-like great auk, which is now extinct. It once nested in large colonies around Iceland. The auk's persecution began, in many parts of the world, before the existence of the true, southern hemisphere, penguins was even recorded. Once abundant and widespread, it was an important part of the human diet at least as far back as 7000 BC. Ancient rubbish tips along the coasts of Iceland, Norway, Denmark, Scotland and Ireland prove it with enormous numbers of the birds' bones. But it was only in the sixteenth and seventeenth centuries that sailors really began to take a heavy toll. The birds made easy prey standing almost a metre high and, although in their element in the sea, completely flightless. The great auk was genuinely believed to have been designed for man's benefit.

Iceland was one of the main strongholds of the great auk, which is now extinct. The world's last two survivors lived on Eldey island, off the south-west coast.

Iceland was one of its main strongholds, though it was also numerous along the coasts of North America and, to a lesser extent, Britain and Scandinavia. Reports from only a few centuries ago tell of the locals on Funk Island, Newfoundland, herding the hapless auks in their thousands into pens and killing them with clubs for their flesh, eggs and feathers.

A major Icelandic colony was destroyed by a volcanic eruption in 1830, by which time the birds were fetching high prices from egg and skin collectors, adding to the pressures on the rapidly diminishing population. The world's last two surviving great auks lived on Eldey Island, off Iceland's south-western tip. On 3rd June 1844, they were discovered by three Icelandic fishermen, who found the breeding pair guarding their single egg. Jon Brandsson and Sigurdur Isleifsson killed the two adult birds with their clubs. Ketill Ketilsson smashed the egg with his boot.

Today, a mounted specimen of the great auk can be seen in the Icelandic Natural History Museum, Reykjavik. It was bought at Sotheby's auction rooms in London for £9,300 in 1971, paid for by public subscription. It was, at the time, the highest price ever paid for a stuffed bird, and a sharp reminder for the people of Iceland.

Incidentally, there is a curious theory that links Iceland's great auks (and probably other auk species) with the discovery of

North America. Vikings in Iceland, already familiar with the birds and aware in a general sense of their migrations, began to take an interest in the seasonal appearances and departures of vast "auk rafts" in their western waters. It would have been a small step for the Vikings to conclude that these birds were travelling to other, similar, lands in the west. Vikings were believed to be resident in Newfoundland – which is precisely where the migrating auks would have led anyone who decided to follow them. It is an interesting possibility.

Nesting as they do in their hundreds of thousands right outside the Icelanders' homes, enormous concentrations of other seabird species around Iceland's coasts have also invited exploitation, as the following table of seabird utilisation over the years shows:

	Egg	Young	Adult
Great auk	X		X
Puffin	★	X	X
Common guillemot	X		X
Brunnich's guillemot	X		X
Black guillemot	X	X	X
Little auk			
Razorbill	X		X
Manx shearwater		★	
Storm petrel			
Leach's petrel			
Arctic tern	X		
Kittiwake	X	X	★
Fulmar	X	X	X
Gannet		X	★
Cormorant	X	X	X
Shag	X	X	X

★ utilised but of low importance.

Eggs of the auks are considered the best, though they are taken much less now than in former times. Arctic tern eggs, on the other hand, have been considered a delicacy for a long time – and egg collecting continues throughout the summer – despite a clause in the bird protection act stating that only eggs from the first nesting attempt can be taken. If they are fresh when removed, the birds will normally lay again.

Puffins are caught in mid-air, from concealed positions on the cliffs, with long poles with nets on one end.

Several terneries have been destroyed because of this and a further large colony, near Blonduos in the north, looks about to vanish.

The eggs of shag, cormorant, fulmar and kittiwake were once taken in large numbers, but not so much these days.

Gannets' eggs have never really been taken, possibly because their early laying coincides with unpredictable and difficult climbing weather, but their chicks have been taken for food for centuries. Eldey Island was a popular destination for hunters but, since it was declared a nature reserve in 1940, this practice has stopped. Traditional cropping still continues on the Westmann Islands, though, where just a small number of young birds are taken in late summer. At that time of year, they weigh even more than their parents.

Puffin chicks were once also taken in large numbers, but this too has almost completely stopped. Adult birds make up most of the catch nowadays. Puffins are eaten smoked or broiled, and Icelanders occasionally use their feathers and down as bedding material. At one time, their remains were even dried and burned as fuel for heating homes. It is estimated that 150,000–200,000 puffins are now taken annually in Iceland. This is an extraordinarily high number and hunting on this kind of scale has certainly been felt, at least in the past, by the puffin population in some areas. In the Westmann Islands during the period 1850 to 1870, puffin numbers declined dramatically and on the islands of Breidafjordur many colonies were destroyed entirely. Burrow netting was eventually banned (except in cases where burrow digging by puffins is thought to affect the breeding of eiders) and a new system, pole-netting, was introduced in

1875. This involves the use of 12-foot poles, with nets on the end, to catch the birds in mid-air from concealed positions on the cliffs. Other puffins are often lured to the catching site by a deceiving row of dead birds, their necks wrung, propped up in a lifelike manner. It increased the proportion of immature birds in the catch (up to a maximum of 93%, in the Westmann Islands) since they are caught in flight from the cliff-tops. The result has been a lessening of the impact on the puffin population.

There are many different methods of catching seabirds, most of which are now illegal. Snare rafts were once popular, particularly around the northern islands of Drangey and Grimsey. Birds such as common guillemots, puffins and razorbills climb onto the floating rafts and are caught by their legs in snares. At times, the birds were entangled on the rafts for days, when weather prevented the hunters' boats from visiting them. These rafts, and the use of snares for seabirds in other situations, have been banned since 1954. Hooks, too, have been banned, which were used to drag young and adult puffins out of their burrows. So has the use of baited hooks, which were sometimes used to catch gannets and kittiwakes.

Iceland's current bird protection act now only allows the more humane killing methods and the ones which are better from a conservation point-of-view. The shooting of auks at sea is practised widely, especially in the latter half of winter and early spring, and adult shags and cormorants are also shot in some numbers. But perhaps the most common method, at least in terms of catch size, is to descend over the cliffs on ropes. Originally, the ropes were held by men sitting on the top but increasingly these days tractors are used, as on Grimsey, or even four-wheel drive cars.

Seabirds' eggs have been collected in vast numbers in the Westmann Islands using the ropes in this way for centuries. They still provide a welcome enrichment of the local diet each spring, and every year voluntary organised groups from Heimaey are sent on dangerous egg-gathering expeditions to outlying islands.

Kittiwake chicks — eggs of this bird were once taken in large numbers, but not so much these days.

The method is also practised in other cliff nesting areas. Expeditions are mounted to collect the eggs, which are then sold as a delicacy in Reykjavik and other larger communities.

Despite the attraction in some areas, the utilisation of seabirds in general for food has declined substantially during this century.

With the possible exception of individual arctic tern colonies, hunting is probably not intense enough now to have any drastic effects on the birds' populations. They are

not such an important source of food as they once were and, in the case of cliff-nesting species, descending the sheer cliffs on a rope is a very difficult and dangerous sport (rather than a necessity), providing an irresistible challenge to fewer people. But there is also a conscious effort to refrain from taking too many. Apart from a few poachers, such as the unscrupulous people who shoot fulmars, kittiwakes and one or two other species on the bird cliffs (which is illegal — the fulmar is protected during the breeding season — and it is illegal to shoot any bird on or near bird cliffs because of the disturbance it creates) most relevant bird protection laws are adhered to. It is, after all, in the islanders' interests to make stocks last.

The last few decades have seen an increase in many seabird populations, though this of course may be circumstantial since no direct link has been established. Gannets, puffins, shags, kittiwakes and fulmars all seem to be increasing towards their former population levels. Again, though, the fulmar has been increasing steadily all over the North Atlantic during the past 250 years, possibly because of the new and rich food supply provided by the offal from fishing boats. If there is a link, population increases among the auks — that one would expect — do not seem to have come. It may be that it is taking them longer to "recover".

Seal Hunting

Seal hunting has been practised by farmers along the coast since the beginning of settlement in Iceland. The whole seal was used, both for food and to make clothing. Very large numbers were still being taken earlier this century but the size of the hunt decreased gradually until about 1970. As the table shows, since then the annual catch has fluctuated between four and seven thousand seals (mostly harbour seal pups).

They are no longer killed for their furs. The fish industry companies claim that

SEALING IN ICELAND 1971—82

	1. Harbour seal			2. Grey seal			
Year	Pups	Adults	Total	Pups	Adults	Total	Grand Total
1971	5,126	—	—	557	—	—	6,894
1972	6,237	—	—	415	—	—	6,930
1973	5,995	—	—	483	—	—	6,803
1974	5,534	—	—	406	—	—	6,240
1975	6,111	—	—	122	—	—	6,673
1976	5,895	—	—	274	—	—	6,470
1977	5,705	—	—	96	—	—	6,601
1978	4,030	356	4,386	93	102	195	4,581
1979	4,278	317	4,595	201	179	380	4,975
1980	3,357	295	3,652	54	114	168	3,826
1981	2,511	429	2,940	3	139	142	3,082
1982	2,367	634	3,001	1,154	488	1,642	4,643

NB A small number of unspecified arctic seal species are included in the grand total figures; most of these were adults. Preliminary unpublished figures for 1983 suggest a grand total of 4—5,000, though the number of adults is proportionately higher than in previous years.

they have a heavy impact on commercially important fish stocks, they damage fishing gear and, most importantly, they have a role as hosts in the spreading of the cod worm, **Phocanema decipiens.** They estimate that their industry is losing 200 million krona per year because of cod-worm and are therefore determined to maintain Iceland's seal population at a low level. They do not, however, know if this is necessary, how many need to be killed, or what proportion of adults and pups to take, in order to achieve this. Nearly everyone agrees that seals harbour codworm — but the correlation between the level of infection in fish and the seal population is highly controversial.

There has never been a general law against sealing in Iceland (though at the time of writing it is being debated in Parliament) and there are no quotas or regulations. There is, however, one local law (a ban on seal hunting with a gun in inner Breidafjordur) and fishing laws such as one which states that all seals can be exterminated from fishing lakes and rivers. Not surprisingly, sealing is a very controversial issue both within the country and with other countries. Indeed, it would probably have stopped completely in 1981, due to protests from conservationists abroad which resulted in a slump in the market, if it was not for the fact that since 1982 the larger fishery export and fish-processing companies in Iceland have been paying bounties for all seals killed. Hunters simply have to produce a lower jaw as proof of a kill, to claim their money. The bounty scheme has kept sealing in Iceland a profitable industry, despite the fact that skin prices have dropped to such an extent that it would otherwise not be financially viable. But in the first year of the bounty system, all the seal corpses were left lying around on the beaches. A public outcry led to the introduction of a system, in operation now, whereby the whole animal (minus only the lower jaw) is mashed up in a machine grinder and fed to fur farm foxes. The hunters are paid a set fee per kilo of "seal mash".

Ironically, the only research on sealing — and the effects of seals on fisheries — is being entirely carried out and paid for by the very same non-governmental agencies that are funding the bounty scheme to keep sealing going. Moral, though not financial, support comes from the Ministry of Fisheries. In the meantime, they maintain that decreased hunting will lead to a larger seal population — and therefore more codworm in fish — so the killing will continue.

International Environmental Legislation

In addition to fisheries agreements and others, Iceland has signed and ratified four key international environmental laws and conventions:

1 The Convention on Wetlands of International Importance Especially as Waterfowl Habitat ("Ramsar"). The Convention came into force on 21st December 1975 and has the objective of stemming the progressive encroachment on and loss of wetlands. This includes habitats as diverse as mangrove swamps, peat bogs, water meadows, tidal flats and mountain lakes. Almost 300 wetland sites, covering almost 20 million hectares, have been included in Ramsar's "List of Wetlands of International Importance". At the time of writing, Iceland has listed one site — part of the Myvatn-Laxa Region — which was listed at accession on 2nd December 1977. Recent and proposed developments in energy utilisation, industry, communications and farming potentially threaten Iceland's wetlands. There is therefore a strong need for protective measures and a strong participation in international co-operation such as the Ramsar Convention offers.

2 The International Convention for the Protection of Birds. The Convention itself came into force on 17th January 1963 and requires its parties to protect all birds at least during the breeding season, migratory birds during the period of return to their nesting areas, and species threatened with extinction throughout the year.

3 The International Convention for the Regulation of Whaling (ICRW). This Convention was signed in Washington DC on 2nd December 1946 and came into force on 10th November 1948. It has overseen most of the world's whaling activities from its entry into force to the present day. ICRW established the International Whaling Commission (IWC) which meets annually and adopts regulations on catch quotas, protected species, whaling methods etc.

4 The International Convention on the Law of the Sea. Iceland was a prime mover at the Law of the Sea Conference and became a signatory on 10th December 1982. It has far-reaching implications for the future management of more than half of the world's surface. It covers territorial zones, the continental shelf, navigation, rights of passage and the conservation of marine resources, and is unprecedented in treating marine resources as the "common heritage of mankind".

The Washington Convention on International Trade in Endangered Species of Wild Fauna and Flora (CITES) which regulates international trade in wildlife species, has not yet been signed by Iceland but, since it has now been translated into Icelandic for consideration, there are good indications that it may become a signatory in the not-too-distant future.

Whaling

There are probably more divisions of opinion on whaling than on any other conservation issue in Iceland. The decision of the International Whaling Commission (IWC) to suspend all commercial whaling from 1985/86 met with an assortment of contrasting views from the Icelanders. But, while the country voted against this indefinite "pause" in Brighton, England, in July 1982, it did not file an objection to the final decision and is therefore, in theory, bound by it.

All IWC member nations have 90 days to lodge an objection to a vote, which then allows them to continue in spite of the majority agreement. Several nations did object — even though there is no scientific evidence for setting any safely sustainable catch quotas above zero. The IWC itself has no power to enforce such an agreement and it relies entirely on bilateral external pressures from member countries.

Iceland's decision not to object was dramatic, as it followed many hours of angry debate in the Icelandic parliament. Four members of the foreign relations committee of parliament warned that a United States conservationist boycott of Icelandic fish and the threat of an official trade embargo from abroad could cripple Iceland's fragile economy. Others pointed out the moral aspects of whaling and the strong opposition from abroad. The parliamentary vote was televised and just minutes before the deadline 29 members voted to oppose the objection; 28 voted for it.

Iceland was the only whaling nation at the time to take a democratic decision to get out of whaling. The other governments succumbed to various kinds of internal and external pressures.

In the eyes of the world's conservationists, the result was an important and responsible move by Iceland. There was a minor setback early in 1984 when another motion was forwarded in the Icelandic parliament calling for the government to seek ways to evade the commercial whaling moratorium. But it was rejected and taken no further. And there has been one other attempt to continue whaling since then. At the time of writing, the outcome of this is uncertain.

A few centuries ago, there were so many whales in the coastal waters around Iceland that seafarers could judge the proximity of land by their presence, just as they could by the presence of birds. Indeed, one of the reasons Iceland was colonized in the first place was the rich "supply" of whales. Even today, it is possible to see a number of different species from the coast, particularly in the south, though their numbers have decreased considerably.

The Basques were probably the first foreign people to kill whales in the area using proper sea-going vessels. They were cer-

Among the many laws and regulations for Iceland's whaling operations is one which says that no more than 26 hours may elapse from when the whale is harpooned to the time it arrives at the processing station.

tainly working there as long ago as 1600, if not a good deal earlier. The Dutch and French arrived in the 17th century but disappeared almost as soon as they came, when the Right whale populations they sought declined dramatically. Around this time, the Icelanders themselves were engaged only in small-scale inshore whaling for food. But their hunting techniques, right up to the middle of the 18th century, were not always successful. Tiny boats were used, allowing the hunters to attack only those whales entering the fjords. The harpooner was brought as close to the animal as possible to throw his weapon, then they all rowed back to shore as quickly as they could and waited. No line was attached, so it was touch and go whether the quarry was ever collected. Unless it died fairly quickly, it was impossible to keep a track of it in its death throes. Harpoons were marked and registered and, although the owner of the land where the dead animal was washed ashore usually kept most of the whale, the harpooners did have a claim to part of it.

The most dramatic change took place in 1864, when a Norwegian named Svend Foyn developed a cannon which fired an explosive harpoon. This weapon precipitated such an enormous increase in whaling everywhere that nearly a million whales were killed worldwide during the ensuing 70 years.

In 1883, the Norwegians (who had been experiencing a progressive decline in whale catches off their own northern coasts) decided to have a go. By establishing Iceland's first ever whaling station, at Alftafjordur on the west coast, they invaded the country's hitherto abandoned waters in force.

During the following years, many more stations were opened on the west coast. All of them flourished and the catches were enormous. Detailed information on catch size and species for that period is not known, but the fin and blue whales almost certainly figured prominently. Between 1889 and 1900 no fewer than 1296 whales were brought to a single station.

To Icelanders of the time, whales sometimes filled a desperate need for food, particularly in hard years. So much so that an Icelandic word, "hvalreki", used today to describe "a godsend", literally translated means "a stranded whale". But whaling was also probably a commercial venture, since historical records state that the industry was for baleen oil more than anything else.

The following years saw many more land-based whaling stations established by the Norwegians in Iceland. But towards the end of the century their vessels had to go further and further out to sea and several stations had to move to the east coast in their constant search for quarry. This move successfully increased catch numbers and, by 1902, a peak of 30 boats were operating from Iceland, catching around 1300 whales a year. But the increased catches were short-lived and, from 1902 onwards, a great depletion of stocks became apparent. Just ten years later, in 1912, only 152 whales were caught. In the light of this, whaling off Iceland would have ceased anyway, though it was formally forbidden by Icelandic law in 1915.

But the Norwegians reappeared in 1929, this time with floating factory ships. These were operating in many areas of the North Atlantic and included the old grounds off Iceland in their travels. This prompted the Icelanders themselves, in 1935, to re-establish land-based operations from the original western fjords. It was a small-scale effort, which lasted for just five years, involving only two or three boats which were catching a total of 120 whales each year. The main species involved at this time were: fin (81%), sperm (11%), sei (2%), blue (6%) and only two humpbacks.

In recent years, the whaling industry in

Iceland has been based at one major whaling station (operating on a commercial basis for only two species) and half a dozen small-scale operations (with fishing boats under 30 tons) landing only minke from coastal waters in the north. Icelandic minke whaling was unregulated until the 1974 season and catch limits were not introduced until 1977, when a quota for 200 was allocated. To avoid competition, a seasonal quota system for each catcher boat was introduced in 1981. Hvalfjordur, which was opened in 1948 after a brief interval in whaling during the Second World War, is the main station. Situated 60 miles north of Reykjavik, on Iceland's spectacular south-western coast, it had a quota for 100 sei and 167 fin in 1984, and 38 sei and 161 fin in 1985. The entire North Atlantic quota for minke whales for 1985 was set at 1177; Iceland was allowed to take roughly 150 of these. Despite the fact that oceanographic conditions in Iceland are so variable (frequent fogs or unusually windy summers can reduce the catch considerably) IWC quotas have normally been reached.

Laws and regulations for Iceland's whaling operations are not as severe as in its fishing industry, and they are only properly enforced at Hvalfjordur, where accurate log books are kept. These are delivered to the Ministry of Fisheries for inspection at the end of each season. The station is open to visits by foreign scientists, though only those approved by the Icelandic Government and the IWC. Whalers are prohibited to hunt calves or accompanied cows — the crews receive none of their usual bonuses if milk is found in a cow's teats — and each boat is banned from bringing in more than four whales (depending on the species) at any one time, since the meat is primarily for human consumption and needs to be fresh. It would be a waste if there were too many whales waiting for flensing. In addition, no more than 26 hours may elapse from when the whale is harpooned to the time it arrives at the processing station, though there are good commercial reasons for this. The IWC says that all baleen whales (except minke) must be fully processed — so they must arrive in a good state — and the Japanese industry insists that they be processed quickly for meat exports. The station works closely with the Icelandic Marine Research Institute, which advises the Government.

The industry currently provides about 230 people with employment, some of them students from the University of Iceland working for the summer only. They usually set out on the evening of the first Sunday in June. The season lasts until the latter half of September.

Since no sophisticated tracking equip-

Hvalfjordur, situated 60 miles north of Reykjavik, is the site of the main whaling station in Iceland.

ment is used, the animals have to be seen before harpooning. The harpoon is aimed immediately in front of the flippers, so that it enters either the lungs, heart or spinal region. The grenade at its tip consists of a sack of black powder, in a steel container equipped with spikes, and a detonator which is screwed into the harpoon itself. Roughly two or three seconds elapse from the time the harpoon hits the whale to when the grenade explodes, and then it takes considerably longer (no-one knows exactly how long) for them to die.

The whales are then inflated with air, tied to the ship and brought back to Hvalfjordur station for processing. There to greet them are massive flocks of gulls and fulmars — and dozens of tourists. Thanks to coach tours advertised in Reykjavik ("Whaling station tour — whale permitting") the station attracts them as readily as the geysers and the smoking volcanoes.

The catches (in recent years exclusively fin, sei, minke and, until 1982 — when they were protected — sperm) are processed into whale oil, whale meal and frozen products, though, in the case of minke, everything except the meat is discarded and wasted. Today all the frozen products that are not consumed locally are exported to Japan, which reported imports of over 4,000 tonnes of frozen whale products from Iceland in 1982, for human consumption. The whale oil and whale meal is used locally or exported to Europe. The best of the minke, caught at the smaller stations, is also exported to Japan and, to a smaller extent, to Norway, for human consumption. Some is still eaten in Iceland. Whale products accounted for 1.6% of Iceland's total exports in 1983.

Each year, the Icelandic authorities also grant permission exclusively to the Marine Zoo at Hafnarfjordur, just outside Reykjavik, to capture about five or six live killer whales in waters around the country, for marine zoos in other parts of the world. In effect, it has been the sole source of these animals for licensed zoos anywhere, and there is no doubt that the revenue of the

whale sales keeps the Marine Zoo afloat financially. The US Government did grant a licence for ten to be captured off the coast of Alaska in 1984, for San Diego's "Sea World", but, after long battles, this has effectively been withdrawn.

The killer whale's size, combined with its intelligence, makes capture difficult – but ironically, these are exactly the same characteristics which make them so sought after by aquaria. Hunters cruise off Iceland's south coast during late summer, trailing vessels that are seining herring, a favourite prey of the killer whales. When the herring come up to the surface at night, they are pursued by the killer whales – often enticed by herring fishermen who free fish from their nets. It is relatively easy to find the whales but capturing them alive, using a net, is more than difficult. The animal is hoisted onto the deck with special apparatus and placed in a steel tank lined with wet styrofoam for the trip to port. Until shipment (by air) can be arranged, the captured killer whales are kept in pools at the Zoo. Since 1976, the Marine Zoo has exported over 35 of them, most recently to Japan, San Francisco and Vancouver.

This operation, criticised all over the world, still continues. The whales are being kept in cramped conditions – but are accustomed to vast open spaces. One such animal arrived in Holland early in 1984 and is now on show at the marine museum in Harderwijk. She has been named Gudrun, after the vessel which captured her off the north coast of Iceland. On average, captive killer whales like her have a life span of 3.1 years. In the wild they can be expected to live for 50–70 years.

Fishing

The only serious clashes Iceland has had with other countries for centuries have centred on fish.

During the early 1970s, in what became known worldwide as the "Cod Wars", the Icelanders fought long and hard to extend their fishing limits to 200 miles. It was a

Gudrun the killer whale, at a Marine Zoo in Iceland, shortly after being captured by the vessel after which she was named.

Rich fishing banks constitute the very foundation of Iceland's economy. This herring boat is fishing near the coast of the eastern fjords.

desperate – and successful – bid towards safeguarding diminishing fish stocks in Icelandic waters.

Marine fish are the country's economic lifeblood and efficient fisheries are essential to provide adequate foreign exchange earnings. Iceland's own fishermen, operating the most sophisticated fishing fleet in the world, were taking only about half the total catch of the area, and they didn't want to see the stocks reduced by other nations, such as Britain.

Iceland has no resources of oil or minerals and the climate makes it impossible to grow any but the hardiest of crops. Indeed, most things have to be imported: oil, steel, timber, many foodstuffs, construction equipment, machinery, cars, all kinds of raw materials and finished products . . . the list is almost endless. So to a very large extent, these imports have to be paid for by exports of fish and fish products, which are responsible for about 70% of the country's total exports. Most towns and villages in Iceland base their economy entirely on fish and together they make their country more dependent on fisheries than any other nation in the world.

The first fishing limit in Iceland was 3 miles from the shore. This was then extended, first to 4 in 1952, then 12 in 1958, then 50 miles in 1972. Besides the Icelanders, there were British, East and West German, Soviet, Polish, Belgian and other large fishing fleets putting pressure on the over-exploited fishing grounds around the coast. Herring was virtually wiped out, important herring fisheries collapsed and even now, after years of a total ban on herring fishing, only a very limited quota is al-

Unloading redfish, among the most valuable species of fish caught in Icelandic waters. Annual catches of all fish species together are in the order of 1.5 million metric tonnes.

lowed. Cod, too, was seriously threatened and a quota on each year's fishing had to be enforced. Indeed, the mortality in the Icelandic cod stock, mostly as a result of fishing, had become the highest in the whole North Atlantic. Capelin and other species are still similarly close to the danger line — so much so that there is now a virtual ban on fishing capelin in Icelandic waters. Total catch in 1981 was 640,000 tonnes; in 1983 it was just 13,000 tonnes.

Britain, Germany and other countries, however, did not acknowledge the right of Iceland over the 200-mile limit it was seeking. This resulted in the so-called Cod Wars. It was only after a long shotless sparring fight with ships from other nations, and lengthy diplomatic negotiations, that Iceland did gain full control over the 200-mile fisheries jurisdiction in 1977. The total fishing zone around Iceland now covers an area of 758,000 square kilometres. Foreign fishing in these waters is now limited to a handful of Faroese, Norwegian and Belgian vessels.

There is still, despite the "victory", a serious risk of the Icelanders themselves overexploiting their fish resources. The supply of fish is not inexhaustible. Although the Marine Research Institute in Reykjavik annually advises how much of each species should be caught, the final decision is always a political one and regularly exceeds the limits advised by the experts. The argument given is that increasingly colder waters around Iceland have affected fish distribution and are the cause of declining catches instead. However, some further conservation measures have been incorporated, such as steps to protect the haunts of immature fish and an increase in net

mesh size, in an increasingly determined effort to reverse the disastrous trends of the past.

Freshwater fishing, certainly the most popular sport in Iceland, is very carefully monitored. The fish are caught and farmed for commercial purposes and Iceland's magnificent salmon stocks attract large numbers of native and foreign anglers. As a result of the Freshwater Fisheries Law of 1932, a directorate of freshwater fisheries was eventually established in 1946, under the auspices of the Ministry of Agriculture. Following this, increasing protective measures were introduced, with changes to the original law, in 1957. This led to regulations on netting and angling. Angling is limited to 12 hours a day in each river, between 0700 and 2200, usually with an enforced break in the middle of the day. The owners of rivers have also formed fishing associations for each river (now over 150 throughout the country) to ensure, with the help of water bailiffs, that too many rods are not fishing each beat.

Salmon is the main species of interest. Ocean ranching has made great strides during the last few years and there are so many smolt-rearing stations for salmon in Iceland that, in the future, their production could well exceed local demand. Furthermore, Iceland is probably unique in having a total ban on catching salmon in coastal waters, a measure which ensures a higher recovery rate from the sea than is possible in other countries.

Wetland drainage and dredging

Human interference with Iceland's wetlands has been significant. Horrific drainage programmes have taken place and these days a large proportion of all wetlands (especially lowland meadows) have been damaged or destroyed. Other industrial and agricultural developments and their accompanying road construction could seriously affect several major sites in the future.

Thjorsarver is probably the most threat-

Salmon fishing is one of the most popular sports in Iceland.

Fishing for trout through the ice, in the middle of Lake Myvatn.

ened to date, by flooding as a result of the construction of a dam for a hydro-electric power scheme; but concern is also growing about the future of the Olfusforir area not far from Reykjavik and, also, Lake Myvatn.

Increased urbanisation in the surroundings of Lake Myvatn, entailing industrial use of diatomite (by dredging large areas of the lake), increased use of fertilisers, and increased tourism have all brought about considerable changes and problems to the local environment. The main problem now is the mining of the diatomaceous sediment of Myvatn, which has been carried out using a hydraulic suction dredge since

1967. Hundreds of thousands of tons of dry sediment have been taken from the lake and the operation currently proceeds at several times more than the natural rate of deposition. Not only is this changing the morphological characteristics of the lake, but it is also adversely affecting its nutrient chemistry.

Soil Erosion and Land Reclamation

Most people understand the importance of conserving a productive lake or fish stocks. Substantial funds are devoted to researching fisheries and their management, and there are strict, albeit sometimes optimistic, regulations on fishing. But few people really understand the problems of soil erosion – even though it is probably the most serious and important environmental hazard in Iceland today. Many even deny that erosion is a problem at all, others blame it on the climate or volcanism. It is true that a combination of factors make the Icelandic soil, which already has a low percentage of clay and therefore has a weak structure, very vulnerable to erosion. Volcanic eruptions spread large quantities of ash over the countryside and completely cover the vegetation and eventually mix with the soil. Ashfalls and volcanic lavaflows have resulted in great damage to the vegetation over the centuries. Even Iceland's cool climate doesn't help, leading to slow chemical weathering and decomposition of organic matter. The result is a coarse and immature soil with a high content of inorganic matter; easy prey for the strong mechanical weathering forces dominant over most of the country. Then there are other natural influences, such as glacial rivers and glaciofluvial activities, which have also kept extensive areas clear of vegetation.

But there is no question that man has been the primary cause of erosion. The soils are not vulnerable unless the vegetation cover is lost – and glacial activities are only partly to blame. In Iceland, the vegetation has had to face man's destructive logging and over-grazing by his animals since he first set foot in the country. His horses, cattle, pigs, goats and, particularly, sheep have roamed freely amongst the delicate vegetation since the 10th century and such over-grazing has led to deterioration of the plant cover and a reduction in root growth and in the number of plant species. Before man arrived, there were no mammalian herbivores in Iceland – their arrival inevitably resulted in sudden and great damage.

At Thingvellir, on 27th July 1974, the occasion of the 1,100th anniversary of the settlement of Iceland, the Althing (Icelandic Parliament) passed a resolution allotting a special endowment to be used for land reclamation purposes and to halt the erosion of the island. Some areas have already been protected from grazing, and reafforestation programmes using conifers have begun. The Icelandic Forestry Society boasts 7,000 members and planting trees has almost become an obsession in some parts of the country. But the tide has hardly been turned.

Livestock still ranges freely all over the place. Farmers have grazing rights virtually everywhere and it is usually impossible for the Nature Conservation Council to get sheep off land it wants to protect. The only exceptions are cultivated land (which is usually fenced off), Thingvellir, Skaftafell (apart from a handful of sheep and horses) and a few small areas which have been protected by the Soil and Land Conservation Society and the Forestry Service. Jokulsargljufur National Park and most of the nature reserves are heavily grazed and suffer from erosion, although some stock-proof fencing is planned.

In the 1,100 years since Iceland was settled, more than half the vegetation cover has been lost. And the soil is literally being blown away. In the last few years a new threat has appeared which is actually increasing the rate of erosion of the past. Due to the lack of forests and fences, four-wheel drive vehicles can be driven virtually everywhere – including over vulnerable plant cover. The effect of this "free-range tourism" is similar to over-grazing. Efforts to introduce a new law on off-road driving have been underway since 1982.

In the 1,100 years since Iceland was settled, more than half the vegetation cover has been lost – and the soil is literally being blown away.

A great deal can be done to stop erosion. In some cases, protection from grazing is sufficient to restore the vegetation, if the deterioration is not too advanced. New plant growth can be established with fertilization and seeding on previously eroded land. Lymegrass can be used to halt sand-drift, since its deep root system stabilizes the sand in readiness for other species. Trees and other plants can be imported from other countries (with similar growth conditions) to play an important role in soil conservation too. They provide it with organic matter, which later becomes available as nutrients to other plants, and they give shelter to the ground vegetation. Alaskan lupin, which grows well in Iceland without fertilization, is a good example of this. Irrigation can also help in land reclamation work – increased soil water level goes some way towards preventing soil erosion.

But land reclamation and soil conservation is costly; and what little legislation there is is difficult to enforce. The result is that Iceland's annual net soil loss is still considerable. Soil destruction is still taking place on such a catastrophic scale that it has even been suggested that radical measures have to be taken if the country is to continue to be habitable.

CHAPTER 9

TRAVEL HINTS

PREPARATIONS

1) Passports and visas

A valid passport is necessary for all travellers visiting Iceland, except for those of Danish, Faroese, Finnish, Norwegian or Swedish nationalities. A visa is required from some countries, though none in Western Europe, or from Canada or the USA. Other visitors should check with an Icelandic embassy or consulate well in advance.

2) Health

No special health inoculations or vaccinations are required or recommended for visitors to Iceland. However, those arriving within a certain number of days of leaving or transiting through areas of the world infected by certain diseases (especially smallpox, yellow fever and cholera) may need proof of vaccination for entry.

3) Other restrictions

For health and other reasons, it is illegal to bring live animals and birds, uncooked meat and meat products, eggs and other poultry products, butter, medicines (except small amounts for personal use) and, of course, narcotics, poisons, firearms and ammunition, into Iceland. It is also prohibited to bring in fishing equipment (including waders and rubber boots) which has been used while angling abroad, unless the equipment has been disinfected according to specific Icelandic rules.

HOW TO GET THERE

1) By Air

All international flights are into Keflavik International Airport, about 50 kilometres west of Reykjavik. It is unique in having a duty-free shop which is open to **arriving** passengers as well as those departing!

ICELANDAIR (or Flugleidir, as it is known to the Icelanders) operates regular jet services to Iceland from the following cities: London, Glasgow, Copenhagen, Stockholm, Gothenburg, Oslo, Faroe Islands, Frankfurt, Luxembourg, Paris, Narssarssuaq, New York, Chicago, Baltimore, Detroit, Orlando, Salzburg and Bergen.

SCANDINAVIAN AIRLINES SYSTEM (SAS) operates regular jet services to Iceland from Copenhagen, Oslo and Stockholm, in co-operation with Icelandair.

EAGLE AIR operates regular jet services to Iceland from Amsterdam, Dusseldorf and Zurich.

Connecting flights are available from a number of other major cities (such as, in the case of Icelandair, several places in California) and there is an enormous range of travel packages and attractive excursion fares to choose from, for individuals, families and groups. These are worth investigating as they often allow considerable savings on normal one-way and return fares.

For passengers travelling between Europe and the USA, Icelandair also offers a special stopover rate, allowing up to 72 hours in Reykjavik en route. For a very modest extra charge, this includes accommodation at the first class Hotel Loftleidir, all necessary transfers, continental breakfast, sightseeing and considerable discounts on domestic air fares, car rental and souvenir shopping. As far as travel bargains go this particular offer is outstanding. Most Icelandair flights between Europe and the USA make brief transit stops at Keflavik Airport in Iceland, anyway, but these barely allow enough time to do a bit of duty-free shopping.

Transportation to and from Keflavik Airport is simple. Immediately after customs clearance for each flight into the airport, there are bus departures from outside the airport terminal non-stop to Reykjavik. The 45-minute journey takes you along the coastline to Reykjavik Town Terminal, which adjoins the main lobby of Hotel Loftleidir. Conversely, buses for the airport leave the terminal about 1¾ hours before flight departures. Regular buses and taxis connect the Loftleidir with the rest of Reykjavik.

2) By Sea

SMYRIL LINE (FAROESE COASTAL LINE) operates a weekly service in the summer, for about 1,000 passengers and 250 cars, on four routes from Seydisfjordur on the east coast of Iceland to the Faroe Islands, the Shetlands (Scotland) with connecting passages from the mainland, Bergen (Norway), and to Hanstholm (Denmark).

ONCE YOU ARE THERE

1) Language

Icelandic is the national language. However, virtually everyone speaks both Danish and English, which are compulsory subjects in Icelandic schools. Icelandic itself is believed to have changed very little from the original tongue spoken by the Norse settlers. It has two letters of its own: þ like "th" in "thin" and ð, which is pronounced as the "th" in "them".

Preceding pages: At Breidamerkurlon, south of Vatnajokull, icebergs calve into a lagoon and begin their voyage seaward.

2) Money

The Icelandic monetary unit is the "krona" (kr), which is equal to 100 "aurar". Coins are 10, 5 and 1 krona, and 50, 10 and 5 aurar. Banknotes are 50, 100, 500 and 1,000 krona.

Visitors are allowed to bring a limited sum of krona into the country, and any sum of foreign currency. Travellers' cheques or cash can easily be changed into krona at the airport, banks, major hotels and even some restaurants and travel bureaux. International credit cards are accepted all over the country.

Inflation in Iceland is currently very high, so it would be unrealistic to attempt to give any guide to exchange rates.

3) Time

Iceland is on Greenwich Mean Time (GMT) all year round.

4) Electricity

220 volt, 50 Hz, AC.

5) Business hours

Most shops and offices are closed at weekends. Shops are generally open from 9 am to 6 pm from Monday to Friday, and some from 9 am to noon on Saturdays. Souvenir and hotel shops often have extended hours. Newsagents, or "sales windows" selling magazines, tobacco and sweets are usually open until 11.30 pm daily. Banks are open from 9.15 am to 4 pm from Monday to Friday and, in addition, from 5 pm to 6 pm on Thursdays. Offices are generally open from 9 am to 5 pm on weekdays only.

6) Film

Film in Iceland is very expensive — so always take plenty with you — and bear in mind the astronomical number of photogenic subjects! Think of the minimum number of films you are likely to use — then double it.

7) Tipping

There is no tipping in Iceland — more often than not, tips will be returned.

8) Names

Very few Icelanders have original surnames, so it can often be difficult to fathom out the telephone directory, which lists people by their first names. This is why Icelanders call each other by their first names — not because they all know one another — though, nevertheless, this often seems to be the case! Most people have a patronymic rather than a family surname. For example, Sigurdsson, means the son of Sigurdur, and Finnbogadottir means the daughter of Finnbogi.

9) Clothing

The weather in Iceland is very changeable. The basic clothing necessities, at any time of the year, are a sweater, rainproof jacket and sturdy shoes. Jeans are not very good as they can be freezing cold when wet and take a long time to dry. Also, the most popular participation sport in Iceland is swimming — and there are ample opportunities for bathing in water from the warm springs or in the many pools — so swimming gear should be taken whatever the time of year.

WHERE TO STAY

Reykjavik is certainly the best central base for exploring Iceland — most trips and travel systems start and finish in the capital — but there is a sufficient range of accommodation all over the country to suit all pockets and all tastes.

1) Hotels and guesthouses

Hotels are available at convenient locations right the way around the country's ring-road, though there is nowhere to stay in the interior. Hotel Edda is probably the best known chain of hotels outside Reykjavik and Akureyri, offering motel-like accommodation (as well as sleeping bag facilities), during summer months, as well as restaurants, shops and often swimming pools. This kind of hotel offers the traveller good service at a reasonable price and is usually located on the outskirts of a town or a village.

The Loftleidir, in Reykjavik, which doubles its purpose as the Town Terminal, has to be the best hotel in the country. It certainly has excellent facilities, including one of the best restaurants in town, a cafeteria, indoor swimming pool (the water is drawn from hot springs — as it is for all the showers), sauna, sunlounge and souvenir shop.

If you do not already have a hotel reservation when you arrive in the country (and it is advisable to book stays in Reykjavik in advance, particularly in the height of the season) contact the information service at the Loftleidir for information and bookings for any other hotel in the country.

Incidentally, breakfast is rarely included in the hotel price, particularly in Reykjavik. The only exception to this rule is in the case of some private houses which offer clean, homely and low-priced accommodation — and a hearty Icelandic breakfast to boot. In Reykjavik, particularly, guest houses providing cooking facilities are also available. Again, ask at the Loftleidir for information.

2) Camping

With a small population, few towns and so much land, Iceland offers ample scope for camping. Vast areas of the interior are completely uninhabited and have no hotels, so camping is the **only** way to stay in many parts of the country. Despite the rough terrain, indeed because of the rough terrain, suitable sheltered spots can be found fairly easily in most places.

Camping is prohibited in very few parts of the country, such as in certain sections of National Parks, but these areas are normally signed. If in doubt, consult the local warden beforehand or get permission from the NCC. Other than that, there are no restrictions, though it is always good manners to request the permission of the local farmer (which is usually readily given) especially if you are in the immediate vicinity of a farm, or on any fenced or cultivated land.

The number of well-equipped campsites, for those who wish to avoid roughing it too much, is limited. There are only about a dozen designated sites in the interior, the rest being well-distributed around the ring-road, and in Reykjavik and Akureyri. A few of these are well-equipped — luxurious even — but many are not, even though the settings are often fabulous. One particular word of warning: facilities shown in the guides to be available are **not** always provided directly at the site, but more often in the local village or town. This is particularly the case with swimming pools, showers, stores, restaurants, and garages, but also even toilets in some cases.

It is possible to hire tents, camping equipment, sleeping bags and foam mattresses in Reykjavik, and near some campsites around the ring-road.

3) Other accommodation

Buildings which are boarding schools (such as the Edda hotels) during winter become transformed in summer, taking on the temporary job of guest-houses. Cheap overnight accommodation for travellers with their own sleeping bags is also available at certain summer hotels and hostels. And there is something similar to the Youth Hostels Association or the YMCA/YWCA, known as the Bandalag Islenzkra Farfugla. The BIF, which has its headquarters in Reykjavik, provides cheap accommodation in hostel dormitories, in nearly a dozen of the main towns.

Tourists huts in uninhabited areas may also be used by hikers, for a small fee, providing they are not already occupied by organised groups, which always take precedence. You must take your own sleeping bags and provisions and closely observe the regulations posted inside. These huts, which belong to the Ferdafelag Islands, the Touring Club of Iceland, are not intended for stays of longer than three nights.

You may also come across rescue huts, which have been erected by the Slysavarnafelag Islands, the Life Saving Association. Provisions, food and equipment are placed in them for use by travellers only in extreme emergency, and it is strictly forbidden to enter them unless circumstances are dire.

GETTING AROUND

1) By Air

Land communications are not always easy in Iceland, regularly hindered as they are by mountains, glaciers, lava-beds, deeply indented coastlines, sudden snowstorms and heavy rains.

No wonder, then, that flying is the typical Icelandic way of travelling. It is the most convenient way, the quickest — and not always the most expensive. It enables you to visit more places in less time, the only disadvantage being that you miss everything there is to see on the way. You can, however, be treated to a series of magnificent vistas on a clear day from the air, if you are lucky.

Air transport began in Iceland as early as 1919, but was not fully organised until 1937 when Icelandair was formed and started its internal air services which have continued to this day.

The centre for all domestic air services, Reykjavik Domestic Airport, is just a few minutes drive from downtown Reykjavik. Icelandair, the main carrier, has regular scheduled services from Reykjavik to a number of points elsewhere in the country — to all the major regional gateways — as well as some of the "toy" landing strips!

Eagle Air, also based at Reykjavik Airport, also flies large aircraft to outlying

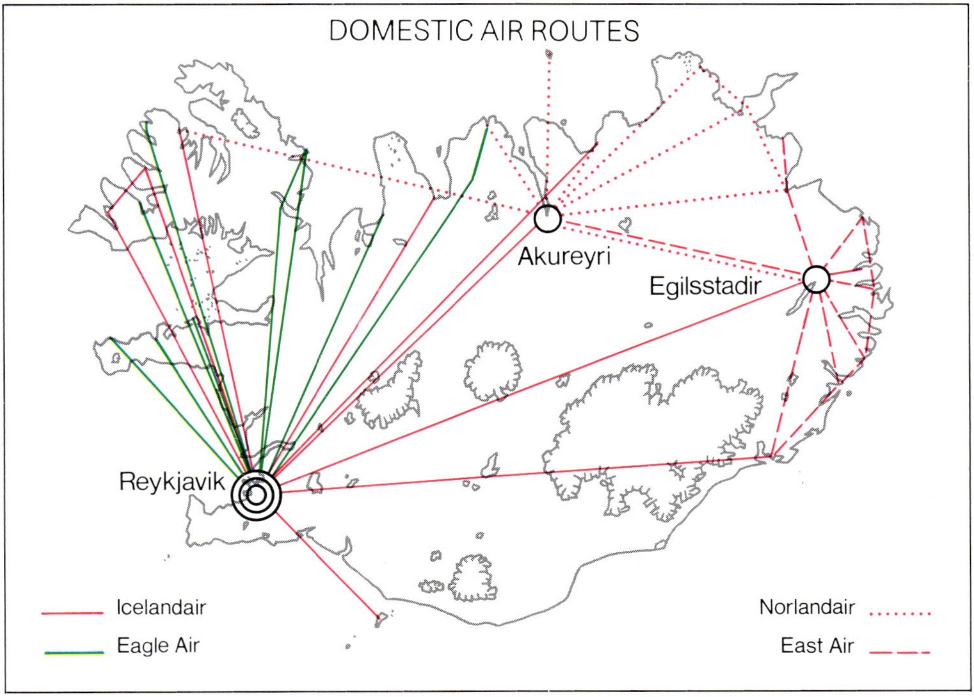

areas. In addition, the airline Ernir is based in Isafjordur, Flugfelag Austurlands in Egilsstadir, and Flugfelag Nordurlands in Akureyri, all adding to the choice of internal routes.

Bus services link most outlying districts to their nearest air-strip.

A complete range of Air Rover tickets, Triangular Flights and other special offers are available to tourists, as well as Air-Bus Rovers and other co-operative packages. As a result, air fares compare well with those for overland transportation. There are offices and agents for booking these in most of the main towns.

In addition to the regular scheduled flights (which put Reykjavik in contact with most inhabited parts of Iceland within just two hours) it is also possible to take circular air tours and sightseeing flights to suit individual requirements, weather permitting.

2) By car or motorcycle

Bearing in mind that the wilderness is vast, traffic minimal, services few and far between and the weather unpredictable, travelling around Iceland by car is enormous fun. It is an experience you will never forget, albeit a very expensive one. Indeed there are few other places in the world where you can drive past and through such varied landscapes — green valleys, fjords, volcanoes, lava deserts and glaciers — in the space of just a few days.

Petrol prices are amongst the highest in Europe, and hiring a car for more than a few days (if you drive a reasonable distance) can easily break the bank. But the freedom and sense of adventure can very nearly make you forget to worry about financing it. Driving in Iceland is almost an adventure on its own.

Roads

Until the turn of the century there were no roads to speak of in Iceland. Horses were practically the only means of transport besides boats. Organised road building did not actually begin until about 1900 and, even then, the first attempts were intended only for horse-drawn traffic. But the car was introduced in 1913 and, by 1930, the most important districts had been successfully linked by roads.

Even so, it was only in 1974 that the most difficult 34-kilometre stretch around Iceland's perimeter was completed, at last enabling Icelanders to drive all the way round their country. Before the ring-road was completed big rivers, several feet deep, had to be forded and everyone made their own precarious route across the sands and plains. Not uncommonly, road signs like "many vehicles have been destroyed at-

An economical way to travel in a country where petrol prices are amongst the highest in Europe.

tempting to ford this river" prompted travellers to revise their schedules.

These days, all the rivers and streams are bridged. You can now drive in either direction, from Reykjavik to Reykjavik, to reach any district along the 1,446 kilometre route. Even that is no mean feat considering some of the terrain.

You can drive for hours without seeing another car, even though the "main" roads are fairly well travelled. But the lack of traffic also has something to do with the fact that, outside the main towns, only a few hundred kilometres of roads (about 10% in all) are surfaced. Potholes, grooves, boulders, loose gravel and many other (usually unexpected) obstacles are the order of the day. Heavy rains can make the roads positively hazardous but, after no rain for a long time, they become a rally driver's dream of dusty, winding, narrow, hilly tracks. Being followed by a thick cloud of dust can make one **feel** like a rally driver — even if only doing 30 kph!

Travelling time is something to bear in mind when planning a route. With all the general hazards, and roads winding a tortuous path around fjords and deep valleys or up steep mountain slopes, you can forget about speed right away. Somehow, the Icelanders manage to negotiate "their" roads at an enviable rate, but the average tourist attempting to follow suit often ends up in a ditch or with a puncture. Indeed, there are probably as many punctures in Iceland as there are puffins. So always check that you have a puncture outfit (and a spare tyre!) before you set off. Besides, take Iceland at a rush and your broken springs condemn you to spend a day waiting for another car to come along and a week or more organising the repair.

So, although the actual mileage one has to cover to get around Iceland is small in comparison with larger countries, it takes a lot longer than a glance at the map might lead you to believe to complete the trip. Three or four hundred kilometres in a day and you have something to boast about.

Anyway, speed should not be the main

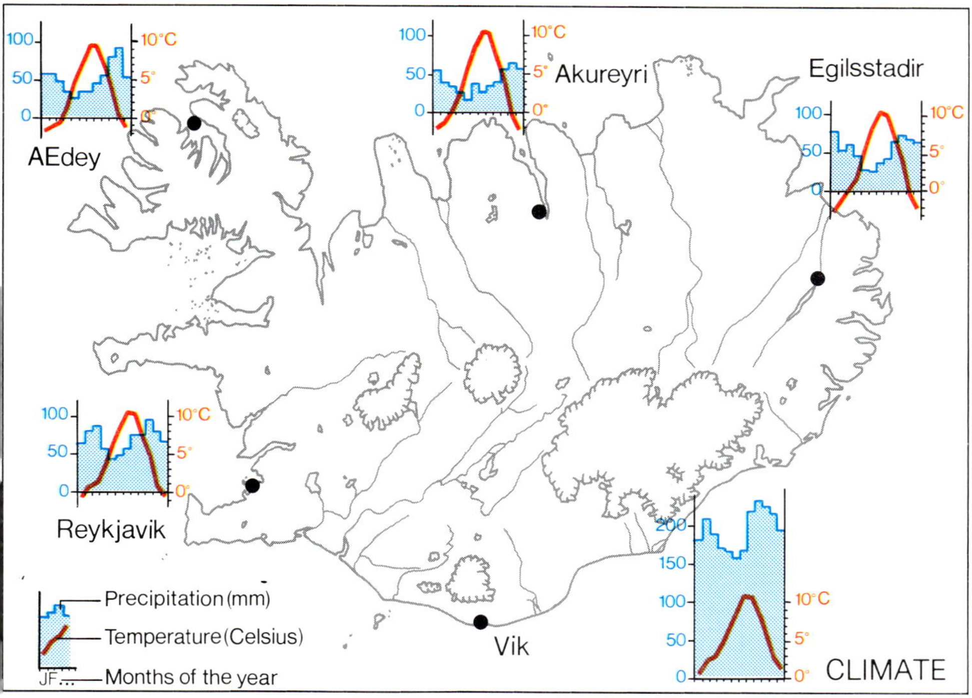

object of the exercise. There is too much variety in the scenery, too many new things to look at and so much wildlife to look for, to worry about speed. A new world in new surroundings opens out over every hill and around every corner — and there are plenty of those! Thus allowing for stops and detours, it is not a good idea to leave less than a complete week for the round trip. Otherwise, you will constantly be pining for more time.

The ring-road (or road "I") closely follows the coastline, missing out only the western fjords. Work is currently in progress to include this spectacular and impressive section, distinctively absent from the present system, although reachable via other routes.

Around the ring-road, a two-wheel drive vehicle is fine during the summer. There are still no "ordinary" roads going all the way into the interior, although some (such as to Gullfoss and Great Geysir) are every bit as good as much of the ring-road. Many cross-country routes can be undertaken in four-wheel drive vehicles, such as jeeps or mountain buses but, even so, highland tracks are usually only passable in high summer, July to August, due to snow and mud at other times of the year.

Before heading for the interior, it is a good idea to check on road conditions beforehand. The Information Desk in Reykjavik town centre is very good in this respect, and usually has the necessary information. Always double-check locally, though. Many areas are effectively closed to **all** vehicles for up to eight months of the year. Never attempt to drive along a track which is not marked on a map, unless it is obvious

Until the turn of the century, there were no roads to speak of in Iceland. Today, it is possible to drive all the way round the country — through some of the most beautiful scenery anywhere in Europe, such as this region in the north-west only a few kilometres from the Arctic Circle.

that it has been frequently travelled before. It is easy — and common — for travellers to get bogged down in mud or wet sand, unable to move. Also, never attempt to cross a river which you cannot wade across. Glacial rivers are very unstable and always dangerous, so should always be treated with the utmost caution.

Those are all the do's and don'ts. One thing is for sure — don't let them put you off. Thousands of people travel around Iceland's 11,000-kilometre road system every year without the slightest problem and the temptation to drive into some of the remotest corners on earth is just too much to resist. Remember to take a valid driving licence from your country of residence and an international licence special for Iceland.

Hiring a car

Hiring a car in Iceland is expensive, but more convenient and less worrying than taking your own. Some excellent budget offers, however, have recently been introduced and these are worth investigating. It is possible to hire a whole range of different vehicles, from a Volkswagen Golf (undoubtedly the most popular choice amongst visitors) to mini-buses or deluxe four-wheel drives. A few firms allow you to leave the car in another town without drop-off charges. In the summer, and on the main roads, two-wheel drives are quite satisfactory. If you can afford it, four-wheel drives are obviously better and they are equipped for highland driving and have a luggage rack, extra fuel tank and other "extras". If you have even more money, modern chauffeur-driven cars can be hired for up to five people.

Usually, there is a 24-hour daily rate (which should include insurance — but check this) and an extra charge for every kilometre travelled. It is the kilometre rate which makes it so expensive to travel any distance. Petrol is not included in the charge, and damage caused by off-road driving and by crossing rivers and streams is not covered by the insurance. There is currently also a 25 per cent sales tax, which is not included, so take this into account as well. Incidentally, if you are driving yourself, as most people do, remember to name every member of the party who is likely to take a turn with the driving on the insurance form before you go. Trailers are available on request and usually at no extra charge.

Taking your own car

Car ferries operate to Iceland from Scotland, Norway, Denmark and the Faroe Islands. It is not expensive and there are several ways of getting bargain fares, according to the number of passengers. In the short-term, taking your own car saves a great deal of money on expensive car hire, but in the long-term the benefit is probably outweighed by the inevitable knocks and bangs it will suffer before arriving home again considerably the worse for wear. Nature is irrevocably boss and it takes no notice of car health.

A non-resident bringing a private vehicle into Iceland must present the vehicle's registration book, an international motor insurance card and a special International Driving Licence. The vehicle cannot be kept in Iceland for longer than three months and may not be loaned, rented or used for any transportation against payment.

Traffic hints

The maximum speed in urban areas is 45 kph (30 mph), in rural areas 70 kph (45 mph). Traffic police use radar, and fines can be heavy if these limits are greatly exceeded. The use of safety belts in the front seats of cars is compulsory. A person with even a modest blood alcohol content (for example, equivalent to a single whisky) is not allowed to drive. Driving under the influence of alcohol can bring heavy penalties and loss of insurance of your car, if you have an accident. Drivers must have a valid International Driving Licence (a special one for Iceland) and must be over 20. Always drive on the right. Driving off roads and tracks is prohibited.

Since most roads have a gravel surface

and can be very dusty, there is an unwritten rule to keep headlights on when driving outside towns, even in broad daylight. For the same reason, check that there is plenty of windscreen wash fluid before setting off. Finding your way out of Reykjavik can be very difficult to say the least – so set off well-armed with maps. Once en route, a compass is useful.

Potholes, grooves, boulders, loose gravel, flooded roads and streams and many other (usually unexpected) obstacles are the order of the day for travellers in many parts of the interior of Iceland.

Filling stations

Petrol stations are marked on most road maps and occur at fairly regular intervals along the ring-road. No petrol, oil or other provisions can be obtained in the interior. Most of these stations have toilets, food, car-cleaning sprays and other facilities. They are normally open from 7.30 am until 9.15 pm, on a daily basis, but close for lunch (11.30 am to 1 pm) on Sundays. In Reykjavik, some filling stations offer all-night self-service facilities. Outside Reykjavik, a few filling stations are open until 11.30 p.m.

Taxis

Taxis are available in all the main towns, 24 hours a day. They are used extensively in all weathers and rates are comparable to those in most European countries. They can also be hired for extended trips into the country to places of interest far from town – such as Gullfoss, Geysir and Thingvellir. All taxis are owner-operated, but charge uniform fares – you pay what the meter shows at the end of the trip. It is often possible to arrange a flat rate for sight-seeing tours.

3) By train

Don't even try — there aren't any.

4) By coach and bus

A range of private companies operate bus services out of Reykjavik and Akureyri and, to a lesser extent, out of Egilsstadir and Isafjordur. They run throughout the country to even the remotest places, at least during the summer. Municipal bus transport is well developed in the capital and in Akureyri, running all year round.

Travelling around by bus offers excellent value for money. If you don't want to spend much — and don't mind missing out on a tour guide — it is easy to take scheduled buses from Reykjavik, for example, to all the main attractions like Gullfoss, Great Geysir, and Thingvellir. For a longer trip, it is only eight hours travelling time between Reykjavik and Akureyri — and then a simple connection to places like Myvatn and the north-east.

If you plan to travel a lot on the buses, it is possible to buy discount tickets (available at the BSI bus terminal in Reykjavik) offering unlimited travel on any scheduled route for 1, 2, 3, or 4 weeks. Known as the Omnibus Passport, it allows you to get off wherever you like and whenever you like, since the drivers will stop anywhere on their routes by request.

Alternatively, the Fullcircle Passport offers a full-circuit ticket without a time limit, which is a relatively cheap way of travelling all around the country at your own pace. It is the longest bus route in the world.

There are also special Air-Bus Rover tickets, allowing an inexpensive combination of flying and busing.

5) By sea

Towns and villages dot most of the irregular coastline of about 6,600 kilometres — but passenger services by sea are few and far between. The main internal ferry services are between Reykjavik and Akranes (four or five times daily); and Thorlakshofn (connected to Reykjavik by bus) and Heimaey, on the Westmann Islands (daily). Both carry passengers and cars.

Otherwise, with a few minor exceptions, if you want to sail from one Icelandic harbour to another, do not be surprised if you are told to go via Copenhagen!

6) By horse

In the olden days, when travelling abroad was only possible for the very few who had the means to spend considerable time on such pursuits, "tourists" who came to Iceland normally hired a guide and a team of horses, in order to get the extraordinary feeling of the unspoiled, spectacular Icelandic countryside.

These days, pony trekking is still possible, for trips of a few hours, a day or several weeks. Iceland must be one of the most ideally-suited places in the world for this kind of holiday. For information on holidays of this kind, or for short trips, contact The Icelandic Horse Hire Service (Islenska hestaleigan sf.) Hlidarvegur 38, 200 Kopavogur, Iceland, tel: 43420. They cater for beginners, experts and anyone and everyone in between.

7) Hiking

There are numerous opportunities for long distance hikes in Iceland. All of them require good equipment and a high level of expertise — and you need to be in fairly good shape. Touring clubs in Iceland offer a variety of hikes and similar tours, under experienced leadership, to nearly all parts of the country.

It is sometimes possible to join regular groups of Icelanders on walking tours, if numbers permit. Contact the Touring Club of Iceland (Ferdafelag Islands), Oldugata 3, tel: 11798 or 19533, or Outdoor Life (Utivist), Laekjargata 6-a, tel: 14606.

For information on glacier walking contact Joklarannsoknarfelag Islands (the Icelandic Glaciological Society) in Reykjavik. Always seek their advice before considering any kind of trip or ascent upon glacier. Previous planning and study is essential.

ORGANISED SIGHTSEEING

There is a tremendous selection of day trips in Iceland, and sightseeing tours to local places of interest are available from most of the larger towns. Without a doubt, these tours offer the easiest and most informative way of seeing many parts of the country, even if they are a little lacking in a sense of adventure.

The most active operator of these short tours is Reykjavik Excursions, a joint venture of several travel agencies (including Icelandair's Travel Service) operating from the capital. There are information and booking offices at Gimli, Laekjargata 3 (tel 28025) near the Information Kiosk and Taxi Rank, and at Hotel Loftleidir (tel 621011). Tours are operated seven days a week, from May to September inclusive, with a free pickup service at all hotels and guesthouses in Reykjavik. A small selection remain in operation for the rest of the year, weather permitting.

Some examples of the kind of tours they have on offer are: Reykjavik City Sightseeing (2.5 hours), offering a basic conducted tour of the city (though one of the best ways to see Reykjavik is on foot, armed with a street map); Pony Trekking, offering a three hour taste of riding Iceland horses with an expert; The Golden Circle (9 hours) offering an excellent day excursion to Gullfoss, Great Geysir, Thingvellir and other places of interest in the south-west; Westmann Islands, offering a magnificent round-trip by air (with the option of returning by boat to view the bird cliffs) and a guided tour of Heimaey; Akureyri and Lake Myvatn by air and bus; Aerial Sightseeing; and even a day in Greenland, visiting Kap Dan on the spectacular east coast.

Other excursion operators offer everything from a flight over the Arctic Circle to half-day trips across Vatnajokull, the largest ice-cap in Europe, in a snowmobile.

Discounts for most of these trips are available for stopover passengers.

One day tours can be great fun and offer the chance to learn something about the

One of Vatnajokull's icy fingers, Skaftafellsjokull, extends southward along the eastern side of Skaftafell National Park.

place and get one's bearings — but they rarely allow much time to look for wildlife.

ALL-INCLUSIVE HOLIDAYS AND LONGER TRIPS

There are literally dozens of tour operators, in the States, Iceland, the UK and other European countries, offering all-inclusive tours to Iceland or long overnight trips once you are there. Many of these offer excellent value for money. They are certainly the easiest and safest way to travel, often while maintaining a sense of adventure and the chance to **experience** the real Iceland.

The agencies offer a range of holidays from "Breakaway Weekends" to two or three centre holidays or escorted camping tours lasting several weeks. Many of these specialise in ornithology or geology or one or two of several other popular pursuits — and special tours or expeditions can be organised on request. There are too many variations and possibilities even for their own brochures to cover, so the remainder of this section is intended only as an indication of the kind of thing to look for and expect.

For camping tours, which are nearly always under the leadership of professional guides, you certainly do not need to be an experienced camper, though you must not mind roughing it a bit, should be in fairly good health, be prepared to lend a hand when needed and, above all, have a spirit of adventure — regardless of weather.

Having said that, as the advertising blurb will tell you, they are designed to take the discomfort and work out of camping. They

do just that. On most of them a special kitchen bus follows the passenger vehicle, in which all your meals are prepared. The buses are modern, specially designed and constructed high-clearance vehicles for rough overland use, thus enabling you to cross otherwise impossible terrain. They are equipped with radio-telephones, and with experienced drivers and expert guides. You will cross raging rivers, pass glacial lakes with floating icebergs, cause minor dust storms in lava deserts, and camp in some of the most spectacular places in the world, amongst the majestic mountains, volcanoes and glaciers of the otherwise "out-of-bounds" interior.

Camping safaris certainly offer the opportunity to go off the beaten track into the interior, following unclear paths, rough lava beds, unbridged rivers and soft sandy beds that you otherwise probably wouldn't experience. And all the sights of interest are pointed out to you! Do not be disappointed, though, if the programme has to be changed without warning — a fairly common occurrence, due to changing road and weather conditions.

Pony trekking, glacier walking and cave explorations are among the many adventure holidays and tours available in Iceland.

Such all-in camping trips usually cover the cost of everything, including food and camping gear. Do not forget to take plenty of films, though, as there is no chance at all of buying any en route. You would not be the first person to run out halfway through the holiday!

For the less adventurous, there are a range of other organised holidays, based on every type of accommodation from 1st class hotels to private houses or farmhouses (where you may be expected to help with the harvest!). Many of them offer ex-

cellent discounts on accommodation and food for children sharing a room with their parents.

There are fly-drive holidays, which cover the cost of flights to and from Iceland and car hire while you are there. Multicentre holidays are also popular, for example Reykjavik plus Akureyri plus Isafjordur, or any one of numerous other combinations.

A final point about "package tours" is that they are usually a lot cheaper than 100% "do-it-yourself" holidays and, if you so wish, can still leave you with a great deal of freedom.

Some Useful Addresses

1 Nature Conservation Council. Established in 1956, the NCC is the official government body for the conservation of flora and fauna in Iceland, landscape conservation, promotion of recreational enjoyment of the countryside and for organising all the associated scientific work. It is in control of all nature protection matters in Iceland and administers all the national parks (except Thingvellir) and other protected areas. The NCC employs only four full-time staff, with some short-term or seasonal personnel such as summer wardens in the National Parks.

Address: Hverfisgata 26, Reykjavik.

2 National Research Council. An official government body, the NRC oversees all scientific research in Iceland, and organises all necessary permits for work of this kind by people from abroad. Composed of 21 members designated by Parliament, research institutions, industrial organisations and the University of Iceland, its chairman is the Minister for Culture and Education. Its objectives and activities include strengthening and coordinating applied and basic science research in Iceland; studies for the utilisation of the country's natural resources for new industries; raising funds for research activities; promotion of a scientific and technical information service; and the promotion of Icelandic participation in international co-operations. A five-man Executive Committee carries out administrative functions, with the assistance of a director, four staff and two secretaries.

Address: Laugavegur 13, 101 Reykjavik.

3 Department of Biology, University of Reykjavik. Wide-ranging research and study subjects including birds, ecology, genetics and freshwater biology.

Address: Grensasvegur 12, 108 Reykjavik.

4 Icelandic Museum of Natural History, Reykjavik. Founded in 1889, the Museum became a state institution in 1947. Its main objectives are: to carry out basic research on nature in Iceland; to establish and preserve scientific collections of botanical, geological and zoological specimens (especially from Iceland); and to keep exhibits which are on display for the general public. It has seven staff and three part-time assistants, and three departments: Botany, with many activities centred on mapping the vascular and bryophyte flora of Iceland and on short-term environmental studies; Geology, with a wide range of research projects, for example mapping the petrological distribution pattern of recent basaltic rocks; and Zoology, with a variety of research projects, including mapping and censusing seabirds, ecological research on seabirds, systematic research on insects and the mapping of their distribution, and ecological studies of reindeer. The Zoology Department is also the centre for bird ringing in Iceland. The exhibition room is located at 11b Hverfisgata, Reykjavik.

Address: Laugavegur 105, 105 Reykjavik.

5 Museum of Natural History, Akureyri. Founded in 1951, the Museum is active in various branches of nature research in northern Iceland, and is a centre for mycology in the country. Since 1970, it has also been the centre for nature conservation in northern Iceland, and there are occasional exhibits specifically on this subject. The permanent exhibits in-

clude a complete collection of native birds and eggs, containing all nesting birds of the country. A variety of fishes, shells and other sea animals is also exhibited, as well as selected examples of Icelandic stones and minerals. The flora of Iceland is represented in the form of pressed plants.

Address: Hafnarstraeti 81, 600 Akureyri.

6 Iceland Tourist Board.

Address: Laugavegur 3, 101 Reykjavik.

7 The Marine Research Institute. This is an independent governmental organisation working under the Ministry of Fisheries. It has a staff of about 100, of which 25 are scientists in various fields of marine research. Four research vessels are in operation and there are three affiliate offices in Isafjordur, Husavik and Hornafjordur. The main work of the MRI involves: overseeing regulations regarding fisheries; investigations into the state of stocks of commercial marine animals (invertebrates, fish and mammals) including the effects of fisheries on these stocks and the influence of environmental changes on distribution, growth and abundance; predictions on stock sizes and catches; advice on quotas and regulations; detection of new fishing grounds and the distribution of marine animals (such as capelin or deep sea shrimp) of commercial importance; the development of new or improved fishing gear; and mariculture.

Address: Skulagata 4, 101 Reykjavik.

8 Botanical Garden, Akureyri. Founded in 1912, this beautiful garden presents living examples of Iceland's Arctic flora, as well as other plants that can be grown at this northern latitude. A living museum of almost all native plants of Iceland has been maintained since 1957 and most of the 3000-odd plant species cultivated in the garden are labelled by name.

Address: Hafnarstraeti, near Eyrarlandsvegur, 602 Akureyri.

MAPS OF ICELAND

1:1,000,000
General map of the whole island, with most roads, towns and villages, farms and distances marked. Ideal for long-distance route planning but needs to be supplemented with more detailed maps.

1:500,000
Excellent road map, with east and west Iceland on opposite sides. Distinguishes hard from gravel road surfaces, summer-only and 4-wheel-drive tracks, unbridged and bridged rivers etc; also shows filling stations, kilometre distances, hotels, campsites, emergency huts, farms, views etc.

1:250,000
The main touring maps, dividing the country into nine separate sheets, and showing good detail with virtually all farms by name.

1:100,000
A series of 87 sheets covering the whole country. A few are pre-war, but most are post-war revisions, and many quite recent.

1:50,000
Two series, one of 117 sheets mostly pre-war and now discontinued (though most are still available), and the other more recent but only covering the extreme south-west of the country. The Myvatn, Hekla and Westmann Islands sheets from the first series have, however, been updated (late 1970s) and are readily available.

1:25,000
Available for Thingvellir and Skaftafell regions, in fairly recent editions.

All these (and other) maps are available from most bookshops in Reykjavik, Akureyri and elsewhere. Geological, vegetation and 3-D contour maps are also stocked. They can also be obtained from specialist Icelandic travel service stockists abroad, for example Dick Phillips in Cumbria, England.

NB. 1:1,000,000 = approx. 1 inch : 16 miles.

APPENDIX

CHECKLISTS OF THE FLORA AND FAUNA OF ICELAND

The checklists which follow are intended to be used as an indication to the plant and animal species which occur, or have been recorded, in Iceland. They are comprehensive at the time of writing, but bear in mind that, as remote areas become more accessible and as research expertise and interest continually improves, previously unrecorded species are being discovered all the time. An average of four new birds, for example, have been added to the Iceland list almost every year since the Second World War – while the number of insects has almost doubled during the same period.

With the exception of birds, which are better known than any of the other groups, the lists give no indication of the species' abundance or distribution. Some occur in their millions and are found all over the country, while many others have been recorded only once or just a handful of times.

Where there have been unconfirmed reports, or where individual sightings or recordings are particularly controversial (as they often are) the species involved have been omitted. Plant records, in particular, cause endless arguments – as chapter 2 explains.

For all these reasons, the checklists should be used in conjunction with the main text of the book, where many species are discussed in more detail. The order of listing has been chosen individually for each group to facilitate quick reference.

APPENDIX 1: FLOWERING PLANTS

1. Angelica, arch, *Angelica archangelica*
2. Angelica, wild, *Angelica sylvestris*
3. Arrowgrass, marsh, *Triglochin palustris*
4. Arrowgrass, sea, *Triglochin maritima*
5. Aspen, *Populus tremula*
6. Asphodel, Scottish, *Tofieldia pusilla*
7. Avens, mountain, *Dryas octopetala*
8. Avens, water, *Geum rivale islandicum*
9. Awlwort, *Subularia aquatica*
10. Azalea, mountain, *Loiseleuria procumbens*
11. Bartsia, alpine, *Bartsia alpina*
12. Bearberry, common, *Arctostaphylos uvaursi*
13. Bedstraw, Icelandic, *Galium normanii islandicum*
14. Bedstraw, fen, *Galium uliginosum*
15. Bedstraw, lady's, *Galium verum*
16. Bedstraw, marsh, *Galium palustre*
17. Bedstraw, northern, *Galium boreale*
18. Bedstraw, small, *Galium trividium*
19. Beechfern, *Phegopteris connectilis*
20. Bentgrass, brown, *Agrostis canina*
21. Bentgrass, common, *Agrostis tenuis*
22. Bentgrass, fiorin, *Agrostis stolonifera*
23. Bentgrass, large, *Agrostis gigantea*
24. Bilberry, *Vaccinium myrtillus*
25. Birch, downy, *Betula pubescens*
26. Birch, dwarf, *Betula nana*
27. Birdseye, *Veronicella chamaedrys*
28. Bistort, alpine, *Polygonum viviparum*
29. Bistort, amphibious, *Polygonum amphibium*
30. Bittercress, alpine, *Cardamine bellidifolia*
31. Bittercress, arctic, *Cardamine nymanii*
32. Bittercress, hairy, *Cardamine hirsuta*
33. Bitterwort, alpine, *Draba alpina*
34. Bitterwort, arctic, *Draba fladnizensis*
35. Bitterwort, Norwegian, *Draba norvegica*

36. Bitterwort, snow, *Draba nivalis*
37. Bitterwort, twisted, *Draba incana*
38. Bladderfern, brittle, *Cystopteris fragilis*
39. Bladderfern, Dickie's, *Cystopteris dickieana*
40. Bladderwort, lesser, *Utricularia minor*
41. Blinks, *Montia fontana*
42. Bogbean, *Menyanthes trifoliata*
43. Bramble, rock, *Rubus saxatilis*
44. Braya, purplish, *Braya purpurescens*
45. Brooklime, thymeleaved, *Veronica serpyllifolium*
46. Bucklerfern, *Dryopteris dilatata*
47. Bucklerfern, broad, *Dryopteris austriaca*
48. Bucklerfern, northern, *Dryopteris expansa*
49. Bugle, pyramidal, *Ajuga pyramidalis*
50. Burnet, salad, *Sanguisorba officinalis*
51. Bur-reed, floating, *Sparganium angustifolium*
52. Bur-reed, northern, *Sparganium hyperboreum*
53. Bur-reed, small, *Sparganium minimum*
54. Buttercup, arctic, *Ranunculus hyperboreus*
55. Buttercup, creeping, *Ranunculus repens*
56. Buttercup, glacier, *Ranunculus glacialis*
57. Buttercup, meadow, *Ranunculus acris*
58. Buttercup, pigmy, *Ranunculus pygmaeus*
59. Butterwort, alpine, *Pinguicula alpina*
60. Butterwort, common, *Pinguicula vulgaris*
61. Campion, moss, *Silene acaulis*
62. Campion, sea, *Silene vulgaris*
63. Caraway, *Carum carvi*
64. Catchfly, alpine, *Lychnis alpina*
65. Catsfoot, alpine, *Antennaria alpina*
66. Catsfoot, red alpine, *Viscaria alpina*
67. Catstail, alpine, *Phleum commutatum*
68. Catstail, timothy, *Phleum pratense*
69. Chickweed, *Stellaria media*
70. Chickweed, mountain, *Cerastium cerastoides*
71. Cicely, sweet, *Myrrhis odorata*
72. Cinquefoil, alpine, *Potentilla crantzii*
73. Cinquefoil, marsh, *Potentilla palustris*
74. Clawmoss, *Huperzia selago*
75. Clover sp., *Lotus corniculatus*
76. Clover, red, *Trifolium pratense*
77. Clover, white, *Trifolium repens*
78. Clubmoss, alpine, *Lycopodium alpinum*
79. Clubmoss, fir, *Lycopodium selago*
80. Clubmoss, interrupted, *Lycopodium annotinum*
81. Clubmoss, lesser, *Selaginella selaginoides*
82. Coralroot, *Corallorrhiza trifida*
83. Cornel, dwarf, *Cornus suecicum*
84. Cotton-grass, common, *Eriophorum angustifolium*
85. Cotton-grass, Schewchzer's, *Eriophorum scheuchzeri*
86. Couch, bearded, *Agropyron caninum*
87. Couchgrass, *Agropyron repens*
88. Cowberry, *Vaccinium vitis-idaea*
89. Cowwheat, wood, *Melampyrum sylvaticum*
90. Cranberry, *Vaccinium oxycoccus*
91. Cranesbill, wood, *Geranium sylvaticum*
92. Crowberry, *Empetrum nigrum*
93. Crowfoot, three-leaved water, *Ranunculus tricophyllus*
94. Cudweed, dwarf, *Gnaphalium supinum*
95. Cudweed, heath, *Gnaphalium sylvaticum*
96. Cudweed, highland, *Gnaphalium norvegicum*
97. Cudweed, marsh, *Gnaphalium uliginosum*
98. Cudweed, wood, *Omalotheca silvatica*
99. Currant, red, *Ribes rubrum*
100. Dandelion, common, *Taraxacum officinale*
101. Dandelion, northern, *Taraxacum spectabile*
102. Dandelion sp., *Taraxacum croceum*
103. Dandelion sp., *Taraxacum cymbifolium*
104. Dandelion sp., *Taraxacum faeroense*
105. Dandelion sp., *Taraxacum naevosum*
106. Deadnettle, red, *Lamium purpureum*
107. Deadnettle, intermediate, *Lamium molucellifolium*
108. Deadnettle, white, *Lamium album*
109. Deergrass, *Scirpus caespitosus*
110. Dewcup, cluster, *Alchemilla glomerulans*
111. Dewcup, kidney-shaped, *Alchemilla murbeckiana*
112. Dewcup, scalloped, *Alchemilla subcrenata*
113. Dewcup, silvery, *Alchemilla wichurae*
114. Dewcup, slope, *Alchemilla glabra*
115. Dewcup, thread-stemmed, *Alchemilla filicaulis*
116. Diapensia, *Diapensia lapponica*
117. Ditchgrass, *Ruppia cirrhosa*
118. Dock, broad-leaved, *Rumex obtusifolius*
119. Dock, curled, *Rumex crispus*
120. Dock, garden, *Rumex longifolius*
121. Eelgrass, *Zostera marina*
122. Everlasting, mountain alpine, *Antennaria alpina*
123. Eyebright sp., *Euphrasia calida*
124. Eyebright sp., *Euphrasia curta*
125. Eyebright sp., *Euphrasia nemorosa*
126. Eyebright sp., *Euphrasia stricta*
127. Eyebright, cold, *Euphrasia frigida*
128. Eyebright, Davidson's, *Euphrasia davidsonii*
129. Eyebright, round-leaved, *Euphrasia rotundifolia*
130. Felwort, marsh, *Lomatogonium rotatum*
131. Fern, parsley, *Cryptogramma crispa*

132. Fescue, creeping, *Festuca rubra*
133. Fescue, meadow, *Festuca pratensis*
134. Fescue, proliferous, *Festuca vivipara*
135. Fescue, Richardson's, *Festuca richardsonii*
136. Fescue, sheep's, *Festuca ovina*
137. Filmfern, *Hymenophyllum wilsonii*
138. Fireweed, arctic, *Linum angustifolium intermedium*
139. Fireweed, common, *Linum angustifolium angustifolium*
140. Flax, purging, *Linum catharticum*
141. Fleabane, boreal, *Erigeron borealis*
142. Fleabane, dwarf, *Erigeron uniflorum*
143. Fleabane, lowly, *Erigeron humilis*
144. Fleabane, woolly-headed, *Erigeron uniflorus*
145. Flixweed, *Descurania sophia*
146. Flotegrass, *Glyceria fluitans*
147. Fog, Yorkshire, *Holcus lanatus*
148. Forget-me-not, common, *Myosotis arvensis*
149. Forget-me-not, early, *Myosotis ramosissima*
150. Forget-me-not, strict, *Myosotis stricta*
151. Forget-me-not, water, *Myosotis scorpiodes*
152. Forget-me-not, yellow-and-blue, *Myosotis discolor*
153. Foxtail, marsh, *Alopecurus geniculatus*
154. Foxtail, meadow, *Alopecurus pratensis*
155. Foxtail, orange, *Alopecurus aequalis*
156. Garlic, field, *Allium oleraceum*
157. Gentian, autumnal, *Gentianella amarella*
158. Gentian, field, *Gentianella campestris islandica*
159. Gentian, golden, *Gentianella aurea*
160. Gentian, serrate, *Gentianella detonsa*
161. Gentian, slender, *Gentianella tenella*
162. Gentian, small, *Gentianella nivalis*
163. Gold-of-pleasure, common, *Camelina sativa*
164. Gold-of-pleasure, hairy, *Camelina microcarpa*
165. Goldilocks, *Ranunculus auricomus islandicus*
166. Goosegrass, northern, *Phippsia distans borealis*
167. Goosegrass, snow, *Phippsia algida*
168. Grapefern, glossy, *Botrychium simplex*
169. Grapefern, lance-leaved, *Botrychium lanceolatum*
170. Grass, alpine hair, *Deschampsia alpina*
171. Grass, heath, *Sieglingia decumbens*
172. Grass, tufted hair, *Deschampsia caespitosa*
173. Grass, wavy hair, *Deschampsia flexuosa*
174. Grass-of-Parnassus, *Parnassia palustris*
175. Gravelcress, *Cardaminopsis petraea*
176. Groundsel, *Senecio vulgaris*
177. Hardfern, *Blechnum spicant*
178. Harebell, Greenland, *Campanula rotundifolia*
179. Harebell, arctic, *Campanula uniflora*
180. Hawkbit, autumnal, *Leontodon autumnalis*
181. Hawksbeard, marsh, *Crepis paludosa*
182. Hawksbeard, mire, *Taraxacum paludosum*
183. Hawkweed, alpine, *Hieracium alpinum*
184. Hawkweed, blackening, *Hieracium nigrescens*
185. Hawkweed, Icelandic, *Hieracium islandica*
186. Hawkweed, mouse-ear, *Hieracium pilosella*
187. Heath, mountain, *Phyllodoce coerulea*
188. Heather, *Calluna vulgaris*
189. Heathgrass, *Danthonia decumbens*
190. Hempnettle, common, *Galeopsis tetrahit*
191. Henbit, *Lamium amplexicaule*
192. Hollyfern, *Polystichum lonchitis*
193. Holygrass, *Hierochloe odorata*
194. Horsetail, common, *Equisetum arvense*
195. Horsetail, marsh, *Equisetum palustre*
196. Horsetail, northern, *Equisetum arvense boreale*
197. Horsetail, shady, *Equisetum pratense*
198. Horsetail, variegated, *Equisetum variegatum*
199. Horsetail, water, *Equisetum fluviatile*
200. Horsetail, wood, *Equisetum sylvaticum*
201. Icecup, *Beckwithia glacialis*
202. Juniper, *Juniperus communis*
203. Knautia, field, *Knautia arvensis*
204. Knotgrass, common, *Polygonum aviculare*
205. Knotweed, amphibious, *Persicaria amphibia*
206. Kobresia, Bellard's, *Kobresia myosuroides*
207. Koenigia, Iceland, *Koenigia islandica*
208. Ladder, Jacob's, *Polemonium caeruleum*
209. Ladyfern, *Athyrium filix-femina*
210. Ladyfern, lady, *Athyrium distentifolium*
211. Ling, *Calluna vulgaris*
212. Lopgrass, *Bromus hordeaceus*
213. Lousewort, upright, *Pedicularis flammea*
214. Lovage, northern, *Ligusticum scoticum*
215. Lupin, Alaskan, *Lupinus nootkatensis*
216. Lymegrass, European, *Leymus arenarius*
217. Malefern, *Dryopteris filix-mas*
218. Malefern, *Dryopteris abbreviata*
219. Mantle, alpine lady's, *Alchemilla alpina*
220. Mantle, common lady's, *Alchemilla vulgaris*
221. Mantle, Faeroeic lady's, *Alchemilla faeroensis*
222. Marestail, common, *Hippuris vulgaris*
223. Marestail, four-leaved, *Hippuris tetraphylla*
224. Marigold, arctic, *Caltha minor*

225. Marigold, marsh, *Caltha palustris*
226. Matgrass, *Nardus stricta*
227. Mayweed, pineapple, *Matricaria matricarioides*
228. Mayweed, scentless, *Matricaria maritima*
229. Mayweed, sea, *Tripleurospermum maritimum*
230. Meadowgrass, alpine, *Poa alpina*
231. Meadowgrass, annual, *Poa annua*
232. Meadowgrass, arctic, *Poa arctica*
233. Meadowgrass, black, *Poa balfourii*
234. Meadowgrass, blue, *Poa glauca*
235. Meadowgrass, common, *Poa pratensis*
236. Meadowgrass, narrow-leaved, *Poa angustifolia*
237. Meadowgrass, rough, *Poa trivialis*
238. Meadowgrass, spreading, *Poa subcoerulea*
239. Meadowgrass, wavy, *Poa flexuosa*
240. Meadowgrass, wood, *Poa nemoralis*
241. Meadowrue, alpine, *Thalictrum alpinum*
242. Meadowsweet, *Filipendula ulmaria*
243. Milkwort, sea, *Glaux maritima*
244. Millet, wood, *Milium effusum*
245. Moonwort, *Botrychium lunaria*
246. Moonwort, northern, *Botrychium boreale*
247. Moorgrass, blue, *Sesleria caerulea*
248. Moorgrass, white, *Sesleria albicans*
249. Moss, Dovedale, *Saxifraga hypnoides*
250. Moss, stag's horn, *Lycopodium clavatum*
251. Mossplant, *Harrimanella hypnoides*
252. Mouse-ear, alpine, *Cerastium alpinum*
253. Mouse-ear, arctic, *Cerastium arcticum*
254. Mouse-ear, common, *Cerastium fontanum*
255. Mouse-ear, Nordic, *Cerastium fontanum scandicum*
256. Mouse-ear, starwort, *Cerastium cerastoides*
257. Mouse-ear, sticky, *Cerastium glomeratum*
258. Mudwort, *Limosella aquatica*
259. Nettle, burning, *Urtica urens*
260. Nettle, stinging, *Urtica dioica*
261. Oakfern, *Gymnocarpium dryopteris*
262. Oat, *Avena sativa*
263. Oatgrass, false, *Arrhenatherum elatius*
264. Oatgrass, hairy, *Helictotrichon pubescens*
265. Orach, common, *Atriplex patula*
266. Orach, longfoot, *Atriplex longipes*
267. Orach, smoothish, *Atriplex glabriuscula*
268. Orchid, broad-leaved marsh, *Dactylorhiza majalis*
269. Orchid, common spotted, *Dactylorhiza fuchsii*
270. Orchid, frog, *Coeloglossum viride*
271. Orchid, Icelandic frog, *Coeloglossum viride islandicum*
272. Orchid, Icelandic spotted, *Dactylorhiza maculata islandica*
273. Orchid, northern green, *Limnorchis hyperborea*
274. Orchid, white, *Leucorchis albida*
275. Pansy, wild, *Viola tricolor*
276. Paris, herb, *Paris quadrifolia*
277. Pea, marsh, *Lathyrus palustris*
278. Pea, sea, *Lathyrus japonicus maritimus*
279. Pearlplant, knotted, *Sagina nodosa*
280. Pearlplant, snow, *Sagina intermedia*
281. Pearlplant, tufted, *Sagina caespitosa*
282. Pearlwort, alpine, *Sagina saginoides*
283. Pearlwort, procumbent, *Sagina procumbens*
284. Pearlwort, sharp-leaved, *Sagina subulata*
285. Pennycress, field, *Thlaspi arvense*
286. Pennywort, marsh, *Hydrocotyle vulgaris*
287. Pepperwort, *Lepidium campestre*
288. Pigmyweed, *Tillaea aquatica*
289. Plant, oyster, *Stenhammaria maritima*
290. Plantain, common sea, *Plantago maritima maritima*
291. Plantain, great, *Plantago major*
292. Plantain, ribwort, *Plantago lanceolata*
293. Plantain, sea, *Plantago maritima*
294. Polypody, common, *Polypodium vulgare*
295. Pondweed, broad-leaved, *Potamogeton natans*
296. Pondweed, clasping-leaved, *Potamogeton perfoliatus*
297. Pondweed, horned, *Zannichellia palustris*
298. Pondweed, lesser, *Potamogeton pusillus*
299. Pondweed, long-stalked, *Potamogeton praelongus*
300. Pondweed, reddish, *Potamogeton alpinus*
301. Pondweed, slender-leaved, *Potamogeton filiformis*
302. Pondweed, small, *Potamogeton berchtoldii*
303. Pondweed, tassel, *Ruppia spiralis*
304. Pondweed, various-leaved, *Potamogeton gramineus*
305. Poppy, arctic, *Papaver relictum*
306. Poppy, Icelandic, *Papaver radicatum*
307. Poppy, Stefansson's Icelandic, *Papaver radicatum stefanssonii*
308. Primrose, Greenland, *Primula egaliksensis*
309. Primrose, upright, *Primula stricta*
310. Purse, shepherd's, *Capsella bursa-pastoris*
311. Quackgrass, *Elytrigia repens*
312. Quillwort, *Isoetes setacea*
313. Quillwort, lake, *Isoetes lacustris*
314. Quillwort, springspored, *Isoetes echinospora*
315. Redleg, *Polygonum persicaria*
316. Reedgrass, *Phalaroides arundinacea*
317. Ribwort, *Plantago lanceolata*
318. Riverbeauty, arctic, *Epilobium latifolium*
319. Robin, ragged, *Lychnis flos-cuculi*
320. Rockcress, alpine, *Arabis alpina*

321. Rockcress, northern, *Cardaminopsis petraea*
322. Rocket, sea, *Cakile edentula*
323. Rocket, tall, *Sisymbrium altissimum*
324. Rose, burnet, *Rosa pimpinellifolia*
325. Rose, Taeckholm's, *Rosa taeckholmii*
326. Rose, prickly, *Rosa vosagiaca*
327. Roseroot, *Rhodiola rosea arctica*
328. Rowan, *Sorbus aucuparia*
329. Rush, alpine, *Juncus alpinus*
330. Rush, arctic, *Juncus arcticus*
331. Rush, bulbous, *Juncus bulbosus*
332. Rush, chestnut, *Juncus castaneus*
333. Rush, Dutch, *Equisetum hyemale*
334. Rush, heath, *Juncus squarrosus*
335. Rush, highland, *Juncus trifidus*
336. Rush, Iceland, *Juncus arcticus intermedius*
337. Rush, jointed, *Juncus articulatus*
338. Rush, mud, *Juncus gerardi*
339. Rush, thread, *Juncus filiformis*
340. Rush, three-flowered, *Juncus triglumis*
341. Rush, toad, *Juncus bufonius*
342. Rush, two-flowered, *Juncus biglumis*
343. Salt-marsh-grass, common, *Puccinellia maritima*
344. Sandwort, mountain, *Minuartia rubella*
345. Sandwort, Norwegian, *Arenaria norvegica*
346. Sandwort, sea, *Honckenya peploides*
347. Sandwort, two-flowered, *Minuartia biflora*
348. Sandwort, Teesdale, *Minuartia stricta*
349. Saxifrage, alpine, *Saxifraga nivalis*
350. Saxifrage, alpine brook, *Saxifraga rivularis*
351. Saxifrage, arctic brook, *Saxifraga hyperborea*
352. Saxifrage, drooping, *Saxifraga cernua*
353. Saxifrage, foliolose, *Saxifraga foliolosa*
354. Saxifrage, lifelong, *Saxifraga aizoon*
355. Saxifrage, meadow, *Saxifraga granulata*
356. Saxifrage, mossy, *Saxifraga hypnoides*
357. Saxifrage, purple, *Saxifraga oppositifolia*
358. Saxifrage, pyramidal, *Saxifraga cotyledon*
359. Saxifrage, rosy, *Saxifraga rosacea*
360. Saxifrage, slender, *Saxifraga tenuis*
361. Saxifrage, starry, *Saxifraga stellaris*
362. Saxifrage, tufted, *Saxifraga caespitosa*
363. Saxifrage, yellow marsh, *Saxifraga hirculus*
364. Saxifrage, yellow mountain, *Saxifraga aizoides*
365. Scabious, field, *Knautia arvensis*
366. Scurvygrass, common, *Cochlearia officinalis*
367. Scurvywort, *Cochleariopsis groenlandica*
368. Seapink, *Armeria maritima planifolia*
369. Sedge, alpine black, *Carex atrata*
370. Sedge, alpine club-headed, *Carex norvegica*
371. Sedge, alpine loose-flowered, *Carex rariflora*
372. Sedge, bicoloured, *Carex bicolor*
373. Sedge, bog, *Carex magellanica*
374. Sedge, bottle, *Carex rostrata*
375. Sedge, bristle, *Carex microglochin*
376. Sedge, brownish, *Carex brunnescens*
377. Sedge, capitate, *Carex capitata*
378. Sedge, carnation, *Carex panicea*
379. Sedge, club, *Carex buxbaumii*
380. Sedge, common, *Carex nigra*
381. Sedge, curved, *Carex maritima*
382. Sedge, dioecious, *Carex dioeca*
383. Sedge, flea, *Carex pulicaris*
384. Sedge, glacier, *Carex glacialis*
385. Sedge, glaucous, *Carex flacca*
386. Sedge, Goodenough's, *Carex goodenoughii*
387. Sedge, gravel, *Carex glareosa*
388. Sedge, hair, *Carex capillaris*
389. Sedge, hare's foot, *Carex lachenalii*
390. Sedge, hoppner, *Carex subspathacea*
391. Sedge, hudsonbay, *Carex heleonastes*
392. Sedge, large yellow, *Carex flava*
393. Sedge, lesser tussock, *Carex diandra*
394. Sedge, lyngbye's, *Carex lyngbei*
395. Sedge, mud, *Carex limosa*
396. Sedge, nard, *Carex nardina*
397. Sedge, Norway, *Carex mackenziei*
398. Sedge, pale, *Carex livida*
399. Sedge, pill, *Carex pilulifera*
400. Sedge, Porsild's, *Carex krausei*
401. Sedge, red, *Carex rufina*
402. Sedge, rock, *Carex rupestris*
403. Sedge, russet, *Carex saxatilis*
404. Sedge, sheathed, *Carex vaginata*
405. Sedge, small-fruited yellow, *Carex serotina*
406. Sedge, somber, *Carex pallescens*
407. Sedge, star, *Carex echinata*
408. Sedge, stiff, *Carex bigelowii*
409. Sedge, string, *Carex chordorrhiza*
410. Sedge, thick-headed, *Carex macloviana*
411. Sedge, tufty common, *Carex nigra juncella*
412. Sedge, white, *Carex curta*
413. Selfheal, common, *Prunella vulgaris*
414. Shoreweed, *Littorella uniflora*
415. Shorewort, northern, *Mertensia maritima*
416. Sibbaldia, creeping, *Sibbaldia procumbens*
417. Silverweed sp., *Potentilla anserina*
418. Smallreed, narrow, *Calamagrostis stricta*
419. Sneezewort, *Achillea ptarmica*
420. Sorrel, common, *Rumex acetosa*
421. Sorrel, mountain, *Oxyria digyna*
422. Sorrel, sheep's, *Rumex acetosella*
423. Spearwort, adder's tongue, *Ophioglossum azoricum*

424. Spearwort, creeping, *Ranunculus reptans*
425. Speedwell, alpine, *Veronica alpina*
426. Speedwell, common, *Veronica officinalis*
427. Speedwell, marsh, *Veronica scutellata*
428. Speedwell, rock, *Veronica fruticans*
429. Speedwell, water, *Veronica anagallis-aquatica*
430. Spikerush, common, *Eleocharis palustris*
431. Spikerush, few-flowered, *Eleocharis quinqueflora*
432. Spikerush, slender, *Eleocharis acicularis*
433. Spikerush, swamp, *Eleocharis uniglumis*
434. Spleenwort, maidenhair, *Asplenium trichomanes*
435. Spleenwort, forked, *Asplenium septentrionale*
436. Spleenwort, green, *Asplenium viride*
437. Spurrey, cliff, *Spergula salina*
438. Spurrey, corn, *Spergula arvensis*
439. Spurrey, sea, *Spergula marina*
440. Starwort, intermediate, *Callitriche intermedia*
441. Starwort, northern, *Callitriche hermaphroditica*
442. Starwort, peduncled, *Callitriche brutia*
443. Starwort, vernal, *Callitriche verna*
444. Starwort, water, *Callitriche stagnalis*
445. Stitchwort, fleshy, *Stellaria crassifolia*
446. Stitchwort, lesser, *Stellaria graminea*
447. Stitchwort, low, *Stellaria humifusa*
448. Stitchwort, northern, *Stellaria calycantha*
449. Stonecrop, annual, *Sedum annuum*
450. Stonecrop, biting, *Sedum acre*
451. Stonecrop, hairy, *Sedum villosum*
452. Strawberry, wild, *Fragaria vesca*
453. Succisa, Devil's bit, *Succisa pratensis*
454. Sundew, common, *Drosera rotundifolia*
455. Tasselweed, beaked, *Ruppia maritima*
456. Thistle, creeping, *Cirsium arvense*
457. Thrift, *Armeria maritima*
458. Thyme, arctic, *Thymus arcticus*
459. Thyme, hairy, *Thymus praecox*
460. Tillaea, water, *Crassula aquatica*
461. Timothy, *Phleum pratense*
462. Tormentil, *Potentilla erecta*
463. Treaclemustard, hawkweedleaved, - *Erysimum hieracifolium*
464. Trefoil, birdsfoot, *Lotus corniculatus*
465. Trisetum, soft hairy, *Trisetum triflorum*
466. Trisetum, spike, *Trisetum spicatum*
467. Twayblade, *Listera ovata*
468. Twayblade, lesser, *Listera cordata*
469. Twitch, don's, *Agropyron donianum*
470. Valerian, common, *Valeriana officinalis*
471. Velvetgrass, *Holcus lanatus*
472. Vernalgrass, sweet, *Anthoxanthum odoratum*
473. Vetch, bush, *Vicia sepium*
474. Vetch, common kidney, *Anthyllis vulneraria*
475. Vetch, tufted, *Vicia cracca*
476. Vetchling, meadow, *Lathyrus pratensis*
477. Violet, alpine marsh, *Viola palustris*
478. Violet, common, *Viola riviniana*
479. Violet, dog, *Viola canina*
480. Violet, northern marsh, *Viola epipsila*
481. Watermilfoil, loose-flowered, - *Myriophyllum alterniflorum*
482. Watermilfoil, spiked, *Myriophyllum spicatum*
483. Weed, pineapple, *Chamomilla suaveolens*
484. Wheatgrass, bearded, *Elymus caninus*
485. Whitlow-grass, alpine, *Draba alpina*
486. Whitlow-grass, common, *Erophila verna*
487. Whorlgrass, water, *Catabrosa aquatica*
488. Whortleberry, bog, *Vaccinium uliginosum*
489. Willow, arctic, *Salix arctica*
490. Willow, broad-leaved, *Salix callicarpaea*
491. Willow, least, *Salix herbacea*
492. Willow, tea-leaved, *Salix phylicifolia*
493. Willow, woody, *Salix lanata*
494. Willowherb, alpine, *Epilobium anagallidifolium*
495. Willowherb, American, *Epilobium adenocaulon*
496. Willowherb, chickweed, *Epilobium alsinifolium*
497. Willowherb, cliff, *Epilobium collinum*
498. Willowherb, Hornemann's, *Epilobium hornemannii*
499. Willowherb, marsh, *Epilobium palustre*
500. Willowherb, milkyflowered, *Epilobium lactiflorum*
501. Willowherb, rosebay, *Epilobium angustifolium*
502. Wintergreen, arctic, *Pyrola grandiflora*
503. Wintergreen, chickweed, *Trientalis europaea*
504. Wintergreen, common, *Pyrola minor*
505. Wintergreen, serrated, *Orthilia secunda*
506. Woodrush, curved, *Luzula arcuata*
507. Woodrush, manyheaded, *Luzula multiflora*
508. Woodrush, northern, *Luzula confusa*
509. Woodrush, northern manyheaded, - *Luzula multiflora frigida*
510. Woodrush, spiked, *Luzula spicata*
511. Woodrush, sudetan, *Luzula sudetica*
512. Woodsia, alpine, *Woodsia alpina*
513. Woodsia, fragrant, *Woodsia ilvensis*
514. Woodsorrel, *Oxalis acetosella*
515. Yarrow, common, *Achillea millefolium*
516. Yellowcress, marsh, *Rorippa islandica*
517. Yellowrattle, small, *Rhinanthus minor*

APPENDIX 2: INSECTS

		No. of species recorded
1.	Blood-sucking lice (Siphunculata)	3
2.	Mayflies (Ephemeroptera)	1
3.	Dragonflies and damselflies (Odonata)	1
4.	Stoneflies (Plecoptera)	1
5.	Web-spinners (Embioptera)	0
6.	Termites (Isoptera)	0
7.	Zorapterans (Zoraptera)	0
8.	Grasshoppers, crickets and allies (Orthoptera)	1
9.	Stick-insects and leaf insects (Phasmida)	0
10.	Earwigs (Dermaptera)	1
11.	Book-lice (Psocoptera)	7
12.	Bird-lice (Mallophaga)	47
13.	Thrips (Thysanoptera)	5
14.	Bugs (Hemiptera)	48
15.	Lacewings, alderflies and ant-lions (Neuroptera)	1
16.	Beetles (Coleoptera)	160
17.	Strepsipterans (Strepsiptera)	0
18.	Scorpion flies (Mecoptera)	0
19.	Caddisflies (Trichoptera)	11
20.	Butterflies and moths (Lepidoptera)	82
21.	Wingless, soil-living insects (Grylloblattodea)	0
22.	Cockroaches and mantids (Dictyoptera)	5
23.	Jumping bristle-tails, silver fish (Thysanura)	2
24.	Two-pronged bristle-tails (Diplura)	0
25.	Proturans (Protura)	3
26.	True flies (Diptera)	425
27.	Fleas (Siphonaptera)	8
28.	Ants, bees and wasps (Hymenoptera)	230
29.	Springtails (Collembola)	76
		1118

APPENDIX 3: FISH

(Better known English names are included in brackets)

FAMILY:		
PETROMYZONIDAE	1.	*Petromyzon marinus* (sea lamprey)
MYXINIDAE	2.	*Myxine glutinosa* (hagfish)
HEXANCHIDAE	3.	*Hexanchus griseus* (six-gilled shark)
LAMNIDAE	4.	*Lamna nasus* (porbeagle)
CETORHINIDAE	5.	*Cetorhinus maximus* (basking shark)
SCYLIORHINIDAE	6.	*Scyliorhinus canicula* (catshark)
	7.	*Apristurus laurussonii* (deepsea catshark)
	8.	*Galeus murinus*
PSEUDOTRIAKIDAE	9.	*Pseudotriakis microdon* (false cat shark)

CARCHARHINIDAE	10.	*Galeocerdo cuvier* (tiger shark)
	11.	*Galeorhinus galeus* (tope)
SQUALIDAE	12.	*Squalus acanthius* (spurdog)
	13.	*Centroscyllium fabricii* (black dogfish)
	14.	*Centroscymnus coelolepis*
	15.	*Centroscymnus crepidater*
	16.	*Deania calceus*
	17.	*Etmopterus spinax* (velvet belly)
	18.	*Etmopterus princeps*
	19.	*Lepidorhinus squamosus*
	20.	*Scymnodon obscurus*
	21.	*Scymnorhinus lica* (dark charlie)
	22.	*Somniosus microcephalus* (Greenland shark)
RAJIDAE	23.	*Raja clavata* (thornback ray)
	24.	*Raja radiata* (starry ray)
	25.	*Raja hyperborea*
	26.	*Raja batis*
	27.	*Raja nidarosiensis*
	28.	*Raja fullonica* (shagreen ray)
	29.	*Raja spinacidermis* (soft skate)
	30.	*Raja fyllae*
	31.	*Raja lintea* (pale ray)
	32.	*Bathyraja spinicauda*
CHIMAERIDAE	33.	*Chimaera monstrosa* (rabbitfish)
	34.	*Hydrolagus affinis* (deepwater chimaera)
	35.	*Hydrolagus mirabilis* (ratfish)
RHINOCHIMAERIDAE	36.	*Rhinochimaera atlantica* (chimaera)
	37.	*Harriotta raleighana* (longnose chimaera)
ACIPENSERIDAE	38.	*Acipenser sturio* (sturgeon)
ALEPOCEPHALIDAE	39.	*Alepocephalus agassizi*
	40.	*Alepocephalus bairdii* (slickhead)
	41.	*Xenodermichthys socialis*
SEARSIIDAE	42.	*Searsia koefoedi*
	43.	*Holtbyrnia anomala*
	44.	*Holtbyrnia problematica*
	45.	*Maulisia mauli*
	46.	*Normichthys operosus*
	47.	*Sagamichthys schnakenbecki*
CLUPEIDAE	48.	*Clupea harengus harengus* (herring)
	49.	*Sardina pilchardus* (sardine)
	50.	*Alosa fallax fallax* (twaite shad)
GONOSTOMATIDAE (deepsea bristlemouths)	51.	*Gonostoma elongatum*
	52.	*Gonostoma bathyphilum*
	53.	*Cyclothone microdon*
	54.	*Maurolicus mulleri* (pearlside)
STERNOPTYCHIDAE (deepsea hatchetfish)	55.	*Argyropelecus hemigymnus*
	56.	*Argyropelecus gigas*
	57.	*Argyropelecus olfersi*

ASTRONESTHIDAE	58.	*Astronesthes gemmifer*
	59.	*Borostomias antarcticus*
CHAULIODONTIDAE	60.	*Chauliodus sloani* (deepsea viperfish)
STOMIATIDAE	61.	*Stomias boa ferox* (boa dragonfish)
MELANOSTOMIATIDAE	62.	*Trigonolampa micriceps*
MALACOSTEIDAE	63.	*Malacosteus niger*
SALMONIDAE	64.	*Salmo salar* (salmon)
	65.	*Salmo trutta trutta* (trout)
	66.	*Salmo gairdneri* (rainbow trout)
	67.	*Oncorhynchus gorbuscha* (pink salmon)
	68.	*Salvelinus alpinus* (arctic charr)
MICROSTOMATIDAE	69.	*Argentina sphyraena* (argentine)
	70.	*Argentina silus* (great silver smelt)
	71.	*Nansenia groenlandica*
BATHYLAGIDAE	72.	*Bathylagus euryops* (deepsea smelt)
OSMERIDAE	73.	*Mallotus villosus* (capelin)
SCOPELOSAURIDAE	74.	*Scopelosaurus lepidus*
MYCTOPHIDAE (lantern fish)	75.	*Myctophum punctatum*
	76.	*Benthosema glaciale*
	77.	*Ceratoscopelus maderensis*
	78.	*Diaphus rafinesquei*
	79.	*Hygophum hygomi*
	80.	*Lampadena speculigera*
	81.	*Lampanyctus crocodilus*
	82.	*Lampanyctus intricarius*
	83.	*Lampanyctus macdonaldi*
	84.	*Notoscopelus kroeyeri*
	85.	*Protomyctophum arcticum*
	86.	*Symbolophorus veranyi*
ALEPISAURIDAE	87.	*Alepisaurus ferox* (longnose lancet fish)
PARALEPIDIDAE	88.	*Paralepis coregonoides borealis*
	89.	*Paralepis atlantica*
	90.	*Notolepis rissoi*
SACCOPHARYNGIDAE	91.	*Saccopharynx sp.* (swallower)
EURYPHARYNGIDAE	92.	*Eurypharynx pelecanoides* (gulper)
ANGUILLIDAE	93.	*Anguilla anguilla* (eel)
SERRIVOMERIDAE	94.	*Serrivomer beani* (shortnosed snipe eel)
	95.	*Serrivomer parabeani*
NEMICHTHYIDAE	96.	*Nemichthys scolopaceus* (snipe eel)
CONGRIDAE	97.	*Conger conger* (conger eel)

SYNAPHOBRANCHIDAE	98.	*Synaphobranchus kaupi*
NOTACANTHIDAE	99.	*Notacanthus chemnitzii* (snipe eel)
	100.	*Polycanthonotus rissoanus* (short-spined tapir fish)
BELONIDAE	101.	*Belone belone belone* (garpike)
SCOMBEROSOCIDAE	102.	*Scomberesox saurus* (saury pike)
SYNGNATHIDAE	103.	*Entelurus aequoreus* (snake pipefish)
GASTEROSTEIDAE	104.	*Gasterosteus aculeatus* (stickleback)
MACROURIDAE	105.	*Trachyrhynchus murrayi*
(grenadiers)	106.	*Nezumia aequalis*
	107.	*Coryphaenoides rupestris*
	108.	*Coryphaenoides guntheri*
	109.	*Macrourus berglax*
	110.	*Coelorhynchus coelorhynchus*
MERLUCCIIDAE	111.	*Merluccius merluccius* (hake)
GADIDAE	112.	*Gadus morhua morhua* (cod)
	113.	*Boreogadus saida* (polar cod)
	114.	*Gadiculus argenteus thori* (silvery cod)
	115.	*Melanogrammus aeglefinus* (haddock)
	116.	*Merlangius merlangus merlangus* (whiting)
	117.	*Micromesistius poutassou* (blue whiting)
	118.	*Pollachius pollachius* (pollack)
	119.	*Pollachius virens* (saithe)
	120.	*Trisopterus esmarki* (Norway pout)
	121.	*Brosme brosme* (torsk)
	122.	*Ciliata mustela* (five-bearded rockling)
	123.	*Ciliata septentrionalis* (Norway rockling)
	124.	*Molva molva* (ling)
	125.	*Molva dypterygia dypterygia* (blue ling)
	126.	*Phycis blennoides* (greater forkbeard)
	127.	*Rhinonemus cimbrius* (four-bearded rockling)
	128.	*Urophycis tenuis* (white hake)
	129.	*Cnogadus argentatus* (codfish)
MORIDAE	130.	*Antimora rostrata* (blue antimore)
	131.	*Halargyreus johnsonii*
	132.	*Laemonema latifrons*
	133.	*Lepidion eques*
	134.	*Mora moro*
LAMPRIDAE	135.	*Lampris guttatus* (sunfish)
REGALECIDAE	136.	*Regalecus glesne* (ribbonfish)
TRACHIPTERIDAE	137.	*Trachipterus arcticus* (dealfish)
BERYCIDAE	138.	*Beryx decadactylus* (red bream)
	139.	*Beryx splendens* (bream)
DIRETMIDAE	140.	*Diretmus argenteus* (spiny fish)

CARISTIIDAE	141.	*Caristius* sp.
TRACHICHTHYIDAE	142.	*Hoplostethus mediterraneus* (roughfish)
	143.	*Hoplostethus islandicus*
SERRANIDAE	144.	*Dicentrarchus labrax* (bass)
	145.	*Polyprion americanus* (stonebass)
APOGONIDAE	146.	*Epigonus telescopus*
	147.	*Howella brodiei*
CARANGIDAE	148.	*Trachurus trachurus* (scad)
BRAMIDAE	149.	*Taractes asper* (pomfret)
	150.	*Brama brama* (Ray's bream)
	151.	*Pterycombus brama* (bream)
SCIAENIDAE	152.	*Argyrosomus regius* (meagre)
SPARIDAE	153.	*Pagellus bogarareo* (red sea bream)
AMMODYTIDAE	154.	*Ammodytes tobianus*
(sand eels)	155.	*Ammodytes marinus*
	156.	*Hyperoplus lanceolatus*
GEMPYLIDAE	157.	*Nesiarchus nasutus*
TRICHIURIDAE	158.	*Aphanophus carbo* (black-scabbard fish)
	159.	*Benthodesmus elongatus simonyi*
	160.	*Lepidopus caudatus* (scabbard fish)
SCOMBRIDAE	161.	*Scomber scombrus* (mackerel)
THUNNIDAE	162.	*Thunnus thynnus* (tunny)
XIPHIIDAE	163.	*Xiphias gladius* (swordfish)
GOBIIDAE	164.	*Buenia jeffreysii* (Jeffrey's goby)
	165.	*Lebetus scorpioides* (little goby)
CALLIONYMIDAE	166.	*Callionymus lyra* (dragonet)
	167.	*Callionymus maculatus* (spotted dragonet)
ANARHICHADIDAE	168.	*Anarhichas lupus lupus* (catfish)
	169.	*Anarhichas denticulatus*
	170.	*Anartrichas minor*
STICHAEIDAE	171.	*Chirolophis ascanii* (Yarrell's blenny)
PHOLIDAE	172.	*Pholis gunnellus* (butterfish)
LUMPENIDAE	173.	*Lumpenus lampretaeformis lampretaeformis*
(snake blennies)	174.	*Leptoclinus maculatus maculatus*
ZOARCIDAE	175.	*Gymnelus retrodorsalis*
	176.	*Lycenchelys muraena*
	177.	*Lycenchelys sarsi*
	178.	*Lycodes vahli gracilis* (Vahl's eelpout)

	179.	*Lycodes esmarki* (Esmark's eelpout)
	180.	*Lycodes eudipleurostictus*
	181.	*Lycodes frigidus*
	182.	*Lycodes microcephalus* (pale eelpout)
	183.	*Lycodes pallidus pallidus*
	184.	*Lycodes reticulatus* (arctic eelpout)
	185.	*Lycodes rossi*
	186.	*Lycodes seminudus*
	187.	*Lycodes squamivenser*
	188.	*Lycodonus flagellicanda*
	189.	*Lycodonus ophidium*
BYTHITIDAE	190.	*Bythites islandicus*
	191.	*Thalassobathia pelagica*
CARAPIDAE	192.	*Echiodon drummondi* (pearlfish)
CENTROLOPHIDAE	193.	*Centrolophus niger* (blackfish)
	194.	*Hyperoglyphe perciformis* (barrel-fish)
	195.	*Schedophilus medusophagus* (cornish blackfish)
MUGILIDAE	196.	*Chelon labrosus*
	197.	*Mugil chelo* (thick-lipped mullet)
SCORPAENIDAE	198.	*Helicolenus dactylopterus dactylopterus* (blue-mouth)
	199.	*Sebastes marinus* (redfish)
	200.	*Sebastes mentella*
	201.	*Sebastes viviparus* (Norway haddock)
TRIGLIDAE	202.	*Eutrigla gurnardus* (grey gurnard)
COTTIDAE	203.	*Artediellus atlanticus atlanticus* (Atlantic mail-cheeked sculpin)
	204.	*Gymnacanthus tricuspis* (staghorn)
	205.	*Icelus bicornis* (twohorn sculpin)
	206.	*Myoxocephalus scorpius scorpius* (father lasher)
	207.	*Taurulus lilljeborgi* (Norway bullhead)
	208.	*Triglops murrayi* (mailed sculpin)
	209.	*Taurulus bubalis* (sea scorpion)
COTTUNCULIDAE	210.	*Cottunculus microps* (polar sculpin)
	211.	*Cottunculus thomsoni* (pallid sculpin)
	212.	*Cottunculoides subspinosus*
AGONIDAE	213.	*Agonus cataphractus* (pogge)
	214.	*Leptagonus decagonus* (poacher)
CYCLOPTERIDAE	215.	*Cyclopterus lumpus* (lumpfish)
	216.	*Eumicrotremus spinosus* (Atlantic spiny lumpsucker)
LIPARIDAE (snailfish)	217.	*Liparis liparis*
	218.	*Liparis fabricii*
	219.	*Liparis montagui* (Montagu's sea snail)
	220.	*Careproctus reinhardti* (sea tadpole)
	221.	*Paraliparis bathybius*
	222.	*Rhodichthys regina*
SCOPHTHALMIDAE	223.	*Scophthalmus rhombus* (brill)

	224.	*Lepidorhombus whiffiagonis* (sail-fluke)
	225.	*Phrynorhombus norvegicus* (Norwegian topknot)
	226.	*Psetta maxima* (turbot)
PLEURONECTIDAE	227.	*Pleuronectes platessa* (plaice)
	228.	*Glyptocephalus cynoglossus* (witch)
	229.	*Hippoglossoides platessoides limandoides* (rough dab)
	230.	*Hippoglossus hippoglossus* (halibut)
	231.	*Limanda limanda* (dab)
	232.	*Microstomus kitt* (lemon sole)
	233.	*Reinhardtius hippoglossoides* (Greenland halibut)
ECHENEIDIDAE	234.	*Remora remora* (shark-sucker)
MOLIDAE	235.	*Mola mola* (ocean sunfish)
LOPHIIDAE	236.	*Lophius piscatorius* (anglerfish)
HIMANTOLOPHIDAE	237.	*Himantolophus groenlandicus*
CERATIIDAE	238.	*Coratias holboelli* (deepsea angler)
	239.	*Cryptopsaras couesi* (lesser deepsea angler)
LINOPHRYNIDAE	240.	*Linophryne lucifera*
	241.	*Linophryne coronata*

APPENDIX 4: BIRDS

VC — very common wherever habitat suitable
C — common wherever habitat suitable
FC — fairly common wherever habitat suitable
LC — locally common (ie at certain localities)
R — rare
ER — extremely rare
A — recorded only once or twice

		Breeding Season	Winter	Passage Only
1.	Red-throated diver, *Gavia stellata*	FC	FC	—
2.	Great northern diver, *Gavia immer*	R	R	—
3.	Great crested grebe, *Podiceps cristatus*	—	—	A
4.	Red-necked grebe, *Podiceps grisegena*	—	ER	A
5.	Slavonian grebe, *Podiceps auritus*	LC	R	—
6.	Yellow-nosed albatross, *Diomedea chlororhynchos*	—	—	A
7.	Fulmar, *Fulmarus glacialis*	VC	C	—
8.	Manx shearwater, *Puffinus puffinus*	LC	—	—
9.	Great shearwater, *Puffinus gravis*	—	—	R
10.	Sooty shearwater, *Puffinus griseus*	—	—	R
11.	Leach's petrel, *Oceanodroma leucorhoa*	LC	—	—
12.	Storm petrel, *Hydrobates pelagicus*	LC	—	—
13.	Gannet, *Sula bassana*	LC	—	—
14.	Cormorant, *Phalacrocorax carbo*	LC	C	—
15.	Shag, *Phalacrocorax aristotelis*	LC	LC	—
16.	Little bittern, *Ixobrychus minutus*	—	—	A
17.	Bittern, *Botaurus stellaris*	—	—	A
18.	American bittern, *Botaurus lentiginosus*	—	—	A
19.	Squacco heron, *Ardeola ralloides*	—	—	A
20.	Grey heron, *Ardea cinerea*	—	FC-R	—

		Breeding Season	Winter	Passage Only
21.	Night heron, *Nycticorax nycticorax*	—	—	A
22.	Spoonbill, *Platalea leucorodia*	—	—	A
23.	Glossy ibis, *Plegadis falcinellus*	—	—	A
24.	White stork, *Ciconia ciconia*	—	—	A
25.	Whooper swan, *Cygnus cygnus*	C	FC	—
26.	Bewick's swan, *Cygnus columbianus bewickii*	—	—	ER
27.	Mute swan, *Cygnus olor*	*introduced, now extinct*		
28.	Canada goose, *Branta canadensis*	—	—	A
29.	Brent goose, *Branta bernicla*	—	—	FC
30.	Brent goose ssp., *Branta bernicla nigricans*	—	—	A
31.	Barnacle goose, *Branta leucopsis*	ER	—	FC
32.	Greylag goose, *Anser anser*	C	—	—
33.	White-fronted goose, *Anser albifrons*	—	—	FC
34.	White-fronted goose ssp., *Anser albifrons albifrons*	—	—	A
35.	Bean goose, *Anser fabalis*	—	—	A
36.	Pink-footed goose, *Anser brachyrhynchus*	LC	—	—
37.	Snow goose, *Anser caerulescens*	—	—	R
38.	Mallard, *Anas platyrhynchos*	C	C	—
39.	Gadwall, *Anas strepera*	LC	R	—
40.	Pintail, *Anas acuta*	R-FC	—	—
41.	Wigeon, *Anas penelope*	C	FC	—
42.	American wigeon, *Anas americana*	—	—	ER
43.	Teal, *Anas crecca*	C	C	—
44.	Common green-winged teal, *Anas crecca carolinensis*	—	—	A
45.	Blue-winged teal, *Anas discors*	—	—	A
46.	Garganey, *Anas querquedula*	—	—	R
47.	Black duck, *Anas rubipres*	—	—	A
48.	Shoveler, *Anas clypeata*	R	R	—
49.	Shelduck, *Tadorna tadorna*	—	—	A
50.	Tufted duck, *Aythya fuligula*	C	R	—
51.	Scaup, *Aythya marila*	C	R	—
52.	Ring-necked duck, *Aythya collaris*	—	—	A
53.	Pochard, *Aythya ferina*	ER	—	A
54.	Goldeneye, *Bucephala clangula*	—	R	—
55.	Barrow's goldeneye, *Bucephala islandica*	LC	FC	—
56.	Bufflehead, *Bucephala albeola*	—	—	A
57.	Harlequin duck, *Histrionicus histrionicus*	C	C	—
58.	Long-tailed duck, *Clangula hyemalis*	C	VC	—
59.	Common scoter, *Melanitta nigra*	LC	—	—
60.	Velvet scoter, *Melanitta fusca*	—	—	A
61.	Surf scoter, *Melanitta perspicillata*	—	—	A
62.	Eider, *Somateria mollissima*	VC	VC	—
63.	King eider, *Somateria spectabilis*	—	FC	—
64.	Steller's eider, *Polysticta stelleri*	—	—	A
65.	Red-breasted merganser, *Mergus serrator*	C	C	—
66.	Goosander, *Mergus merganser*	R	R	—
67.	Smew, *Mergus albellus*	—	—	ER
68.	White-tailed eagle, *Haliaeetus albicilla*	R	R	—
69.	Black kite, *Milvus migrans*	—	—	A
70.	Sparrowhawk, *Accipiter nisus*	—	—	A
71.	Rough-legged buzzard, *Buteo lagopus*	—	—	A
72.	Honey buzzard, *Pernis apivorus*	—	—	A
73.	Buzzard, *Buteo buteo*	—	—	A
74.	Osprey, *Pandion haliaetus*	—	—	A
75.	Montagu's harrier, *Circus pygargus*	—	—	A
76.	Hen harrier, *Circus cyaneus*	—	—	A
77.	Gyrfalcon, *Falco rusticolus*	FC	FC	—

		Breeding Season	Winter	Passage Only
78.	Peregrine, *Falco peregrinus*	—	—	A
79.	Merlin, *Falco columbarius subaesalon*	C	R	—
80.	Red-footed falcon, *Falco vespertinus*	—	—	A
81.	Kestrel, *Falco tinnunculus*	—	—	A
82.	Ptarmigan, *Lagopus mutus*	VC	VC	—
83.	Water rail, *Rallus aquaticus*	ER	ER	—
84.	Spotted crake, *Porzana porzana*	—	—	A
85.	Corncrake, *Crex crex*	—	—	A
86.	Moorhen, *Gallinula chloropus*	—	—	A
87.	Coot, *Fulica atra*	ER	—	A
88.	Oystercatcher, *Haematopus ostralegus*	C	LC	—
89.	Lapwing, *Vanellus vanellus*	ER	—	A
90.	Ringed plover, *Charadrius hiaticula*	C	—	—
91.	Killdeer, *Charadrius vociferus*	—	—	A
92.	Grey plover, *Pluvialis squatarola*	—	—	A
93.	Golden plover, *Pluvialis apricaria*	VC	—	—
94.	Lesser golden plover, *Pluvialis dominica*	—	—	A
95.	Turnstone, *Arenaria interpres*	—	C	C
96.	Snipe, *Gallinago gallinago*	C	R	—
97.	Jack snipe, *Lymnocryptes minimus*	—	—	A
98.	Woodcock, *Scolopax rusticola*	—	—	A
99.	Curlew, *Numenius arquata*	—	FC	—
100.	Whimbrel, *Numenius phaeopus*	C	—	—
101.	Black-tailed godwit, *Limosa limosa*	FC	—	—
102.	Bar-tailed godwit, *Limosa lapponica*	—	—	A
103.	Wood sandpiper, *Tringa glareola*	ER	—	—
104.	Solitary sandpiper, *Tringa solitaria*	—	—	A
105.	Redshank, *Tringa totanus*	C	LC	—
106.	Spotted redshank, *Tringa erythropus*	—	—	A
107.	Greenshank, *Tringa nebularia*	—	—	A
108.	Broad-billed sandpiper, *Limnicola falcinellus*	—	—	A
109.	Ruff, *Philomachus pugnax*	—	—	A
110.	Lesser yellowlegs, *Tringa flavipes*	—	—	A
111.	Greater yellowlegs, *Tringa melanoleuca*	—	—	A
112.	Long-billed dowitcher, *Limnodromus scolopaceus*	—	—	A
113.	Knot, *Calidris canutus*	—	C	C
114.	Purple sandpiper, *Calidris maritima*	FC	VC	—
115.	Dunlin, *Calidris alpina*	C	R	—
116.	Curlew sandpiper, *Calidris ferruginea*	—	—	A
117.	Little stint, *Calidris minuta*	—	—	A
118.	Sanderling, *Calidris alba*	—	C	C
119.	Pectoral sandpiper, *Calidris melanotos*	—	—	A
120.	White-rumped sandpiper, *Calidris fuscicollis*	—	—	A
121.	Wilson's phalarope, *Phalaropus tricolor*	—	—	A
122.	Grey phalarope, *Phalaropus fulicarius*	ER	—	—
123.	Red-necked phalarope, *Phalaropus lobatus*	C	—	—
124.	Stone curlew, *Burhinus oedicnemus*	—	—	A
125.	Black-winged pratincole, *Glareola nordmanni*	—	—	A
126.	Great skua, *Stercorarius skua*	LC	—	—
127.	Pomarine skua, *Stercorarius pomarinus*	—	—	R
128.	Arctic skua, *Stercorarius parasiticus*	C	—	—
129.	Long-tailed skua, *Stercorarius longicaudus*	—	—	R
130.	Ivory gull, *Pagophila eburnea*	—	R	—
131.	Glaucous gull, *Larus hyperboreus*	C	C	—
132.	Iceland gull, *Larus glaucoides*	—	C	—
133.	Great black-backed gull, *Larus marinus*	VC	C	—
134.	Lesser black-backed gull, *Larus fuscus*	VC	—	—

		Breeding Season	Winter	Passage Only
135.	Herring gull, *Larus argentatus*	C	C	—
136.	Ring-billed gull, *Larus delawarensis*	—	—	A
137.	Common gull, *Larus canus*	R	R	—
138.	Kittiwake, *Rissa tridactyla*	VC	R	—
139.	Black-headed gull, *Larus ridibundus*	VC	FC	—
140.	Laughing gull, *Larus atricilla*	—	—	A
141.	Bonaparte's gull, *Larus philadelphia*	—	—	A
142.	Little gull, *Larus minutus*	—	—	A
143.	Sabine's gull, *Xema sabini*	—	—	A
144.	Ross's gull, *Rhodostethia rosea*	—	—	A
145.	Black tern, *Chlidonias niger*	ER	—	A
146.	Sandwich tern, *Sterna sandvicensis*	—	—	A
147.	Arctic tern, *Sterna paradisaea*	VC	—	—
148.	Forster's tern, *Sterna forsteri*	—	—	A
149.	Great auk, *Alca impennis*	extinct		
150.	Razorbill, *Alca torda*	VC	—	—
151.	Guillemot, *Uria aalge*	VC	VC	—
152.	Brunnich's guillemot, *Uria lomvia*	VC	R	—
153.	Little auk, *Alle alle*	ER	C	—
154.	Crested auklet, *Aethia cristatella*	—	—	A
155.	Black guillemot, *Cepphus grylle*	C	C	—
156.	Mandt's guillemot, *Cepphus grylle mandtii*	—	—	A
157.	Puffin, *Fratercula arctica*	VC	R	—
158.	Wood pigeon, *Columba palumbus*	—	—	A
159.	Feral pigeon, *Columba livia*	FC	FC	—
160.	Turtle dove, *Streptopelia turtur*	—	—	A
161.	Collared dove, *Streptopelia decaocto*	—	—	A
162.	Cuckoo, *Cuculus canorus*	—	—	A
163.	Black-billed cuckoo, *Coccyzus erythrophthalmus*	—	—	A
164.	Scops owl, *Otus scops*	—	—	A
165.	Snowy owl, *Nyctea scandiaca*	ER	ER	—
166.	Long-eared owl, *Asio otus*	—	—	A
167.	Short-eared owl, *Asio flammeus*	R	R	—
168.	Nightjar, *Caprimulgus europaeus*	—	—	A
169.	American nighthawk, *Chordeiles minor*	—	—	A
170.	Swift, *Apus apus*	—	—	A
171.	Alpine swift, *Apus melba*	—	—	A
172.	Roller, *Coracias garrulus*	—	—	A
173.	Hoopoe, *Upupa epops*	—	—	A
174.	Belted kingfisher, *Ceryle alcyon*	—	—	A
175.	Great-spotted woodpecker, *Dendrocopos major*	—	—	A
176.	Yellow-bellied sapsucker, *Sphyrapicus varius*	—	—	A
177.	Wryneck, *Jynx torquilla*	—	—	A
178.	Skylark, *Alauda arvensis*	—	—	A
179.	Shore lark, *Eremophila alpestris*	—	—	A
180.	Short-toed lark, *Calandrella cinerea*	—	—	A
181.	Swallow, *Hirundo rustica*	—	—	A
182.	House martin, *Delichon urbica*	—	—	A
183.	Tree pipit, *Anthus trivialis*	—	—	A
184.	Meadow pipit, *Anthus pratensis*	VC	—	—
185.	Rock pipit, *Anthus spinoletta*	—	—	A
186.	Tawny pipit, *Anthus campestris*	—	—	A
187.	Yellow wagtail, *Motacilla flava*	—	—	A
188.	Grey-headed wagtail, *Motacilla flava thunbergi*	—	—	A
189.	Citrine wagtail, *Motacilla citreola*	—	—	A
190.	Grey wagtail, *Motacilla cinerea*	—	—	A
191.	Pied wagtail, *Motacilla alba yarrellii*	—	—	A

		Breeding Season	Winter	Passage Only
192.	White wagtail, *Motacilla alba alba*	C	—	—
193.	Great grey shrike, *Lanius excubitor*	—	—	A
194.	Red-backed shrike, *Lanius collurio*	—	—	A
195.	Golden oriole, *Oriolus oriolus*	—	—	A
196.	Baltimore oriole, *Icterus galbula*	—	—	A
197.	Starling, *Sturnus vulgaris*	C	C	—
198.	Rose-coloured starling, *Sturnus roseus*	—	—	A
199.	Waxwing, *Bombycilla garrulus*	—	—	ER
200.	Jackdaw, *Corvus monedula*	—	—	A
201.	Rook, *Corvus frugilegus*	—	—	A
202.	Carrion crow, *Corvus corone corone*	—	—	A
203.	Hooded crow, *Corvus corone cornix*	—	—	A
204.	Raven, *Corvus corax*	C	C	—
205.	Iceland wren, *Troglodytes troglodytes islandica*	R	R	—
206.	Dunnock, *Prunella modularis*	—	—	A
207.	Barred warbler, *Sylvia nisoria*	—	—	A
208.	Grasshopper warbler, *Locustella naevia*	—	—	A
209.	Reed warbler, *Acrocephalus scirpaceus*	—	—	A
210.	Sedge warbler, *Acrocephalus schoenobaenus*	—	—	A
211.	Garden warbler, *Sylvia borin*	—	—	A
212.	Blackcap, *Sylvia atricapilla*	—	—	A
213.	Whitethroat, *Sylvia communis*	—	—	A
214.	Lesser whitethroat, *Sylvia curruca*	—	—	A
215.	Willow warbler, *Phylloscopus trochilus*	—	—	A
216.	Chiffchaff, *Phylloscopus collybita*	—	—	A
217.	Wood warbler, *Phylloscopus sibilatrix*	—	—	A
218.	Parula warbler, *Parula americana*	—	—	A
219.	Myrtle warbler, *Dendroica coronata*	—	—	A
220.	Blackpoll warbler, *Dendroica striata*	—	—	A
221.	Yellow-browed warbler, *Phylloscopus inornatus*	—	—	A
222.	Tennessee warbler, *Vermivora peregrina*	—	—	A
223.	Red-eyed vireo, *Vireo olivaceus*	—	—	A
224.	Goldcrest, *Regulus regulus*	—	—	A
225.	Pied flycatcher, *Ficedula hypoleuca*	—	—	A
226.	Red-breasted flycatcher, *Ficedula parva*	—	—	A
227.	Spotted flycatcher, *Muscicapa striata*	—	—	A
228.	Stonechat, *Saxicola torquata*	—	—	A
229.	Whinchat, *Saxicola rubetra*	—	—	A
230.	Wheatear, *Oenanthe oenanthe*	C	—	—
231.	Redstart, *Phoenicurus phoenicurus*	—	—	A
232.	Black redstart, *Phoenicurus ochruros*	—	—	A
233.	Siberian rubythroat, *Luscinia calliope*	—	—	A
234.	Bluethroat, *Luscinia svecica*	—	—	A
235.	Robin, *Erithacus rubecula*	—	—	A
236.	Nightingale, *Luscinia megarhynchos*	—	—	A
237.	Hermit thrush, *Catharius guttatus*	—	—	A
238.	Blackbird, *Turdus merula*	—	FC	—
239.	Fieldfare, *Turdus pilaris*	—	FC	—
240.	Ring ouzel, *Turdus torquatus*	—	—	A
241.	American robin, *Turdus migratorius*	—	—	A
242.	Redwing, *Turdus iliacus*	C	—	—
243.	Song thrush, *Turdus philomelos*	—	—	A
244.	Mistle thrush, *Turdus viscivorus*	—	—	A
245.	White's thrush, *Zoothera dauma*	—	—	A
246.	Great tit, *Parus major*	—	—	A
247.	Tree sparrow, *Passer montanus*	—	—	A
248.	House sparrow, *Passer domesticus*	—	—	ER

		Breeding Season	Winter	Passage Only
249.	White-throated sparrow, *Zonotrichia albicollis*	—	—	A
250.	Fox sparrow, *Passerella iliaca*	—	—	A
251.	Chaffinch, *Fringilla coelebs*	—	—	A
252.	Brambling, *Fringilla montifringilla*	—	—	ER
253.	Bullfinch, *Pyrrhula pyrrhula*	—	—	A
254.	Siskin, *Carduelis spinus*	—	—	A
255.	Greenfinch, *Carduelis chloris*	—	—	A
256.	Redpoll, *Acanthis flammea*	C	C	—
257.	Scarlet grosbeak, *Carpodacus erythrinus*	—	—	A
258.	Crossbill, *Loxia curvirostra*	—	—	A
259.	Parrot crossbill, *Loxia pytyopsittacus*	—	—	A
260.	Pine bunting, *Emberiza leucocephala*	—	—	A
261.	Corn bunting, *Emberiza calandra*	—	—	A
262.	Little bunting, *Emberiza pusilla*	—	—	A
263.	Reed bunting, *Emberiza schoeniclus*	—	—	A
264.	Yellowhammer, *Emberiza citrinella*	—	—	A
265.	Yellow breasted bunting, *Emberiza aureola*	—	—	A
266.	Black headed bunting, *Emberiza melanocephala*	—	—	A
267.	Slate coloured junco, *Junco hyemalis*	—	—	A
268.	Lapland bunting, *Calcarius lapponicus*	—	—	A
269.	Snow bunting, *Plectrophenax nivalis*	VC	VC	—
270.	Indigo bunting, *Passerina cyanea*	—	—	A

NB A number of other records of rarities are being considered for their validity at the time of writing. It is expected that the final count, up to spring 1985, will be 305.

APPENDIX 5: MARINE MAMMALS

1. Right whale, *Balaena glacialis*
2. Bowhead whale, *Balaena mysticetus*
3. Fin whale, *Balaenoptera physalus*
4. Blue whale, *Balaenoptera musculus*
5. Minke whale, *Balaenoptera acutorostrata*
6. Sei whale, *Balaenoptera borealis*
7. Humpback whale, *Megaptera novaeangliae*
8. Northern bottlenose whale, *Hyperoodon ampullatus*
9. Beaked whale, *Mesoplodon sp.*
10. Narwhal, *Monodon monoceros*
11. White whale, *Delphinapterus leucas*
12. Sperm whale, *Physeter macrocephalus*
13. Common or harbour porpoise, *Phocoena phocoena*
14. Longfin pilot whale, *Globicephala melaena*
15. Killer whale, *Orcinus orca*
16. White-beaked dolphin, *Lagenorhynchus albirostris*
17. Atlantic whiteside dolphin, *Lagenorhynchus acutus*
18. Common dolphin, *Delphinus delphis*
19. North Atlantic walrus, *Odobenus rosmarus rosmarus*
20. Eastern Atlantic harbour or common seal, *Phoca vitulina vitulina*
21. Grey seal, *Halichoerus grypus*
22. Bearded seal, *Erignathus barbatus*
23. Hooded seal, *Cystophora cristata*
24. Harp seal, *Pagophilus groenlandicus*
25. Ringed seal, *Pusa hispida*

APPENDIX 6: TERRESTRIAL MAMMALS

1. Arctic fox, *Alopex lagopus*
2. Mink, *Mustela vison*
3. Polar bear, *Thalarctos maritimus*
4. Reindeer, *Rangifer tarandus*
5. Brown rat, *Rattus norvegicus*
6. Black or Ship rat, *Rattus rattus*
7. Long-tailed field mouse, *Apodemus sylvaticus*
8. House mouse, *Mus musculus*

FURTHER READING

Bardarson, Hjalmar R. 1982. Iceland: a Portrait of its Land and People. Hjalmar R. Bardarson.

Escritt, Tony. 1985. Iceland: A Handbook for Expeditions. The Iceland Information Centre.

Fridriksson, Sturla. 1975. Surtsey: Evolution of life on a Volcanic Island. Butterworth & Co Ltd.

Iceland Review, 1963–1985

Jonasson, Petur M. 1979. Ecology of eutrophic, subarctic Lake Myvatn and the River Laxa. Icelandic Literary Society, Copenhagen.

Jonsson, Gunnar. 1983. Islenskir Fiskar. Fjolvautgafan. (Icelandic fish – Icelandic only).

Love, Askell. 1983. Flora of Iceland. Almenna Bokafelagid.

Magnusson, Sigurdur A. 1984. Northern Sphinx: Iceland and Icelanders. Snaebjorn Jonsson & Co.

Njardvik, Njordur P. 1973. Birth of a Nation: the Story of the Icelandic Commonwealth. Iceland Review.

Selected Papers. 1939. The Zoology of Iceland. University of Copenhagen.

Selected Papers. 1975. Iceland 874–1974. Central Bank of Iceland (includes short papers on population, flora and vegetation, animal life on land, life in the Icelandic seas, geology and physical geography).

Selected Papers. 1980. Villt Spendyr. Rit Landverndar 7. Landvernd. (Wild mammals of Iceland – short English summaries only).

Selected Papers. 1982. Fuglar. Rit Landverndar 8. Landvernd. (Birds of Iceland – Icelandic only).

Selected Papers. 1983 onwards. Bliki. (Icelandic birds – short English summaries for some papers only).

Tomasson, Richard F. 1980. Iceland: The First New Society. Iceland Review.

Williams, David. 1985. Iceland: A Visitor's Guide. Stacey International.

Wolseley, Pat. 1979. A Field Key to the Flowering Plants of Iceland. The Thule Press.

Photos	*Page*
Mike Amphlett	69
Hjálmar R. Bárdarson	123
Hans Van Brandwijk	51
Mark Carwardine	112, 115 upper, 147
Grétar Eiríksson	54, 56, 58 upper
Árni Johnsen	48, 102
Sigurgeir Jónasson	Front cover (centre inset), 45, 46, 135, 139, 140
Stephen J. Kasserman	62
Mats Wibe Lund	121
Magnús Magnússon	53 upper
Thórhallur Magnússon	78, 79
Erling Ólafsson	53
Max Schmid	24
Páll Stefánsson	Front cover (except centre inset), 2, 6, 8, 10, 12, 16, 19, 21, 23, 26, 28, 29, 30, 32, 34, 36, 37, 38, 41, 43, 47, 50, 57, 60, 64, 67, 70, 71, 73, 74, 77, 83, 85, 86, 95, 97, 99, 104, 106, 108, 110, 114, 116 lower, 124, 126, 128, 129, 131, 137, 144, 148, 149, 151, 152, 153, 155, 157, 162, 164, 166, 168, 170
Joe Van Wormer	58 lower

Maps drawn by Jean-Pierre Biard